AF621860

on track ...

The Beatles 1967-1970 & Beyond

every album, every song

Alberto Bravin and Andrew Wild

SONICBOND

sonicbondpublishing.com

Sonicbond Publishing Limited
www.sonicbondpublishing.co.uk
Email: info@sonicbondpublishing.co.uk

First Published in the United Kingdom 2026
First Published in the United States 2026

British Library Cataloguing in Publication Data:
A Catalogue record for this book is available from the British Library

Copyright Alberto Bravin and Andrew Wild 2026

ISBN 978-1-78952-650-9

The right of Alberto Bravin and Andrew Wild to be identified
as the authors of this work has been asserted by them
in accordance with the Copyright, Designs and Patents Act 1988.
All rights reserved. No part of this publication may be reproduced, stored in a
retrieval system or transmitted in any form or by any means, electronic, mechanical,
photocopying, recording or otherwise, without prior permission in writing from
Sonicbond Publishing Limited

Typeset in ITC Garamond Std & ITC Avant Garde Gothic
Printed and bound in England

Graphic design and typesetting: Full Moon Media

Cover author photo: Simon Trott

Follow us on social media:
Twitter: https://twitter.com/SonicbondP
Instagram: www.instagram.com/sonicbondpublishing_/
Facebook: www.facebook.com/SonicbondPublishing/

Linktree QR code:

Dedication

Thank you to Nick Jackson, Mark Lewisohn and Gregory Spawton.

For Nicole and Laila.

There's something about a Beatles song, that lives forevermore
The beauty of the harmonies, the sound of the Fab Four
All their music will live on and on...
ELO, 'Beatles Forever' (1983)

And while Lennon read a book on Marx
The quartet practiced in the park...
Don McLean, 'American Pie' (1971)

I don't believe in Elvis
I don't believe in Zimmerman
I don't believe in Beatles
John Lennon, 'God' (1970)

Also by Andrew Wild

Books About Music
Pink Floyd Song By Song (Fonthill, 2017)
Queen On Track (Sonicbond, 2018)
The Beatles: An A-Z Guide To Every Song (Sonicbond, 2019)
Solo Beatles 1969-1980 On Track (Sonicbond, 2020)
Crosby, Stills And Nash On Track (Sonicbond, 2020)
Dire Straits On Track (Sonicbond, 2021)
Fleetwood Mac In The 1970s (Sonicbond, 2021)
Eric Clapton Solo On Track (Sonicbond, 2021)
Eric Clapton Sessions (Sonicbond, 2022)
Phil Collins In The 1980s (Sonicbond, 2022)
The Allman Brothers Band On Track (Sonicbond, 2023)
A Mirror Of Dreams: The Progressive Rock Revival 1981-1983 (Kingmaker, 2024)
Live Aid: The Greatest Show On Earth, 13 July 1985 (Sonicbond, 2024)
Four Sides Of The Circle (Rumble Strips, 2024)
The Beatles On Track 1962-1966 (Sonicbond, 2025 – with Alberto Bravin)
A Playground Of Broken Hearts: The Progressive Rock Revival 1984-1989 (Kingmaker, 2025)
Apple Of My Eye (Sonicbond, 2025)
The Doobie Brothers On Track (Sonicbond, 2026)
Time And Tide: The Songs Of Big Big Train (Kingmaker Publishing, 2026)
The Band On Track (Sonicbond, 2026)

Books About Films
James Bond On Screen (Sonicbond, 2022)

Local History
108 Steps Around Macclesfield (Sigma Press, 1994/2nd Edition, Rumble Strips, 2018)
Exploring Chester (Sigma Press, 1996/Re-Publication, Rumble Strips, 2018)
Ever Forward (MADS, 1997)

Biographies
Play On: The Official Biography Of Twelfth Night (Twelfth Night, 2009)
One For The Record: The Official Biography Of Galahad (Avalon, 2013/2nd Edition, 2018)
His Love: The Art, Music And Faith Of Geoff Mann (Sonicbond, 2023)

Books About Comics
The Perfect Marvel Comics Collection – 1939-1985 (Rumble Strips, 2022)

Plays
The Difficult Crossing (Stagescripts, 2016)
A Difficult Man (Rumble Strips, 2021)

As Editor
Stored In Clocks And Mortal Shadows: Geoff Mann's Poems And Lyrics 1973-1993
(Twelfth Night, 2024)

Foreword

My dad was a big Beatles fan. He worked in London and brought back singles like 'Love Me Do' and 'Day Tripper'. I moved to London in my late teenage years, and it was a good feeling to be close to where it all happened. But I wouldn't say that I was a big fan at that time. I knew all the songs, of course.

When I moved back to Italy to set up my first studio, in 2005 aged 22, I really started to listen to The Beatles properly. I lived in a little apartment upstairs, above the studio. I was given the *Anthology* DVD box set as a gift. This had come out a year or two beforehand and was on a constant loop for months.

And then came the *Love* album in 2006, which is one of my favourites. It focuses on all of those great songs from their last few years as a group and weaves them together into a perfect hour of music. It was this album that turned me back onto The Beatles and it's still one of their best albums for me.

I played in a Beatles tribute band for five years and we needed to deconstruct and learn lots of songs in many styles. It was then that I really began to appreciate their musicianship and craft.

Alberto Bravin, Trieste, 2026

Like Alberto, my introduction to The Beatles came courtesy of my dad – who, in the mid-1970s, proudly purchased one of those massive desk-sized hi-fi systems that looked like it could double as a spaceship control panel. Along with it came the *Red* and *Blue* albums, which basically became the soundtrack to my childhood.

As a student, I owned most of their albums on vinyl, including a vintage 1965 copy of *Rubber Soul* – which I think my dad had borrowed from someone and forgotten to give back. It has now been stolen by my daughter. Then, in the late 1980s, I jumped on the CD reissue bandwagon and finally bought the entire back catalogue.

Fast forward to around 1993, when I decided to channel my inner detective and placed a small ad in *Q* or *Mojo,* hunting for *The Beatles At The Hollywood Bowl*. A local hero responded and, as part of the deal, gifted me – or maybe sold me – a cassette filled with unreleased versions of 'Strawberry Fields Forever' and session outtakes of 'Misery'.

Basically, this was the bootleg equivalent of finding a secret menu at your favourite restaurant. Turns out, there was a whole underground world of live and studio recordings floating around. I collected every last one. This quest lasted 25 years – yes, a quarter-century of chasing Beatles treasure. Along the way, my respect for those original albums and 1960s singles grew, along with my ever-expanding collection of under-the-counter tapes and CDs. But, always, I went back to the original albums and singles. And it's those gems we're here to celebrate in this book because nothing says 'timeless' more than decades of obsessive fandom and questionable storage choices.

Andrew Wild, Rainow, 2025

<table>
<tr><th colspan="2">The Authors’ Twenty Favourite Beatles Songs</th></tr>
<tr><th>Andy’s</th><th>Alberto’s</th></tr>
<tr><td>‘A Day In The Life’</td><td>‘And Your Bird Can Sing’</td></tr>
<tr><td>‘Dear Prudence’</td><td>‘Being For The Benefit Of Mr. Kite!’</td></tr>
<tr><td colspan="2">‘Come Together’</td></tr>
<tr><td></td><td>‘Don’t Let Me Down’</td></tr>
<tr><td></td><td>‘Day Tripper’</td></tr>
<tr><td></td><td>‘Drive My Car’</td></tr>
<tr><td></td><td>‘Eleanor Rigby’</td></tr>
<tr><td></td><td>‘The Fool On The Hill’</td></tr>
<tr><td></td><td>‘Girl’</td></tr>
<tr><td colspan="2">‘Golden Slumbers-Carry That Weight-The End’</td></tr>
<tr><td>‘Here Comes The Sun’</td><td>‘Happiness Is A Warm Gun’</td></tr>
<tr><td>‘Here, There And Everywhere’</td><td>‘In My Life’</td></tr>
<tr><td>‘I Am The Walrus’</td><td>‘I’ve Got A Feeling’</td></tr>
<tr><td>‘I Saw Her Standing There’</td><td></td></tr>
<tr><td colspan="2">‘I Want You (She’s So Heavy)</td></tr>
<tr><td>‘I’ll Be Back’</td><td>‘The Long And Winding Road’</td></tr>
<tr><td>‘Lucy In The Sky With Diamonds’</td><td>‘She’s Leaving Home’</td></tr>
<tr><td>‘Norwegian Wood (This Bird Has Flown)’</td><td></td></tr>
<tr><td>‘Oh! Darling’</td><td></td></tr>
<tr><td>‘Rain’</td><td></td></tr>
<tr><td colspan="2">‘Something’</td></tr>
<tr><td>‘Strawberry Fields Forever</td><td>‘While My Guitar Gently Weeps’</td></tr>
<tr><td>‘There’s A Place’</td><td></td></tr>
<tr><td>‘Tomorrow Never Knows’</td><td></td></tr>
<tr><td colspan="2">‘Within You Without You’</td></tr>
<tr><td>‘The Word’</td><td>‘Your Mother Should Know’</td></tr>
</table>

Preface

Other than George's last-minute strum through 'I Me Mine' and the odd sprinkle of overdubbing, The Beatles recorded their entire EMI/Apple catalogue in just under seven years. That's from 4 September 1962 to 20 August 1969 – 12 albums, 22 singles, two stand-alone EPs and a grand total of 213 songs. Or, to put it another way, your average band's entire lifetime output, plus several greatest hits compilations and still enough time left over for three films, several breakdowns and an unfortunate dalliance with Maharishi-approved facial hair.

That's remarkable enough on its own. But what elevates The Beatles beyond mere mortals is not just the quantity, but the consistent quality – the kind of songwriting and sonic experimentation that makes most other bands look like they're still trying to work out how to plug in an amp. Musical innovation? Check. Artistic evolution? Absolutely. Unrivalled influence? Undeniable. It's impossible to disagree with this assessment – and if you do, well, you're simply wrong. Don't worry, we've all been there.

Of course, the internet – the reliable font of wisdom that it is – occasionally likes to stir the pot with clickbait such as 'The Ten Worst Beatles Songs Of All Time'. Without fail, these lists always include 'Maggie Mae', 'Wild Honey Pie', 'Rocky Raccoon' and 'Revolution 9'. Naturally. One particularly enthusiastic critic – who shall remain nameless to protect their credibility, or what's left of it – once described 'Yesterday' as 'a sickly, mawkish, ubiquitous, unflushable turd' and 'I Want You (She's So Heavy)' as 'a turgid descending riff' that 'alternates between a coma-inducing blues jam and the kind of dirge that should've been left in a rehearsal room with the lights off.'

We, of course, dispute this. Vehemently. Now, it's true that The Beatles occasionally recorded the odd curiosity ('What's The New Mary Jane', we're looking at you). But the idea that 'Yesterday' is anything other than a perfectly formed piece of pop brilliance only proves that even critics can be wrong, loudly and often.

And then there's the equally meaningless 'Best Beatles Songs' lists, which are, by their very nature, entirely subjective and therefore instantly debatable (see our own lists!). Tasked with compiling our personal top 20s, we selected 35 different songs. Entirely subjective, as we say. Only five songs appear on both of our lists: 'Within You Without You', finally recognised as one of the best songs from *Sgt. Pepper*, and four from *Abbey Road*: 'Come Together', 'Something', most of the *Abbey Road* medley (yes, we cheated) and that turgid dirge, 'I Want You (She's So Heavy)'. Indeed, 32 of our combined 35 choices were released between late 1965 and mid-1970, arguably the band's creative and artistic peak.

Then there's the perennial 'boy band' theory – the notion that The Beatles were basically The Backstreet Boys of the early 1960s who discovered LSD and accidentally became artists. Wrong. Spectacularly wrong.

There's also the tiresome argument that Ringo was a bad drummer – likewise very, very wrong – and the still-going conspiracy that Paul is dead, which is not just erroneous but also deeply inconvenient for Sir Paul, who continues to tour quite energetically for a deceased man.

From a technical standpoint, The Beatles recorded most of their finest work using two- and four-track tape, usually under brutal time constraints and with equipment now considered laughably primitive. And yet, within these limitations – or perhaps because of them – they created music that still sounds fresh, vital and, crucially, not like it was recorded in a broom cupboard.

They were, by every conceivable measure, the best band of all time. This is not up for debate.

We've listened to it all – every album, every single, every leftover snippet from an *Abbey Road* session – and in doing so, we've reminded ourselves why we fell in love with this music in the first place: why it still moves us and why it still matters, 60 years later.

on track ...

The Beatles
1967-1970 & Beyond

Contents

Prologue: Paul's Not Dead

A minor accident on 26 December 1965 was the catalyst for one of the most ridiculous conspiracy theories of the last 60 years: that Paul McCartney died in an accident and was replaced in The Beatles by an equally-talented doppelganger called William 'Billy Shears' Campbell, or perhaps Shepherd.

The facts are these.

The Beatles' final UK tour took place between 3 and 12 December 1965. At its conclusion, Paul stayed for a few days in London, attending a preview of Lionel Bart's new musical *Twang!* on 19 December, before heading to Liverpool to spend time with his family. He was accompanied by his friend Tara Browne, a 20-year-old Irish socialite and heir to the Guinness brewing fortune.

'I had a very good friend who lived in London called Tara Browne, a Guinness heir', Paul says in *The Beatles Anthology*. 'A nice Irish guy, very sensitive bloke. I'd see him from time to time and enjoyed being around him. He came up to visit me in Liverpool once when I was there, seeing my dad and brother. I had a couple of mopeds on hire, so we hit upon the bright idea of going to my cousin Bett's house. We were riding along on the mopeds. I was showing Tara the scenery ... and I suddenly had a freeze-frame image of myself at that angle to the ground when it's too late to pull back up again ... I looked at the ground, and it seemed to take a few minutes to think, 'Ah, too bad – I'm going to smack that pavement with my face!' Bang! There I was, chipped tooth and all. It came through my lip and split it. But I got up, and we went along to my cousin's house ... she rang a friend of hers who was a doctor.'

Paul was stitched up, but his memory fails about what happened next.

'In fact, that was why I started to grow a moustache', he said. 'It was pretty embarrassing, because around that time, you knew your pictures would get winged off to teeny-boppery magazines like *16*, and it was pretty difficult to have a new picture taken with a big fat lip. So I started to grow a moustache – a sort of Sancho Panza – mainly to cover where my lip had been sewn. It caught on with the guys in the group: if one of us did something like growing his hair long and we liked the idea, we'd all tend to do it. And then it became seen as a kind of revolutionary idea that young men of our age definitely ought to grow a moustache! And it all fell in with the *Sgt Pepper* thing because he had a droopy moustache.'

He's jumping the gun here. Paul was first photographed with a moustache in November 1966, whilst on holiday. The public learned of this new facial hair as the band reconvened to start work on *Sgt. Pepper's Lonely Hearts Club Band*. In the interim, between Paul's tumble and the arrival of that moustache, The Beatles took part in photograph sessions, made promotional films for 'Paperback Writer' and 'Rain', recorded *Revolver* and toured the Far East and the US.

The Beatles took part in two photograph sessions on 25 March 1966, three months after Paul's accident. One of these was used on the (in)famous 'butcher' sleeve of the Capitol album *Yesterday...And Today.* You need to look closely at the album cover to see that there is scarring on Paul's top lip. His broken tooth is crowned.

The *Revolver* album was recorded between 6 April and 21 June 1966. Promotional films for 'Paperback Writer' and 'Rain' would be filmed in the grounds of Chiswick House on 20 May 1966. Here, Paul's chipped tooth is very obvious, suggesting that the crown didn't hold or was temporary.

At the last session for the album, on 21 June, Paul fell out with the band and left early. Three days later, the band were in Germany. They played shows in Germany (24-26 June), Japan (30 June-2 July), the Philippines (4 July), and after a few weeks' break, their calamitous final tour of the US (12-29 August).

They returned to the UK on 1 September and took an extended break from Beatledom that autumn before jointly returning to EMI on 24 November 1966. It had been five months since they finished 'She Said She Said'.

A few days before Christmas, Paul's friend Tara Browne was driving through South Kensington with his girlfriend, Suki Potier. He was under the influence of alcohol and other drugs and, as some reports suggest, was driving in excess of 100 mph (170 km/h). At the junction of Redcliffe Square and Redcliffe Gardens, Browne's car collided with a parked lorry. He died of his injuries the following day, 18 December 1966. Paul McCartney attended the premiere of the film *The Family Way* later that evening.

And then, on 7 January 1967, Paul was free from other commitments, having spent the previous three evenings recording 'Penny Lane'. According to author Jim Yoakum, McCartney hosted a lively party at his London home with Mick Jagger, Keith Richards, Brian Jones and others. Paul's art dealer friend Robert Fraser was in attendance, as was Fraser's Moroccan-born assistant Mohammed Chtaibi. At some stage, they decided to head to Jagger's Hertfordshire home, The Arthouse, which is about an hour's drive north of Cavendish Avenue. Chtaibi was tasked with driving Paul's customised Austin Mini Cooper and, on route, was involved in a serious incident on the M1. The car was written off, and Chtaibi would need hospital treatment. The car was recognised as McCartney's, and word spread that he had been in an accident. The band's official magazine, *The Beatles Book*, noted in its next issue, published in February 1967: 'Stories about The Beatles are always flying around. A rumour swept London that Paul McCartney had been killed in a car crash on the M1. But, of course, there was absolutely no truth in it at all.'

Unfortunately, the magazine stated that 'The Beatles' Press Officer found out when he telephoned Paul's St. John's Wood home and was answered by Paul himself, who had been at home all day with his black Mini Cooper safely locked up in the garage.'

This was clearly untrue.

So, three motor accidents involving either Paul or one of his associates – all of them resulting in injury or death – took place between December 1965 and January 1967. These three unconnected events were, it seems, the index cases of the Paul-Is-Dead rumours.

John Lennon would write about Tara Browne in 'A Day In The Life', after reading a story in the 17 January 1967 edition of *The Daily Mail*, which reported the ruling on a custody action over Browne's two young children.

> He blew his mind out in a car
> He didn't notice that the lights had changed
> A crowd of people stood and stared
> They'd seen his face before
> Nobody was really sure
> If he was from the House of Lords

That, it seemed, was that, until almost three years later, when a college student in Michigan called into his local radio show.

A Rumour Is Born

Twenty-four-year-old American writer Nicholas Schaffner published his diligently researched and well-received book *Beatles Forever* in 1977. It was critically accepted as a balanced and entertaining look at the band's history and legacy. It is still a terrific read.

Schaffner addresses the Paul-Is-Dead theory. On page 127, he writes:

> On 12 October 1969, disk jockey Russ Gibb of WKNR-FM (Detroit's 'underground' station) received an eerie phone call, which advised him to listen closely to the fade-outs of certain Beatles numbers, and to play others backward. Following instructions, Gibb and his listeners found among other 'clues' that John mutters 'I buried Paul' at the end of 'Strawberry Fields Forever', and that 'Revolution 9's oft-intoned words 'number nine, number nine' become 'turn me on dead man, turn me on dead man' when one spins the *White Album* [*The Beatles*] counterclockwise. By the same process, the message 'Paul-Is-Dead man, miss him, miss him' emerges from the gibberish sandwiched between 'I'm So Tired' and 'Blackbird'. Gibb, smelling a dead, er, Beatle, became the first of many vocal promulgators of Paul's untimely death. Two days later, *The Michigan Daily* ran a review of *Abbey Road* by Fred LaBour that took the form of an obituary, illustrated with a gruesome likeness of Paul's severed head. According to LaBour, the LP cover shows The Beatles leaving a cemetery dressed as a minister (John), an undertaker (Ringo) and a gravedigger (George). Paul is not only out of step with the others, but barefoot, as British corpses supposedly are prone to be buried. A cigarette in his right hand confirms that this is an imposter for the left-handed McCartney. 'One and one and one is three', concluded LaBour, who also cited corroborating 'evidence' on earlier LP sleeves.

Shaffner traced the story to a prank article called 'Clues Hint At Possible Beatles Death'. This was written by Barb Ulvinden and published in the

Northern Star, a student newspaper for Northern Illinois University, on 23 September 1969. It was full of unsubstantiated conjecture and several mistakes (Paul's new wife was 'Jane Eastman', for example, and 'Jane' had previously dated Paul's brother Michael).

In fact, Ulvinden had plagiarised the article, complete with the Jane Eastman error, from 'Is Beatle Paul McCartney Dead?' published in the *Times-Delphic*, the student newspaper of Drake University in Des Moines, Iowa. This was written by Tim Harper, a Drake University journalism student and staff writer for the *Times-Delphic*. Harper, it seems, had heard the story from a local student.

'The story begins with a student named Dartanyan Brown', writes Andru Reeve, who interviewed Brown and Harper for his book *Turn Me On Dead Man: The Beatles And The Paul Is Dead Hoax*. 'Also a struggling musician, Brown shared a residence with his band in Des Moines, Iowa, near the campus. Their house also served as a 'crash pad' of sorts for any itinerant musicians who happened to be passing through town on tour. On any given night, one might find members of The Rotary Connection or Fuse camped out on the living room floor. Impromptu parties and all-night rap sessions were not out of place at Brown's house, and the weekend of 12 September was no exception. Brown returned home from classes that Friday night to find an assortment of long-haired musicians and their girlfriends jamming on acoustic guitars, bongos and maracas. He didn't recognise anyone visiting the house that night, and he never saw any of them again. But when he returned to the Drake campus on Monday morning, he couldn't get one of the girls out of his mind. Brown strolled into the office of the student newspaper, *The Drake Times-Delphic*, where he served as an associate editor. There he discovered the bespectacled sports editor, Tim Harper, sitting alone and puffing thoughtfully on a cigarette. 'What's up, Dart?' Harper greeted him. Dartanyan Brown took a seat next to Harper. 'Had these cats from I don't know where over at the house last night.' 'Any good?' 'Didn't get a chance to catch their gig, but I was rapping with the guitarist's old lady and she was laying this whole trip on me about Paul McCartney being dead.' Harper snubbed out his cigarette. 'Really? He isn't, is he?' No. But check this out! 'Brown relayed the scenario he'd heard from the girl at the party. Harper didn't buy any of it, but thought that it would make a hell of a story for the *Delphic*. Although he was a sports writer and didn't even own a single Beatles album, that didn't stop him from penning the article himself.'

'It was just a joke,' Harper told the *Chicago Sun-Times* on 23 October 1969. 'I was the first one to put it all together. I knew when I wrote the story that it wasn't true.'

The evidence presented in these first two articles was entirely circumstantial. You can read them online.

1 On the front cover of *Sgt. Pepper's Lonely Hearts Club Band*, a 'mysterious hand' is raised over Paul's head. This, it is claimed, is an ancient death symbol

of either the Greeks or American Indians. This is, in fact, the hand from the life-size photograph of the British comedian, singer and actor Issy Bonn, whose face can be seen over McCartney's left shoulder, just in front of Stan Laurel. This is clearly visible in alternative shots of the photographic session.

2 A 'wreath' in the shape of a guitar lies on the grave at the group's feet. Claims that this is 'left-handed' are impossible to substantiate and meaningless.

3 Paul is wearing a black armband in the band photograph in the gatefold. No, he isn't; it's a cloth badge with the crest and initials of the Ontario Provincial Police. Beatles historian and author Piers Hemmingsen confirms that four OPP arm badges were presented as a gift to The Beatles at Malton Airport, now Toronto Pearson International Airport, on Tuesday 28 September 1964, as they were waiting to board a chartered plane to Montreal.

4 On the back cover, John, George and Ringo are facing toward the camera, but Paul has his back turned. So what?

5 Also on the back cover, George is pointing to a phrase from the song 'She's Leaving Home', specifically the opening line, 'Wednesday morning at 5 o'clock as the day begins'. This is true. By implication, this is the time and day of Paul's fatal accident. Paul's moped incident was on 19 December 1975 (a Sunday), Tara Browne's car crash was on 17 December 1966 (a Saturday), and Paul's mini was wrecked on 7 January 1967 (also a Saturday). The supposed date of Paul's accident was Wednesday 9 November 1966 (an extrapolation or origin of the 'mirror across the bass drum' theory). Paul was on holiday in France on 9 November 1966. It was the date that John Lennon first met Yoko Ono, however. Later theorists switched the date to 11 September 1966, clearly confusing the UK/US date format and conveniently linking to another much-debated event from 2001.

6 On the cover of the *Magical Mystery Tour* EP, four men are dressed in animal suits. We can assume that these are The Beatles, as seen in the TV film of the same name. According to these reports, three of the suits are white, the fourth black. It is speculated that Paul is wearing the black costume in the guise of a walrus, and that the walrus is a Viking symbol of death. Not only is the suit not black – it's dark brown – but Paul didn't wear the walrus suit, it was John. There is no evidence that the walrus is a symbol of death in any culture or society.

7 Within 'Revolution No. 9', a voice repeats 'number nine'. When this is played backwards, it is supposed to say 'turn me on, dead man' and 'cherish the dead'. It doesn't. Listen for yourself.

8 In 'Glass Onion', John sings 'and here's another clue for you all: The Walrus was Paul'. Attempting to interpret song lyrics, especially Lennon's in 1967-1968, is a fool's errand.

9 Three of The Beatles went to see Bob Dylan perform at the Isle of Wight Festival on 31 August 1969. Paul was 'conspicuously absent'. This is hardly surprising because his wife Linda had given birth to their first daughter, Mary, on 28 August, three days beforehand.

This was the extent of the 'clues' offered at this time: no Billy Shears, no William Campbell/Shepherd, no gravedigger/priest/funeral director, no 28 IF, no freemasons, no Illuminati.

But the flame had been lit. Russ Gibb was a part-time rock promoter and DJ on WKNR-FM, broadcasting from the Detroit suburb of Dearborn. On the afternoon of 12 October 1969, a student named Tom Zarski called into Gibb's radio show, claiming that Paul McCartney had died and discussed the various clues that could be contrived as evidence.

'Certainly, I had no reason to believe it was true', Zarski told Keener13.com (the website of WKNR-FM). '[I was sure] it was not. Yet, I felt as if I was being sent on some quest. It was either a riddle or maybe some kind of scavenger hunt. I was driven by my own curiosity. I needed an answer.'

According to Andru Reeve, Zarski had first heard the rumour from another student right after the summer break. 'It was one person who did this and he lived in Illinois somewhere', Zarski told Todd Gardner of the website Turn Me On DeadMan.net. '[He] carried the story to me. And for several weeks before my call to Uncle Russ, I'd collected [clues] from various people around the campus. I was a real nerd. Nerds have nothing else to do; they don't have girlfriends, so that's what I did.'

And the focus then shifts from one nerd to another.

'Twenty miles from the studios of WKNR, on the main road that led out of Ann Arbor, University of Michigan,' Reeve writes, 'sophomore Fred LaBour was driving to nearby Jackson to visit with his relatives. Feeling miserable after an argument with his girlfriend, LaBour switched on the car radio so he could lose himself in the music. When he flipped the dial to his favourite station, he lost himself in something else entirely.'

LaBour quickly submitted a 58-column-inch news item to *The Michigan Daily*, the newspaper of the University of Michigan. This was published on 14 October 1969 – two days after Gibb's broadcast – under the heading 'McCartney dead; new evidence brought to light.'

The article was almost wholly fabricated.

> It took about an hour and a half. It's the best bullshit I ever wrote, and it only took me an hour and a half.
> Fred LaBour, quoted in *Turn Me On Dead Man: The Beatles And The Paul Is Dead Hoax*

This is the foundation of much of the spurious information that has since proliferated – with no sources or evidence whatsoever – in the Paul-Is-Dead story. Most of the elements of LaBour's article, many of which have been repeated countless times since, were unsubstantiated products of a vivid imagination. It's very clear from the tone of the article that LaBour was not being serious. 'Thus began the greatest hoax of our time,' he wrote, 'and the subsequent founding of a new religion based upon Paul as Messiah.'

Let's examine the 'new' information from LaBour's article, which opens with the bold statement, 'Paul McCartney was killed in an automobile accident in early November 1966 after leaving EMI recording studios tired, sad and rejected.'

Remember that this was published only two days after the WKNR broadcast. LaBour was either a very knowledgeable, diligent and fast-working researcher, or he simply made up some or all of his article. Several of his statements are provably wrong.

1 According to LaBour, The Beatles were working on a new album in late 1966, 'tentatively entitled *Smile*'. And when The Beatles abandoned the idea, the album (and all recordings made so far) was taken over by Brian Wilson of The Beach Boys, and, as a thank you, The Beatles recorded 'Back In The USSR' in tribute to the American band. Yes, The Beach Boys were working on an album called *Smile* during this period. The Beatles themselves, however, were not recording in early November 1966 – they would start on their next project on 24 November. Paul himself was out of the country until 19 November.

2 McCartney was found 'pinned under his car in a culvert with the top of his head sheared off.' There is no evidence for this.

3 'Lennon's plan was to create a false Paul McCartney, bring him into the group as if nothing had happened and then slowly release the information of the real Paul's death to the world via clues secreted in record albums.' This one sentence from LaBour's article is so laughable as to be dismissed immediately. But here is the source of the ongoing 'Paul was replaced' theory. According to LaBour, a 'Paul look-a-like contest was held and a living substitute was found in Scotland. He was an orphan from Edinburgh named William Campbell.' And here are two words that have fuelled 50-plus years of nonsense. LaBour himself has admitted that 'William Campbell' was a name he made up, based on the name of the famous musician Glen Campbell. If you follow all of the various theories about Paul's replacement, then Campbell was Scottish, Canadian, the real Paul McCartney's older brother (there is no genealogical or documentary support for this), or even Vivian Stanshall, the singer from The Bonzo Dog Doo-Dah Band, who must himself have been replaced as he was active in that band from 1962 to 1970. Later theorists used the name William Shepherd. Neither William Campbell nor William Shepherd has ever been linked to a real person close to The Beatles or any credible historical record.

4 Apparently, Campbell's picture can be found on the lower left-hand corner of the poster included with *The Beatles*. It's not. It's Paul in late 1966.

5 Campbell had 'minor plastic surgery to complete the image.' LaBour doesn't say what was done, where it was done, or who did it.

6 'Voice print studies have confirmed the difference in voice timbre between the original and phoney Paul.' LaBour offers no sources for these, which can

only have taken place in the four weeks since Tim Harper's *Times-Delphic* article (which Harper has admitted was fabricated).

7 Paul is wearing a patch reading 'OPD', meaning 'officially pronounced dead ... used in England similar to our DOA.' No, he isn't, and no, it doesn't.

8 'The medal on his left breast is given by the British Army commemorating heroic death' ... it's Paul's MBE, presented to him on 26 October 1965.

9 This is the first time that anyone suggests that John is saying 'I buried Paul' at the end of 'Strawberry Fields Forever'. It's 'cranberry sauce', clearly heard on the *Anthology 2* alternative mix of the track. Online commenters have suggested that the *Anthology* track has been faked to suit the narrative.

10 There is a photograph of Paul on page three in the booklet of the *Magical Mystery Tour* EP. He is seen behind a sign which reads 'I You Was'. So what?

11 Paul is shown wearing a black rose in the final scenes of *Magical Mystery Tour*. The others wear red roses. Again, so what?

12 The word 'Beatles' on the cover of *Magical Mystery Tour* can be read upside-down in a mirror to reveal a secret phone number. The first digit could be 2, 5, 6, or 8; the second could be 1, 3, or 4; the third could be 0, 1, 4, or 6; and so on. One of the options, 834-7132, belonged to Victor Keegan, a journalist with *The Guardian*, who was subjected to dozens of reverse-charge calls from the US.

13 'Walrus is Greek for corpse.' It's not. Nor is it Greek for carcass, cadaver, body, or remains.

14 'I Am The Walrus' includes a passage from *King Lear*, in which Oswald says, 'O untimely death', and Gloucester responds, 'Is he dead?' This is true. It's well-documented that the passage was mixed into 'I Am The Walrus' by chance on the evening of 29 September 1967, as the play was performed live on BBC radio. 'I never knew it was *King Lear* till years later when somebody told me because I could hardly make out what he was saying', John Lennon said in 1975. 'It was interesting to mix the whole thing with a live radio coming through it.'

15 The collage of photographs included with *The Beatles* 'depicts Paul lying on his back ... possibly deceased in a pool of water, with the top of his head invisible.' Or possibly Paul taking a bath, most likely taken at home by Linda.

16 'John called McCartney 'Prudence' back in the old days...' There is no evidence for this. Prudence Farrow, Mia's sister, accompanied The Beatles to India in early 1968, and the song is named for her.

17 The band are shown on the *Abbey Road* sleeve dressed as characters from Paul's funeral. John is 'dressed in white and is utterly an anthropomorphic God', followed by Ringo as an undertaker, Paul as the deceased and George as a gravedigger. This is all the product of a vivid imagination.

18 "Octopus's Garden' is British Navy slang for the cemetery in England where naval heroes are buried.' It's not.

As can be seen, each of LaBour's claims can be either refuted as undeniably incorrect or dismissed either as conjecture or very dry humour ('Paul was a homosexual, as noted in 'Yellow Submarine', it is plainly yelled, 'Paul's a queer...').

The Paul-Is-Dead myth springs directly from this source. None of what LaBour has written is provable and most of it is absurd.

'And yet the story had legs', writes Nicholas Shaffer. 'Alex Bennett of WMCA-AM (a highly above-ground New York station) turned the controversy into the prime topic of his talk-show (after receiving a call from one Lewis Yager, who claimed to have been awakened in the night by the screams of a Beatlemaniacal girlfriend to whom McCartney's dire fate had been revealed in a dream). Not to be outdone, Bennett's counterpart on WABC quickly did the same. It was only a matter of days before the increasingly complicated tale of Paul's decapitation had swept across the North American airwaves to become the number one topic of discussion and conjecture on campuses and in the 'alternative' press.'

The international press picked up the story. *The Times* of London published an article on 21 October 1969. The wire services AP, UPI and Reuters carried the story on 22 October. Over one hundred newspapers published Paul-Is-Dead articles. *The New York Times*, for example, ran a story under the headline, 'Beatle Spokesman Calls Rumor of McCartney's Death 'Rubbish''. Their reporters had attempted to contact The Beatles for their responses. The band's assistant, Peter Brown, called Paul to ask for a statement for the press. McCartney gave a line borrowed from Mark Twain: 'Rumours of my death have been greatly exaggerated. If I were dead, I'd be the last to know.'

The news broadcasts of the three major American television networks covered the story, as did national magazines such as *Time* and *Life*. None of them seemed to have seen LaBour's *Michigan Daily* article and therefore did not pick up the ironic tone of the writing.

McCartney and his family flew by private jet from London to Glasgow, heading for their farm near Campbelltown.

> Harry Moyes, a veteran photojournalist with the *Glasgow Herald*, had received an anonymous tip that McCartney would be arriving at Glasgow Airport sometime late Wednesday evening, so he staked it out. It took only a few hours for his strategy to pay off. Moyes soon spied Paul and Linda, plus their two children, Heather and Mary, disembarking a private shuttle flight from London.
>
> 'Good evening', Paul said cordially as Moyes began snapping pictures.
>
> 'Have you heard the rumour spreading about you? That you're dead?' Moyes asked on the run.
>
> McCartney shook his head and 'just laughed' as he and his family were hustled into a waiting car.
>
> **Andru Reeve, *Turn Me On Dead Man: The Beatles And The Paul Is Dead Hoax***

That same day, Alex Bennett arrived in London, where he interviewed Ringo Starr, Derek Taylor, Neil Aspinall, photographer Iain Macmillan (who shot the *Abbey Road* sleeve and denied there was any intentional symbolism in it) and, clutching at straws, Paul McCartney's tailor and barber. Starr told Bennett: 'I'm not going to say anything because nobody believes me when I do. If people are gonna believe it, they're gonna believe it. I can only say it's not true.'

The Harvard Crimson, the daily college newspaper of Harvard University, was quick to pick up on Fred LaBour's article. Jeff Magalif's response is dated 23 October and titled 'Clues Do Not A Dead Man Make'.

> It turns out that LaBour is not only a poor writer [Magalif insisted] but somewhat of a liar as well. He has admitted that the entire story is a product of his imagination, based only on assorted clues in Beatles songs and on Beatles albums. He has never met Louise Harrison Caldwell and George Martin's illegitimate daughter, Marian, whom he thanked at the beginning of his story 'for their help'. The account which he put down as the truth was only 'a working hypothesis', he now says.
>
> The *Michigan Daily*'s attitude toward the story is interesting. The paper introduced the article by saying, 'Mr. LaBour says it's all true'. But editorial page editor Steve J. Anzalone said last week that 'we're not trying to pass this off as a news story. I don't know how serious Fred was; I hope most people aren't believing it.'

Magalif admits that 'the clues require a certain degree of imagination to perceive and interpret; that, of course, is where the fun comes in.' He then adds a whole raft of 'new' clues.

> 'Come Together', the first song on [*Abbey Road*], can really seem strange if looked at the right way. One of the possible explanations for The Beatles' 'preoccupation with Paul's death', according to John J. Small, coordinator of WKNR-FM, is that 'Lennon is a self-proclaimed Jesus Christ who has devised a scheme to make the world come together over Paul'. And so: 'One and one and one is three [not four]; got to be good-looking cause he's so hard to see. Come together ... over me'.

Magalif concluded that there were three reasons for the Paul-Is-Dead theory.

> ...that Paul is alive and well and The Beatles are playing a game for the hell of it; that Paul-Is-Dead and The Beatles are hoaxing their fans; Paul is very ill and has been replaced by a double.

There's also a fourth, and it's the simplest: The Beatles had nothing whatsoever to do with this nonsense. If you go looking for a conspiracy theory, you'll surely find one.

Paul himself was at his farm in Scotland, where, on 24 October, he agreed to speak to the BBC's Chris Drake. McCartney said that since getting married six months earlier and becoming a father, he preferred to live a more private life. Not long after, *Life* magazine tracked Paul down in Scotland. Despite being angry at the intrusion, he agreed to an interview. The resulting article went into detail about the supposed clues to Paul's death and appeared as the cover story for the 7 November 1969 issue.

'Perhaps the rumour started because I haven't been much in the press lately', Paul told *Life*. 'I have done enough press for a lifetime, and I don't have anything to say these days. I am happy to be with my family, and I will work when I work. I was switched on for ten years and I never switched off. Now I am switching off whenever I can. I would rather be a little less famous these days. It's all so bloody stupid. I was walking barefoot because it was a hot day. The people who are making up these rumours should look at themselves a little more. There is not enough time in life. They should worry about themselves instead of worrying whether I am dead or not. Can you spread it around that I am just an ordinary person and want to live in peace?'

Life showed a picture of Paul with Linda and their daughters. Coincidentally, there was a car advertisement on the reverse side and, when holding the cover up to a light, this revealed a car superimposed across McCartney's chest so that the top of his head was blocked out. This provided another basis for insinuation and innuendo.

The cover of the 29 November 1969 issue of *Rolling Stone* announced, 'Paul is not dead', and you might have expected the story to wither at this point. However, those with too little time on their hands would look back at other Beatles album sleeves for further 'clues': apparently, rather than just owning up or saying nothing, the other three Beatles were trying to bring Paul's death and replacement to the attention of the world via a series of hints hidden within the artwork of their recent albums, and in clever twists of the lyrics of their songs.

These are best seen in the book *The Walrus Was Paul* (R. Gary Patterson, 1996), which takes a tongue-in-cheek, 208-page look at the various clues and theories at that time. Here are our favourites.

1. The album *A Collection Of Beatles Oldies* shows a picture of Paul with a car 'running off the road into the figure's head'.
2. 'Some investigators claimed that Paul's profile appeared to be haphazardly pieced in with the other Beatles full-face on [the *Revolver*] cover.' *Revolver* was released on 5 August 1966, three months before Paul was supposed to have died.
3. Paul is not wearing a hat on the front cover of *Help!*...
4. On the cover of *Rubber Soul*, The Beatles 'with sombre faces [are] looking down into a grave or coffin.'
5. The yellow wreath in the shape of a guitar on the cover of *Sgt. Pepper's Lonely Hearts Club Band* spells out 'Paul'.

6. If you hold a straight-edged mirror to the centre of the bass drum on the cover of *Sgt. Pepper's Lonely Hearts Club Band,* 'a hidden message appears'. The message is I ONE IX HE ^DIE
   'This is a direct reference to the supposed fatal car crash of 9 November 1966 ... the diamond points directly at the victim.'
7. In a scene in *Magical Mystery Tour*, John is seen in front of a sign, 'the best way to go is by M&D Company' ... 'the rumour suggested that the M&D Company was a funeral home in Britain.'
8. The white cover of *The Beatles* 'seems to be a reference to the traditional colour of mourning in some countries.'
9. Four photographs were included with *The Beatles*. 'If you look closely enough, you can see scars along Paul's upper lip', Patterson says. 'Was this ... a clever attempt to disguise a double?'
10. 'The back cover of *Abbey Road* presented a series of dots that appear to form the numeral 3.' Or 8, or the letter S.
11. The cover of *Let It Be* shows photographs of John, Paul and George in profile with a white background, 'while Paul faces the camera with a blood-red background.'

Another 'clue' was the Volkswagen Beetle with the registration plate LMW 281F. That's two-eight-one F, not 28 IF. Theorists said this is a hint that Paul McCartney would have been 28 years old if still alive when *Abbey Road* was released in September 1969. Paul was born in June 1942 and was therefore still 27 years old. And LMW means 'Linda McCartney Weeps'...

'Truly, the Paul-Is-Dead saga boasted enough literary references and multilingual puns to do James Joyce proud', wrote Nicholas Shaffer in 1977. 'As a matter of fact, one erudite Beatlemaniac detected a clue in 'I Am The Walrus's 'goo goo goo joob' chorus; in *Finnegan's Wake*, these are Humpty Dumpty's last words before he takes a fall and cracks his head. Someone could base a whole book on the rumour – if no one has already.'

Andru Reeve spent years researching the Paul-Is-Dead theory. His book, *Turn Me On Dead Man: The Beatles And The Paul Is Dead Hoax*, first published in 1994, is a sober, accurate and detailed work that should have been the final word on the story.

The last time that all four Beatles were together in the recording studio was 20 August 1969. Two days later, the final group photograph session chronicled four weary and miserable men in the house and grounds of John's estate, Tittenhurst Park. George, especially, looks as if he'd rather be anywhere else. The last time that all four musicians would be in the same room was at Apple in London for a business meeting. This happened the week before the release of *Abbey Road*, between 15 and 19 September.

> I want a divorce. Like the one I got from Cynthia.
> John Lennon, 20 September 1969

By the end of October 1969, Paul was a resident in Scotland with Linda, Heather and two-month-old Mary, fighting off depression and wondering what to do next. Encouraged by his wife, McCartney began to consider a future outside The Beatles. The family returned to London shortly before Christmas and Paul immediately started to record the songs that would make up his first solo album, *McCartney*.

That, it seems again, was that.

Almost 30 years after the story first broke, Ernst E Schultze published the novel *Carry That Weight: The Story Of The Beatles,* which presents an alternative reality in which The Beatles replaced Paul McCartney with a look-alike. As a 'what if?' yarn, it's good fun. By the end of the 1990s, the Paul-Is-Dead story was firmly within the world of fiction, where it belongs.

But then came the internet...

One can spend days chasing rabbits down the ever-more-bizarre holes in the World Wide Web. One of these offers, presumably in jest, one thousand anagrams of the phrase 'turn me on, dead man' ... 'to use in your Paul-Is-Dead research'. We could argue that 'Paul McCartney' is an anagram of 'Mac pantry clue', evidence that Paul McCartney choked to death on a late-night cheese and onion sandwich.

People actually believe this stuff, even now.

The uncontrollable proliferation of social media has meant that every theorist can put forward their increasingly bizarre claim without any kind of substantiation. And, as all Paul-Is-Dead theories are bogus, none of the claimants can agree on anything.

Quite simply, it all began in 1969, and everything builds upon those first, disproven college articles.

'It's the most stupid rumour I've ever heard', John Lennon said when he himself called into the same radio station where the Paul McCartney conspiracy first blew up. He denied hiding messages in Beatles songs and repudiated any symbolism on the band's album covers. 'What did we do?' Lennon asked. 'Stuff him and shave him? How could we do it? I don't understand what it's all about.'

Two years later, speaking to ***Rolling Stone***, Lennon went further, 'That was bullshit, the whole thing was made up. We wouldn't do anything like that. Some people have got nothing better to do than study Bibles and make myths about it, and study rocks and make stories about how people used to live. It's just something for them to do. They live vicariously.'

The psychologists Ralph Rosnow and Gary Alan Fine, in their book *Rumour And Gossip: The Social Psychology Of Hearsay* (1976), expand on this, spending some time evaluating the Paul-Is-Dead story.

> The mistrust of the establishment media leads to the question of how truth can be gauged by the rumour's audience [they wrote]. The 'standard' measure of truth, 'If I read it in the newspaper, it must be true', is not always reliable or valid. Routine assumptions about practical epistemology are

> also being questioned. This attitude makes clear that truth is only accepted when it is consistent with one's frame of reference. Information is processed in light of the assumptions one holds about the nature of the world, for knowledge is culturally determined. What is truth to one person may be part of a massive conspiracy to another. Most people who heard the McCartney rumour probably did not believe that he had actually been killed, although many may have considered the possibility. Whatever the explanations, it became the foundation for fantasy that swept across American adolescent society, developing from a basic core, adding numerous variants, deviations and new explanations as each person and group attempted to make sense of the evidence at hand.

Fifty years after that assessment, the story, like Paul himself, is very much alive.

So, How Did Paul Die?

As the story goes, Paul McCartney had been upset by the band at a recording session on Wednesday, 9 November 1966. He had driven off at speed and died in an accident.

It's documented that Paul did indeed angrily leave one of the band's recording sessions in 1966 – on 21 June 1966 – for 'She Said She Said'. On 9 November, however, Paul was on holiday in France with Jane Asher and Mal Evans. They travelled to Kenya for several days and returned on 19 November, just ahead of the first session for 'Strawberry Fields Forever'.

A remarkable book was published on 9 September 2009. It was surely no accident that this was timed to coincide with the considerable publicity that accompanied the release of *Beatles Rock Band* and two box sets of the entire remastered back catalogue.

The Memoirs Of Billy Shears was 'was created with the talents of 'poet-encoder', Thomas E. Uharriet.' Here's where the story gets more and more absurd. Uharriet describes his work as 'decod[ing] the teachings of Jesus, Krishna, Huang Po and Lao Tzu, bringing that brilliance of the ancient Eastern world to his modern Western audience.'

According to the publishing blurb, *The Memoirs Of Billy Shears* (which has 666 pages, naturally), was 'crafted with poetic brilliance' and 'conveys the historical message utilising multiple methods of encoding and decoding to uncover gnostic, numerological, mythological and cultic symbology [sic] with layered meaning that pulls you in deeper with each reading.'

Right.

The foreword is credited to George Martin's eldest son, Gregory.

'Gregory knew the original Paul personally', the book says. Maybe, but in January 1967, when Paul's car was destroyed on the M1, Gregory Martin was only nine years old.

That Fred LaBour's original *Michigan Daily* article credited 'George Martin's illegitimate daughter Marian' (who doesn't exist) as well as George Harrison's sister Louise Caldwell, then a resident of St. Louis, is another spurious attempt at adding legitimacy to these claims. It's a badly written screed that has zero credibility other than as a piece of easily-disproved fluff.

The book very carefully makes no claim to be anything other than pure invention. Nevertheless, many easily-led readers have taken this for the truth: read the Amazon reviews for some eye-opening claims, such as 'after reading it, I cannot imagine ever thinking that the pre-1966 Paul McCartney is the same person as the man we know as Paul McCartney ... they are as different as night and day, their looks, their music and their personalities.'

Make of that what you will, but don't waste your time buying that book: just remember that famous quote attributed to Abraham Lincoln about fooling people some or all of the time.

And then, in 2017, Auriga Books of Edmunds, Washington, published *Plastic Macca* by Tina Foster. Foster is, to quote her own book, 'an expert in the field of doubles research, especially Paul McCartney.' So, a self-appointed 'expert'. Throughout, she calls the post-1966 musician either 'Faul', as in 'fake Paul', or 'McCartney II'.

We'll take three examples. 'A couple of years later ... McCartney married Linda Eastman, which was thought to be proof that he was not the real Paul' (p. 9). Foster does not explain who thought this, or why it was thought to be 'proof'. Later, 'In the 'Hey Jude' *Smothers Brothers* TV performance from 1968, it appears that he was wearing a face mask based on the unnatural corners of the mouth' (p. 122-123). This is simply ludicrous. And 'another trick to enhance the likeness between the original and the imposter is to stretch or compress photographs' (p. 131). The exact reverse is also true.

This hefty, 500-page self-published book is a masterpiece, but not for its literary merits. Over half of the book is taken up with footnotes – 2,678 in total. Many of these reference Foster's own blog, links to websites without primary source references, or spurious YouTube videos. It's impossible to take this book seriously. Yet people do.

Other sources insist that 'Faul' practiced the Paul role in private and in public for *two years*, evidenced by Faul appearing as Paul in Beatle concerts in both 1965 and 1966, and permanently in Seattle during the 1966 American tour. There are YouTube videos that show 'proof' of this.

It was such a stroke of luck for the surviving Beatles to find, in just a couple of months, someone who looked exactly like Paul McCartney, had his voice, was one of the world's best bass players (and left-handed, too) and was a hugely talented composer. What are the odds?

Paul's Not Dead

Conspiracy theories often rely on confirmation bias, cherry-picking ambiguous statements, or supposed 'clues'. The very concept of Paul McCartney's replacement is utterly ridiculous.

Paul has been publicly active for 60 years since 1966: recording, touring, giving interviews and performing live. He has unmistakable vocal and musical talent. There is, frankly, no credible evidence of a shift in musical ability, vocal tone, or artistic style across Paul's career. Natural evolution and developing maturity as a writer and performer are all we need to consider.

Furthermore, there are no reliable witnesses, documents, or whistleblowers supporting the claim that Paul died and was replaced. McCartney has worked with literally thousands of people in his lifetime and not a single legitimate insider – not one –has come forward with convincing evidence.

As discussed earlier, the supposed clues in Beatles album covers and lyrics can be attributed to over-interpretation – to a phenomenon called apophenia, seeing patterns where none exist. John Lennon himself stated that 'I buried Paul' was actually 'cranberry sauce' (and you can hear him say exactly that on outtakes) and that the rumours were ridiculous. John, known for his candour, never acknowledged any replacement and was reconciled with his childhood friend during the last few years of his life.

It's unfeasible that an auxiliary could match Paul's voice, mannerisms, musicianship, songwriting ability and public persona over many decades, or to have been well-trained in Paul's pre-1966 personal and career minutiae to be able to provide fluent interview answers into his 80s. To pull off such a switch would require the cooperation or silence of not only his bandmates, management, family and the press (and the British press are notorious for digging up the merest hint of celebrity dirt), but other agencies such as the UK government, who approved Paul's knighthood in 1997. This level of deception is not only unprecedented but unsustainable.

A theory that claims that George Harrison hinted at Paul's death in subtle ways is not supported by verified interviews, footage, or biographies. *The Last Testament Of George Harrison* (2005) is a hoax video disgracefully and falsely presenting itself as a deathbed confession.

No one has provided solid evidence or a credible, consistent, verifiable background of William Campbell Shears (or Shepherd).

In short, the counterarguments rest on a combination of common sense, observable reality, scientific analysis and the implausibility of the alternative. The 'Paul-Is-Dead' theory is a great example of how conspiracy theories can take root in cultural imagination, even when all evidence is to the contrary.

And, notwithstanding anything whatsoever that would be accepted as legal proof, there is one inequitable fact that cannot be challenged. Paul has eyes that are out of line. His left eye is slightly lower than his right. This is evident in every photograph of him since he was a child. This is a physical attribute that is impossible to fake. His son, James, has the same physical quirk as did his paternal grandfather, Joseph McCartney (born in 1866).

So, on 29 November 1966, James Paul McCartney, very much not dead, would join his bandmates John, George and Ringo at EMI Studios in London to commence their next recording project. Somewhat ambitiously, they expected to record a single in time for the Christmas market.

Barbara Suczek, a graduate student at the University of California, published her own conclusions in the *Journal Of Contemporary Ethnography* in April 1972, 'The Curious Case Of The 'Death' Of Paul McCartney'.

> On the basis of a quick rundown of press reports [she wrote], it can be roughly estimated that the period of intense public excitement, at least the period during which the news media were actively contributing to it, lasted for approximately two months, reaching a peak in early November [1969]. After the last week of November, interest seemed to peter out, the most likely explanation being that public interest had been diverted by the approach of the holiday season. There was a brief afterglow on 23 February 1970, in a TV skit on *Rowan And Martin's Laugh-In*:
>
> Angel I: Is there any truth to the rumour that Paul McCartney is still alive?
>
> Angel II: I doubt it. Where do you think we get these groovy harp arrangements?

1967

'Strawberry Fields Forever' b/w 'Penny Lane' (Single)

UK: 17 February 1967. US: 13 February 1967.
Chart positions. UK: 2. US: 1.

By the end of November 1966, The Beatles as a collective had not been seen in public since their return from their final tour three months before. They had enjoyed an extended break from Beatledom that autumn. John flew to Germany to take part in a film called *How I Won The War*. George went to India for five weeks to meet with and learn from Ravi Shankar. Paul wrote the themes for the soundtrack for *The Family Way* and went on holiday to France and Kenya (or died in a car crash, depending on who you believe). Ringo stayed at home with his one-year-old son Zak after a short trip to see John in Spain, where film production had moved in mid-October. The Beatles jointly returned to EMI on 24 November 1966. Their previous session was on 21 June 1966, five months beforehand, when they had recorded 'She Said She Said'.

The media were prepared to write the band's epitaph. A syndicated United Press International (UPI) story headlined 'Beatles Getting Bored: Drift Towards Breakup' had been published around the world on 10 November. 'The signs are that The Beatles, over the loyal opposition of thousands of fans, are moving toward an oft-voiced ambition: to develop their individual talents individually.'

Ringo was quoted thus, 'I have no idea what our future plans are...'

Exactly two weeks later, he had his answer. The Beatles were back in the studio after their longest-ever gap between recording sessions. Without the instant news we expect today, entertainment magazines around the world continued to peddle theories and misinformation. *KRLA Beat*, published on 3 December 1966, said, 'Three years after instigating an entire era, The Beatles are breaking up. At least, that's the consensus among London music observers and those close to the princes of pop. The word came as a whisper at first, but subsequent statements by Brian Epstein and The Beatles themselves have given the speculation certainty.'

The Beatles, meanwhile, had entered Studio Two at EMI with the intention of recording a song written by John Lennon during his recent time in Spain. Ahead of this session, according to engineer Geoff Emerick, 'John Lennon was even more agitated than usual. 'Look,' he said to George Martin, 'it's really quite simple. We're fed up with making soft music for soft people, and we're fed up with playing for them, too. But it's given us a fresh start, don't you see?' From the expression on his face, it was clear that George Martin didn't see. 'We can't hear ourselves onstage anymore for all the screaming,' Paul interjected earnestly, 'so what's the point? We did try performing some songs off the last album, but there are so many complicated overdubs that we can't do them justice. Now we can record anything we want, and it won't matter. And what we want is to raise the bar a notch, to make our best album ever.' Another blank look from George Martin. I could tell what he was thinking.

Whoever heard of a band that only makes records but doesn't promote them by doing concerts? Lennon persisted, talking rapid-fire – a sure sign that he was starting to get annoyed. 'What we're saying is, if we don't have to tour, then we can record music that we won't ever have to play live, and that means we can create something that's never been heard before: a new kind of record with new kinds of sounds."

The *Time* review of this 'new kind of record', *Sgt. Pepper's Lonely Hearts Club Band*, confirmed that The Beatles had met their objective: 'From the first mewings of 'I Want To Hold Your Hand', The Beatles have developed into the single most creative force in pop music. Wherever they go, the pack follows. And where they have gone in recent months, not even their most ardent supporters would ever have dreamed of. They have bridged the heretofore impassable gap between rock and classical, mixing elements of Bach, Oriental and electronic music with vintage twang to achieve the most compellingly original sounds ever heard in pop music.'

The Beatles re-contracted with EMI in January 1967. This new deal, which ran until 1976, stipulated that Capitol was no longer permitted to re-work the band's albums – from now on, The Beatles' albums were standardised across the world. This didn't stop Capitol from creating new compilations such as *Magical Mystery Tour* and *Hey Jude,* but the running order of the next five albums between 1967 and 1970 was presented as The Beatles intended.

At the beginning of 1967, however, EMI wanted a new single. Two tracks earmarked for The Beatles' forthcoming album were hastily paired as a double A-side, slated for mid-February. It marked the first new Beatles music in half a year, and with hindsight, stakes a claim as arguably their finest single – bold and inventive but unmistakably theirs.

'Strawberry Fields Forever' (Lennon, McCartney)

Recorded 24, 28, 29 November, 8-21 December 1966. John Lennon – vocals, rhythm guitar, bongos, Mellotron; Paul McCartney – Mellotron, bass, piano, guitar, timpani, bongos; George Harrison – lead guitar, slide guitar, swarmandal, timpani, maracas; Ringo Starr – drums, percussion; Mal Evans – tambourine; Neil Aspinall – güiro; Terry Doran – maracas; Tony Fisher, Greg Bowen, Derek Watkins and Stanley Roderick – trumpet; Joy Hall, Derek Simpson and Norman Jones – cello.

'Wherever you find The Beatles at their most seemingly experimental,' writes Alan W Pollack, 'you almost always find them also at their most traditionally conservative. Here, in 'Strawberry Fields Forever', underneath whatever else is 'far out', you find mostly a folk-ballad-like form with a late-breaking tip of the hat to the pop song format.'

He's absolutely right. 'Strawberry Fields Forever' has its origins in Santa Isabel, Spain, where John spent two weeks for the shooting of the film *How I Won The War*. A series of six demo recordings, just John and his guitar, reveals the compositional process of a folk ballad in action. The first take is little more than two repeats of what would become the second verse, although the lyrics and chord progression are yet to be finalised, even in this short snippet. Only the line I think 'it must be high or low' would progress to the final version, preceded here by the self-examining 'there's no one on my wavelength'.

Once again, Lennon expresses his self-doubt, seen earlier in 'Help!', 'Nowhere Man' and 'I'm A Loser' (and in his future solo songs 'Mother', 'God', 'Jealous Guy' and 'Isolation'). Take 2 has a variant vocal melody and the words now include 'that is you can't, you know, tune in, but it's all right' and the phrase 'it's not too bad'. Take 3 is now recognisably the verse section from 'Strawberry Fields Forever', with both 'no one I think is in my tree' and the chorus chords, without words as yet, making their first appearances. Take 4, thrillingly has 'let me take you down' in the chorus. By the end of this sequence, John has worked out the full structure, two verses of lyrics and, in a real frisson moment, the first use of the song's title.

John returned to the UK on 7 November and, before band sessions recommenced two weeks later, he would record a second series of demos at home in Kenwood. He is still working out the lyrics. 'I cannae do it!' he mutters in a cod-Scottish accent. For one take, he tries a finger-picking guitar arrangement which is beyond him. 'It doesn't work like that', he tells himself. The full chorus is in place, but the lyrics for the third verse are yet to be written. John took this simple acoustic arrangement into EMI on 24 November.

The song in its final structure has a drifting, uncertain quality – John is questioning perception, memory, even his own sense of reality. Lines like 'nothing is real' and 'I think I know, I mean, er, yes, but it's all wrong' are pure Lennon: self-aware but tangled up in doubt. He's retreating to childhood imagery (the orphanage garden he used to play in) as a way of grappling with identity, confusion and not quite fitting into the adult world.

'Strawberry Fields Forever' would take many hours to perfect. Several variants have been officially released.

Take 1 (24 November) can be found on *Anthology 2* and, in a different mix, on the deluxe edition of *Sgt. Pepper's Lonely Hearts Club Band*. Notably, it features the Mellotron for the first time – a curious piece of early analogue sampling tech that had only been around a few years. One of the first pop records to use it was Manfred Mann's 'Semi-Detached, Suburban Mr. James', recorded in August 1966 and released that October, opening with the very same flute setting that would later grace 'Strawberry Fields Forever'. The Beatles would return to the Mellotron across four other tracks in 1967: 'Being For The Benefit Of Mr. Kite!' (February-March), 'Only A Northern Song' (February-April) and both 'I Am The Walrus' and 'Flying' (September). Meanwhile, Mike Pinder of The Moody Blues put it through its paces across *Days Of Future Passed*, recorded between May and November, effectively cementing the instrument's role in early progressive rock – a path soon followed by the likes of King Crimson, Yes and Genesis.

Take 4 (28 November) is available on the deluxe edition of *Sgt. Pepper's Lonely Hearts Club Band*. Subsequent overdubs, labelled take 7, added a second vocal, piano and bass to take 4. This is also available on the Super Deluxe edition of *Sgt. Pepper's Lonely Hearts Club Band*.

A remake (8 December) comprised 16 new takes numbered nine to 24. About one minute of take 24 is edited with take 7 on *Anthology 2*. Cello and brass overdubs were added on 15 December, with the result now listed as take 26. A new remix of this is available on the deluxe edition of *Sgt. Pepper's Lonely Hearts Club Band*.

As every Beatles fan knows, 'Strawberry Fields Forever' is stitched together from three sections. In 1966, that meant literal scissors and tape, not Pro Tools. On 22 December, takes 7 and 26 were mixed – one sped up, the other slowed down – until their pitches and tempos roughly aligned. These speed variations are most noticeable on John's vocals, which are simultaneously sweet, creepy and trippy.

Engineer Geoff Emerick then spliced the pieces into a seamless whole. The *Sgt. Pepper* Super Deluxe set lets us hear those source takes, and pin down exactly which fragments were used.

- 0:00 to 0:55 of the single edit is 0:12 to 1:07 of take 7 (the first 12 seconds are George Martin's remix announcement)
- 0:55 to 0:59 of the single edit is 1:29 to 1:33 of take 7, a four-second bridging edit as the take goes straight into the second verse here ('no one I think is in my tree')
- The remainder is from take 26 (from 00:24, cross-faded on 'going to')
- The single edit has a false fade-out between 3:16 and 3:45.

That's the technical stuff. How does this song make us feel, close to 60 years after its release?

'Strawberry Fields Forever' is complex and intense. And yet brilliantly commercial. Some of the chord changes are outrageous. It heralded a giant leap, sonically and structurally, from 'Nowhere Man' and 'In My Life', recorded just over one year previously. It's quite simply one of the greatest songs ever recorded. Does any more need to be said?

A promo film was shot at Knole Park, Sevenoaks, on 30 and 31 January 1967, directed by Peter Goldmann. This is now often regarded as one of the most innovative pre-MTV promo films of the period, especially in the context of the Musicians' Union restrictions on miming for television.

'Penny Lane' (Lennon, McCartney)

Recorded 29 December 1966 – 17 January 1967. Paul McCartney – vocals, pianos, bass, harmonium, tambourine; John Lennon – backing vocals, piano, guitar, congas, handclaps; George Harrison – backing vocals, lead guitar, handclaps; Ringo Starr – drums, handbell; George Martin – piano; Ray

Swinfield, P. Goody, Manny Winters – flutes, piccolos; David Mason – piccolo trumpet; Leon Calvert, Freddy Clayton, Bert Courtley, Duncan Campbell – trumpets, flugelhorn; Dick Morgan, Mike Winfield – oboes, cor anglais; Frank Clarke – double bass

John's use of the name of a Salvation Army children's home close to his childhood home has led to suggestions of 'Strawberry Fields Forever' being part of a planned 'concept album' of childhood memories. Lennon and McCartney had discussed the idea of writing a quasi-musical about their early days in Liverpool. As John told *Rave* magazine in February 1964, 'Paul and I want to write a stage musical. That's a must. Maybe about Liverpool.'

The first draft of 'In My Life' from *Rubber Soul* includes the lines

Past the tram sheds with no trams
On the 5 bus into town
Past the Dutch and St Columbus
To the Dockers Umbrella that they pulled down

In December 1965, the month that *Rubber Soul* was released, Paul said to *Flip* magazine, 'I like some of the things The Animals try to do, like the song Eric Burdon wrote about places in Newcastle on the flip of one of their hits ['Gonna Send You Back To Walker', the B-side of 'Baby Let Me Take You Home']. I still want to write a song about the places in Liverpool where I was brought up. Places like the Docker's Umbrella, which is a long tunnel through which the dockers go to work on Merseyside, and Penny Lane near my old home.'

Paul was always competitive and, just five days after starting work on 'Strawberry Fields Forever', he brought 'Penny Lane' into the studio. As with Strawberry Fields, which backs onto John's childhood home in Woolton, Penny Lane is an actual place in Liverpool, a street and a shopping area a couple of miles north of Allerton and a familiar location to both John and Paul when they took the bus to school or into the city centre. This anchors both songs to real places, overlaid with vivid psychedelic lyrical imagery. In 'Penny Lane's slightly surreal snapshot of Liverpool life, McCartney's lyrics drift between the ordinary and the whimsical: bank clerks (or the same one, three times), a barber shop and a fireman become characters in a quietly magical tableau. Fictional characters set in real places. Nothing is quite as it seems. The banker in the 'pouring rain' beneath 'blue suburban skies' is joined by a pretty nurse who 'feels as if she's in a play', with the kicker, 'she is anyway'. The melody bubbles with warmth and there's a sense that the song now exists in a space between nostalgia and invention.

The song is a masterpiece, not only of composition but of production, too. The influence of *Pet Sounds* is surely strong. 'Penny Lane' was recorded in ten separate sessions across four weeks. Paul McCartney is at the height of his powers here.

- Thursday 29 December 1966 – Paul recorded a basic piano track in six takes. That same evening, he added two further piano passes, adding flourishes and counterpoint to different parts of the track. One of these, the 'Mrs Mills' upright, was recorded at half-speed, and the other was treated to heavy tremolo through a Vox amplifier. Harmonium, also through the Vox, and Ringo's drums (accenting specific parts of the song) helped to fill all four tracks. Note that there was no 'basic track' recorded by the entire band, as with the other songs recorded so far for this project. The song at this stage can be heard on the Super Deluxe edition of *Sgt. Pepper's Lonely Hearts Club Band.*
- Friday 30 December 1966 – a mono tape reduction of work so far freed up three tracks. This was labelled take 7. Paul and John added their vocals, and the track was put to one side for almost a week.
- Wednesday 4 January 1967 – Paul re-recorded his lead vocals, replacing those from 30 December, whilst John added piano and guitar. All of these overdubs would be subsequently replaced.
- Thursday 5 January 1967 – new vocals from John and Paul replaced the previous vocal tracks from the day before.
- Friday 6 January 1967 – Paul added his complex and fluid bass guitar performance on one of the free tracks. This must rank as one of his greatest basslines. We have written previously about Paul's mastery of that instrument. Here, the bass is more than just the foundation for the song – that's the piano – but the bass guitar is a technically intricate yet breathtakingly lyrical counterpoint. It fits the song with uncanny precision, the mark of a true musical virtuoso. George, Ringo and John overdubbed guitar, drums and congas onto the final remaining free track. A tape reduction and remix placed all instruments together onto one track with all vocals on a second, freeing two tracks for further overdubs. Two more pianos were added along with backing vocals and handclaps. A snippet from this overdub session later surfaced on the Super Deluxe edition of *Sgt. Pepper's Lonely Hearts Club Band*, offering a tantalising glimpse into the creative machinery behind this very fine song.
- Monday 9 January 1967 – Following a third reduction mix to create a new take 9, session musicians added wind and brass instruments.
- Tuesday 10 January 1967 – More backing vocals (Paul, John and George), chimes (Paul) and a handbell (Ringo).
- Thursday 12 January 1967 – Further orchestral overdubs: trumpets, oboe, cor anglais, plus double bass playing a sustained low note in the penultimate verse. The horns were heavily compressed to give a satisfying crunchy sound, almost distorted. The song was mixed to mono at this point, and one of these, RM7, has appeared on bootlegs.
- Tuesday 17 January 1967 – The final addition of the prominent piccolo trumpet.

All of these were squeezed onto four tracks ahead of three mono mixes on 17 January – one of which was issued a promo in the US and includes an extra

piccolo trumpet flourish by David Mason at the end – and three further mono mixes on 25 January. For the record, these are the contents of the final master tape.

Track 1: three pianos, two tambourines, two drum overdubs, harmonium, bass, guitar and congas.
Track 2: backing vocals, chimes, hand bell, trumpet, cor anglais, oboe, double bass, piccolo trumpet.
Track 3: flugelhorn, piccolo trumpet, flute.
Track 4: lead and backing vocals.

The song was not mixed in stereo until 1971. In the meantime, American listeners were treated to a horrible, muddy mock stereo mix on the *Magical Mystery Tour* album. The best mix, to our ears, is Giles Martin's from 2017. This is clean and clear, and the drums have a satisfying snap.

'Penny Lane' is polished, beautiful, charming and meticulously arranged, yet somehow retains the intimacy of a diary entry or glimpses through a window on the top deck of the number 86 bus.

British listeners weren't entirely sure what to make of The Beatles' new single. It debuted at number five on 23 February, only to stall stubbornly at number two for three weeks, held hostage by the insipid charms of Englebert Humperdinck's 'Release Me'. The chart around it was a peculiar menagerie of polite, middle-of-the-road pop: Vince Hill, Ken Dodd, Harry Secombe, Tom Jones, Jim Reeves and The Seekers jostled for attention. The Beatles' innovation feels almost alien by comparison.

Sgt. Pepper's Lonely Hearts Club Band

UK: 26 May 1967. US: 2 June 1967.
Chart positions. UK: 1. US: 1.

Sgt Pepper's Lonely Hearts Club Band redefined the LP as an art form.

Four years before *Sgt. Pepper*, The Beatles were still a beat group – albeit an unusually talented one who happened to write most of their own material. Two guitars, bass and drums remained the framework. *Sgt. Pepper*, often treated as a seismic break, actually follows on quite logically from *Revolver*.

Songs like 'Lovely Rita', 'Good Morning Good Morning' and 'Fixing A Hole' don't stray too far from what we heard on their previous album. Most of the songs on *Sgt. Pepper* aren't so different in construction from those on *Revolver*. The presentation is another matter entirely. What changes here is the scope. The Beatles' music pops out of its old clothes and dresses itself in new ones: Indian classical on 'Within You Without You', music hall pastiche on 'When I'm Sixty-Four', psychedelia on 'Lucy In The Sky With Diamonds', orchestral bombast on 'A Day In The Life', parping brass on the title track. Where the album is most successful, we feel, is when it is at its most experimental.

The so-called concept – a fake band playing songs about The Beatles' Liverpool childhoods – was only ever half-formed and half-successful. We could argue that 'Magical Mystery Tour', 'Your Mother Should Know' and 'Fool On The Hill' would fit right into a series of songs recalling childhood. But these were a few months away.

What *Sgt. Pepper* ultimately delivers isn't narrative cohesion but a dazzling exercise in production and arrangement. That, more than the loose conceit of any 'concept', is why the album still stands apart. George Martin's orchestrations, first glimpsed on 'Yesterday' and 'Eleanor Rigby', are now integral to several songs, giving the album weight and texture. The result pushes The Beatles toward the territory we'd later call 'rock'. Today, we see *Sgt. Pepper* as a statement album – but so, in hindsight, were both *Revolver* and *Rubber Soul*. At the time, though, only *Pepper* made the claim loudly enough that nobody could miss it.

Furthermore, it's not too far a stretch to suggest that *Sgt Pepper's Lonely Hearts Club Band* initiated or at least embodied the counterculture, an anti-establishment ethos that led to the riots of 1968 and the emerging belief that rock music could be seen as serious art. Indeed, the album's cover, a collage of cultural icons – from Marx to Marilyn Monroe to Bob Dylan, along with several Indian spiritual figures chosen by George Harrison – was, for the first time, part of the total artistic statement.

Both the underground and mainstream press publicised The Beatles as leaders of youth culture, just six months after writing them off. Peter Clayton in *Gramophone* was bang on in his review when the album was released.

'*Sgt Pepper's Lonely Hearts Club Band* is [he wrote], like nearly everything The Beatles do, bizarre, wonderful, perverse, beautiful, exciting, provocative, exasperating, compassionate and mocking. More than either of their previous adventurous LPs – *Rubber Soul* and *Revolver* – you'll have to give this one time to grow on you. I think you will find it's worth it. You may at first be fascinated by, say, 'Lucy In The Sky With Diamonds', but that's just a string of pretty images which, if they mean anything at all, are important only to their creators; this sort of thing, in any case, is surprisingly easy to do. The marvellous tracks, to my mind, are the apparently simple ones, like 'A Little Help From My Friends', and the astonishing 'She's Leaving Home', a documentary verse story of infinite knowingness and breathtaking melodic charm. Or the mickey-taking ones like 'Being For The Benefit Of Mr Kite!', with its fairground noises and Victorian handbill language. And what about 'When I'm Sixty-Four'? On the face of it, a pastiche of mid-30s George Formby, it nevertheless has a kind of gentle affectionateness about it – and a certain meaty substance – which raises it well above mere kidding. Another track I keep going back to is 'Fixing A Hole', an engaging tune that alternately lollops and soars. There's plenty of electronic gimmickry on the record (the transistors are really overworked on the track the BBC has banned, 'A Day In The Life'), but that isn't the heart of the thing. It's the combination of imagination, cheek and skill that makes this such a rewarding LP. By the way, owners of automatic cut-outs are in danger of missing the final sounds on side two, some weird gibberish which fills the centre circle like a tape loop.'

Some other critics did not quite know what to make of it. *Sunday Times*' music columnist Derek Jewell wrote, 'The new LP ... is remarkable. Listening to its strange cadences, the sitar passages, its almost atonal propensities, the learned critic might easily assume derivations ranging from English 17th century music to Richard Strauss ... But the influences are likelier to be music hall artists of the last 25 years, and the images which Lennon and McCartney retain of their Liverpool childhood – of places, priests, old women, young girls ... *Pepper* is a tremendous advance, even in the increasingly adventurous progress of The Beatles. Some of the words are splendid urban poetry, almost metaphysical in 'Lucy In The Sky With Diamonds'. The tone is humorous, sympathetic, sceptical and often self-mocking. Musically, it is always stimulating. There won't, though, be much dancing done to *Pepper*. The Beatles are now producing performances, not music for frugging to. Will the kids follow?'

Sgt. Pepper's Lonely Hearts Club Band arrived as both a statement and a spectacle. But, over the years, it has lost some of its sheen. It's no longer regarded as the best album of all time, nor even the best by The Beatles. Yet, in 1967, no other album had attempted such creative ambition, achieved such technical innovation, or powered such cultural reach. Before *Sgt. Pepper*, popular music was seen largely as youth entertainment. After *Sgt. Pepper*, it could be experimental, intellectual and culturally significant.

In the end, *Pepper* may no longer sit atop greatest album lists, but that misses the point. For us, its value is in the way it threw the doors open for what pop music could be: how it dared to make the world pay attention. That's the part that hasn't aged a bit.

And for those reasons, it still demands your attention.

'Sgt. Pepper's Lonely Hearts Club Band' (Lennon, McCartney)

Recorded 1 and 2 February, 3 and 6 March 1967. Paul McCartney – lead vocals, bass, lead guitar; John Lennon – backing vocals, rhythm guitar; George Harrison – backing vocals, lead and rhythm guitar; Ringo Starr – drums; George Martin – organ; Neill Sanders, James W. Buck, Tony Randell and John Burden – French horns.

The sounds of a chattering audience and an orchestra tuning up introduce this churning, chugging title track and overture. Paul is on fire, both vocally and on guitar. Take 1, released in 2017, is sloppy but exciting, and by take 9, they are super-tight even if, as yet, they don't know how to end it. Superimpositions of bass guitar and Beach Boys-tight harmony vocals completed work on the tracks for now. French horns and lead guitar were added on 3 March, and the sound of the cheering crowd, taken from unreleased recordings at the Hollywood Bowl, was mixed in three days later.

It's not a complicated song: a simple rocker to get things moving.

A deft edit moves the performance directly into 'With A Little Help From My Friends'. This was the first time that The Beatles used this trick – two years later, the second side of *Abbey Road* would be constructed from such technical sleights of hand.

'With A Little Help From My Friends' (Lennon, McCartney)
Recorded 29-30 March 1967. Ringo Starr – lead vocals, drums, tambourine; John Lennon – backing vocals, rhythm guitar, cowbell; Paul McCartney – backing vocals, piano, bass; George Harrison – backing vocals, lead guitar; George Martin – Hammond organ, harmonium.

Ringo's showcase, 'With A Little Help From My Friends', was recorded in two sessions.

On 29 March, the band completed several takes of this new song with Paul on piano, Ringo on drums, John on cowbell, George on guitar and George Martin playing harmonium. The first two takes, already sounding very strong, were released in 2017. Take 10 was chosen as the best, and the vocals were added, with Ringo's lead and the band's backing all recorded together, then double-tracked. This completed a busy day's work. The following day, overdubs of further backing vocals (the 'Billy Shears' part, thus igniting that ridiculous conspiracy theory), Hammond organ and timpani for the introduction, snare drum and bass guitar completed the recording.

What resulted was a feel-good tune, brilliantly sung by Ringo – even if his final note seems carefully coached. The lyrics have unusual depth, and the Q&A backing vocals, in particular, are marvellous.

The refrain 'I get by with a little help from my friends' uses a musical technique called a plagal cadence. This is when the song moves to the IV chord (A in this case) before moving back to the root (E). Every time they sing the 'with a little help...' line, that IV-I motion gives that resolution its warm, communal feel. This same trick is used in later songs such as 'Hey Jude' – the long outro ('na-na-na...') which cycles through IV to I – and the chorus of 'Let It Be'. All three of these songs were written by Paul McCartney.

We should also mention several important covers. Both Young Idea and Joe Brown recorded the song in 1967, reaching number ten and number 32 in the summer of 1967. These followed The Beatles' arrangement closely, even if Brown sounds like he's singing 'with a little help from my fringe'. Joe Cocker's 1968 version is a radical re-arrangement, changing the tempo and time signature, and reworking the chords in the middle eight ('do you need anybody?'). Paul McCartney paid tribute to Cocker and the song in 2019: 'I was especially pleased when he decided to cover 'With A Little Help From My Friends', he told *Billboard*, 'and I remember him and [producer] Denny Cordell coming round to the studio in Saville Row and playing me what they'd recorded and it was just mind-blowing. They'd totally turned the song into a soul anthem, and I was forever grateful to him for doing that.' Cocker's version of the song reached number one on the UK Singles Chart in

November 1968. His memorable performance at Woodstock in 1969 would be preserved as a highlight of the film *Woodstock*.

Twenty years after Cocker's number one, Scottish band Wet Wet Wet recorded their own chirpy version, using The Beatles' arrangement, for the album *Sgt. Pepper Knew My Father*. This album also includes covers by artists as diverse as The Fall, Sonic Youth, The Wedding Present, Billy Bragg and an aspiring pop star from the small village of Timperley called Frank Sidebottom. This was the first of Wet Wet Wet's three number one singles.

Finally, in 2004, the UK duo Sam & Mark from the TV series *Pop Idol* also topped the UK singles chart for a single week with their own slightly cheesy electro-pop cover version. This we can safely ignore, but it's proof that you can't put a great song down.

'Lucy In The Sky With Diamonds' (Lennon, McCartney)
Recorded 28 February, 1-2 March 1967. John Lennon – double-tracked lead vocals, maracas, guitar; Paul McCartney – backing vocals, Lowrey organ, bass; George Harrison – acoustic guitar, tambura, lead guitar; Ringo Starr – drums; George Martin – piano.

> I liked 'Lucy In The Sky With Diamonds' a lot. John always had a way of having an edge to his songs. I particularly liked the sounds on it, where I managed to superimpose some Indian instruments onto the Western music. There were specific things that I had written, like 'Within You Without You', to try to feature the Indian instruments, but under normal circumstances, that wouldn't work on a Western song like 'Lucy', which had chord changes and modulations (whereas tamboura and sitars stay in the same key forever). I liked the way the drone of the tamboura could be fitted in there.
> George Harrison, *The Beatles Anthology* (2000)

The timeless 'Lucy In The Sky With Diamonds' still sounds as fresh as the day it was recorded. And just because John always denied that the title was drug-related, it's impossible to believe that the song itself isn't. Is it easy to overestimate the influence of drugs on The Beatles' songs? 'Just about everyone was doing them in one form or another', Paul told *Uncut* in 2004. 'We were no different.'

We can point to 'Day Tripper' and 'Got To Get You Into My Life' in 1965-1966 for certain. And this fabulous song, too. Drugs definitely cracked doors open for The Beatles – new textures, odd turns of phrase, the 'what if we...?' spirit. But those doors were already ajar. The Beatles were restless and curious long before the acid tabs showed up. If you listen across their catalogue, the real through-line isn't the chemicals, it's their ear for melody and their competitive streak with each other. Drugs might have loosened some edges, but the architecture of the songs – their hooks, the chord progressions, the emotional precision – that's craft and instinct, not chemistry.

As with many of John Lennon's songs, 'Lucy In The Sky With Diamonds' feels pieced together from separate sections. The introduction is played on a Lowrey organ – again, it's Paul who adds the opening hook to a Lennon song (see 'Strawberry Fields Forever'). The verse, with its spacey vocals, plays around the notes of a single chord. The bridge ('newspaper taxis') lifts by a tone (from A to Bb), but John sings almost on a monotone. Paul's bass here is phenomenal, a career standout. And so far we've been in waltz time, but with three wallops, Ringo takes us into the common time chorus: louder and rockier.

Note also how George's guitar doubles the vocal melody in the bridges. 'You'll hear me try and play the melody on guitar with John's voice,' he told *Guitar World* in 1992, 'which is what the instrumentalist does in Hindustani vocal music.'

Listen again to notice the structure change in the final verse, when 'and you're gone' goes straight to the verse, missing the reprise of the bridge section. There's so much going on here, but none of it seems contrived.

Take 1, released in 2017, sounds exactly like Oasis. We recommend Elton John's six-minute cover version from 1974, which features guitar and vocals by a certain J. Lennon.

'Getting Better' (Lennon, McCartney)

Recorded 9-10, 21 and 23 March 1967. Paul McCartney – double-tracked vocals, Pianet, bass, handclaps; John Lennon – backing vocals, rhythm guitar, handclaps; George Harrison – backing vocals, lead guitar, tambura, handclaps; Ringo Starr – drums, congas, handclaps; George Martin – piano, Pianet.

There is an Indian mood to 'Getting Better', with a drone-like quality to the guitar and electric piano (a Hohner Pianet) in the verses, a tambura buzz on the last verse and congas giving a very definite Bollywood feel. George Martin bashes the piano strings with a hammer in the closing moments.

Paul's bassline is again inventive and energetic, adding a swing to Ringo's hi-hat flourishes. The vocals and lyrics add a clear message of Macca optimism ('I've got to admit it's getting better'), balanced by a touch of Lennon cynicism ('it can't get no worse').

As a piece in its own right, the song is agreeable but far from essential. What lends it a degree of curiosity is the provenance of its title. During drummer Jimmy Nicol's short association with The Beatles in June 1964, Lennon and McCartney frequently enquired about how he was managing. Nicol's habitual response – 'It's getting better' – would ultimately provide the phrase that endured.

'Fixing A Hole' (Lennon, McCartney)

Recorded 9 and 21 February 1967. Paul McCartney – lead vocals, harpsichord, bass; John Lennon – backing vocals, bass; George Harrison – backing vocals, lead guitar, maracas; Ringo Starr – drums; George Martin – harpsichord.

This song can't quite settle on a single identity. Its verses lean toward a Gershwin-flavoured mix of jazz and blues, while the bridge shifts gears entirely, adopting the stately stride of a torch-song march.

For a minor track, it's impeccably arranged, including inventive backing vocals in the second bridge and George's guitar solo, a rarity in 1967, which is beautifully constructed and performed against the beat. We particularly like the rhyme in 'And it really doesn't matter if I'm wrong I'm right, where I belong, I'm right, where I belong' – even if the lyrics themselves have no big meaning. Listen, though, to George's counterpoint guitar underneath.

'Fixing A Hole' was the first time that The Beatles went to an outside studio to record for EMI.

'Quite often Paul had a song suddenly come to him,' George Martin wrote in *Summer Of Love*, 'and while it was fresh in his mind, he would want to crystallise it. He could not write music, so apart from scribbling down the lyrics and noting a few chord changes underneath, there was no other way for him to be sure of grabbing the song while it was there in his head, other than by recording it. Normally, Abbey Road [EMI Studios] moved heaven and earth to accommodate The Beatles in their hour of need. Nevertheless, the studios and staff could hardly be kept idle in case a Beatle had a flash of inspiration. Although there had been talk of finally building a recording studio solely for The Beatles – grabbing studio reservations ahead of any others was becoming a bit of an embarrassment – nothing had come of it. It so happened that all the studios were in use that particular night, 9 February: there was no room for them at the inn. We had to find a studio, and quickly, while Paul had the urge. The one we found, Regent Sound in Tottenham Court Road, was little more than a demonstration studio, in the heart of Tin Pan Alley. It was a low-ceilinged, boxy little room with a low-ceilinged boxy little sound to it. On top of this, we weren't allowed to take our engineers with us: Geoff Emerick was employed by [EMI] in those days and contractually prevented from recording elsewhere. A man called Adrian Ibbetson was head of Regent Sound then, so he did the recording.'

Take 1 is already advanced, comprising harpsichord (George Martin), bass and vocals (Paul), drums (Ringo) and maracas (John). George added his short but glorious solo on his Fender Stratocaster, double-tracked (1:16 to 1:31). An attempt to record a new backing track (listed as take 3) was released in 2017, but it's ramshackle and was left incomplete.

There was an unusual visitor at this session, as reported by Miles in *Many Years From Now*.

'A guy arrived at my front gate, and I said, 'Yes? Hello', because I always used to answer it to everyone. If they were boring, I would say, 'Sorry, no', and they generally went away', Paul told Miles. 'This guy said, 'I'm Jesus Christ.' I said, 'Oop', slightly shocked. I said, 'Well, you'd better come in then.' I thought, 'Well, it probably isn't. But if he is, I'm not going to be the one to turn him away.' So I gave him a cup of tea, and we just chatted, and I asked,

'Why do you think you are Jesus?' There were a lot of casualties about then. We used to get a lot of people who were maybe insecure or going through emotional breakdowns or whatever.'

Paul took the man to that evening's recording session.

'I said, 'I've got to go to a session, but if you promise to be very quiet and just sit in a corner, you can come.' So he did, he came to the session, and he did sit very quietly, and I never saw him after that. I introduced him to the guys. They said, 'Who's this?' I said, 'He's Jesus Christ.' We had a bit of a giggle over that ... But that was it. Last we ever saw of Jesus!'

'She's Leaving Home' (Lennon, McCartney)

Recorded 17 and 20 March 1967. Paul McCartney – lead vocals; John Lennon – backing vocals; Erich Gruenberg, Derek Jacobs, Trevor Williams, José Luis García – violin; John Underwood, Stephen Shingles – viola; Dennis Vigay, Alan Dalziel, Peter Halling – cello; Gordon Pearce – double bass; Sheila Bromberg – harp.

The Beatles were streets ahead of everyone else with this timeless, peerless song. Like 'A Day In The Life', 'She's Leaving Home' was inspired by a story in the *Daily Mail*. A story published on 27 February 1967 under the headline 'A Level girl dumps car and vanishes' told how Melanie Coe left home without telling her parents.

'I cannot imagine why she should run away', her father said in the article. 'She has everything here ... even her fur coat.'

'I was 17 by then and ran away, leaving a note, just like in the song', Coe told *The Guardian* in 2008. 'I went to a doctor, and he said I was pregnant, but I didn't know that before I left home. My best friend at the time was married to Ritchie Blackmore, so she hid me at their house in Holloway Road. It was the first place my parents came to look, so I ran off with my boyfriend, who was a croupier, although he had been 'in the motor trade' like it says in the song. I think my dad called up the newspapers – my picture was on the front pages. He made out that I must have been kidnapped because why would I leave? They gave me everything – coats, cars. But not love. My parents found me after three weeks, and I had an abortion.'

Remarkably, Melanie Coe had met Paul four years beforehand when she had been presented with a Beatles album as a prize for dancing on *Ready Steady Go*.

'She's Leaving Home' takes the 'Yesterday' arrangement, replacing guitar with harp and doubling the string section to an octet. Harpist Sheila Bromberg – the second woman to appear on a Beatles song after cellist Joy Hall performed on 'Strawberry Fields Forever' – was a session musician for popular artists such as Frank Sinatra, Bing Crosby, the Bee Gees, Dusty Springfield and Sammy Davis Jr. She played harp on the soundtracks for the James Bond films *Dr. No* and *Goldfinger*. The arranger was Mike Leander, who had arranged the strings on recordings by Ben E. King and The Drifters, employed because Paul was 'itching to get on with it'. Leander's strings are reserved and much less innovative than those by George Martin, such as 'Eleanor Rigby', the contemporary 'Within You Without You' and, yes, 'Yesterday'.

The basic track was recorded in six takes on 17 March 1967. Three days later, Paul and John added their vocals. Paul's lyrics are mature and filmic, like a screenplay.

Silently closing her bedroom door
Leaving the note that she hoped would say more

Paul has credited John with the composition of the 'Greek chorus', the beautiful counterpoint vocals, 'We gave her most of our lives ... We gave her everything money could buy'. The combination of voices is exquisite.

There is an odd quirk in the original mono and stereo mixes. In mono, 'She's Leaving Home' is sped up a tone, from E to F.

Both of your authors are the fathers of daughters. This might colour our response to this song, perhaps. But as parents, you do all that you can for your kids. And sometimes it's not enough, and you cannot understand why. These feelings are articulated brilliantly in this perfect song.

'Being For The Benefit Of Mr. Kite!' (Lennon, McCartney)
Recorded 17 and 20 February, 28, 29 and 31 March 1967. John Lennon – lead vocals, Hammond organ, harmonica; Paul McCartney – bass, lead guitar; George Harrison – harmonica, tambourine, backing vocals, shaker; Ringo Starr – drums, tambourine; George Martin – piano, harmonium, Lowrey organ, Wurlitzer organ, Mellotron, Hammond organ, glockenspiel; Mal Evans – bass harmonica; Neil Aspinall – harmonica.

1967 seemed to celebrate Victoriana. This song is one of the reasons.

The lyrics, famously, were taken almost verbatim from a poster for an appearance by Pablo Fanque's Circus Royal in Rochdale on 14 February 1843. John Lennon purchased the wall-hanging print at an antiques shop in Sevenoaks during the filming of a promotional film for 'Strawberry Fields Forever' on 31 January 1967. Lennon told David Scheff of *Playboy* in 1980 that he still had it in his New York home. 'Everything from the song is from that poster,' he said, 'except the horse wasn't called Henry.' The horse was called Zanthus, 'well known to be one of the best Broke Horses in the world!'

Take 4, released in 2017, is already tight. George Martin is on harmonium, Paul on bass and Ringo on drums. The released version is based on take 7, but with a new (excellent) lead vocal from John and additional backing vocals. The Beatles had quite a simple basis for an unusual and idiosyncratic new song; everything else was included to add colour to the basic track. The production work on this song is simply marvellous. Overdubs included harmonica (George Harrison, Mal Evans and Neil Aspinall), guitar (Paul), the organ solo (George Martin, 1:16 to 1:26), glockenspiel and a melange of sound swirling effects comprising cut-up recordings of fairground organs and calliope music.

At the end, the song simply swells and ends. It's as though the sound rises to the surface, bubbles briefly and vanishes before you can quite catch hold of it.

'Within You Without You' (Harrison)

Recorded 15 and 22 March, 3 April 1967. George Harrison – lead vocals, tambura, sitar, swarmandal, acoustic guitar; Anna Joshi and Amrit Gajjar – dilruba; Natwar Soni – tabla; Buddhadev Kansara and Neil Aspinall – tambura; Erich Gruenberg, Alan Loveday, Julien Gaillard, Paul Scherman, Ralph Elman, David Wolfsthal, Jack Rothstein and Jack Greene – violins; Reginald Kilbey, Allen Ford and Peter Beavan – cellos.

There are songs that announce themselves, bold and immediate, and then there are songs that quietly insist you listen on their own terms. 'Within You Without You' belongs emphatically to the latter category.

For decades, 'Within You Without You' languished in the critical wilderness, dismissed as a quirk, a five-minute distraction awkwardly lodged at the start of side two, conveniently skippable *en route* to the jaunty familiarity of 'When I'm 64'. Yet, for those willing to linger, the track reveals itself as one of The Beatles' most audacious and enduring achievements. Both of your authors, unapologetically, place it firmly within their personal top 20s.

And here's the rub: 'Within You Without You' seems forever destined to fall between two stools: love it or loathe it. George Martin, in his memoir *Summer Of Love*, neatly encapsulates its defiance of convention: "Within You Without You' is obviously a long way from your normal Western pop song. It has no harmonic structure, no chords and it doesn't modulate as Western songs generally do.'

The song is based on the Khamaj scale of Indian music. To Western ears, Khamaj sounds close to a major scale, but with one important twist: the 7th note is often flattened (lowered slightly). In simple terms, if a regular major scale feels bright and straightforward, Khamaj adds a softer, more romantic or wistful colour. We have noted elsewhere that the flattened seventh (♭7) is *everywhere* in The Beatles. It's one of the main reasons so many Beatles songs have that mix of brightness and emotional looseness: see also 'Norwegian Wood (This Bird Has Flown)', 'Hey Jude', 'Tomorrow Never Knows', 'She Said She Said', 'Paperback Writer', 'Lucy In The Sky With Diamonds' and others.

Why do we love 'Within You Without You'? Several reasons. First, it is George Harrison: every song he offered was, in its way, a marvel of the offbeat, the cleverness threaded through sincerity. Second, it is endlessly intriguing – a Liverpudlian bus driver's son meditating on the profound, drawing on Indian classical traditions with uncanny fluency. Third, it is a triumph of instrumentation, invention and studio craft.

Despite George being the only band member present on the song, it is entirely, unmistakably Beatles. Harrison's voice, tender and deliberate, floats above a meticulously arranged constellation of sound. The tamboura anchors tonality; the tabla suggests pulse; the dilruba converses with the strings, which themselves offer both counterpoint and resonance. Alan W. Pollack's notes on the instrumental section – where the dilruba and sitar trade antiphonal lines while the strings punctuate with pizzicato percussiveness – reveal just how extraordinary the arrangement is: a hybrid language of East and West, ancient and modern.

The laughter at the end was added during mixing and, according to discographical sources, came from Abbey Road's sound-effects tape library recording; the point was to lighten the almost liturgical gravity of the piece. It is also worth noting that the string overdub was the final element recorded for *Sgt. Pepper*.

The meticulous layering of timbre and rhythm produces a track of astonishing clarity and focus. Misunderstood in its own time, the song's production has aged with uncanny freshness. Its gentle insistence on a different rhythm, a different tonal logic, continues to resonate with anyone willing to abandon expectation.

'Within You Without You' has quietly, yet profoundly, influenced generations of musicians in exploring the intersections of pop, psychedelia and world music – from the chamber-pop textures of Radiohead's later work to Devendra Banhart's gentle psych-folk and the meditative, sitar-infused explorations of modern psych-pop. Were it released today – say, on a Tame Impala record – it would scarcely raise an eyebrow.

We recommend finding a quiet room, with no distractions, and listening to 'Within You Without You' on headphones – Giles Martin's 2017 mix, ideally.

'When I'm Sixty-Four' (Lennon, McCartney)

Recorded 6, 8, 20 and 21 December 1966. Paul McCartney – lead vocals, piano, bass; John Lennon – backing vocals, guitar; George Harrison – backing vocals, guitar; Ringo Starr – drums, chimes; Robert Burns and Henry MacKenzie – clarinet; Frank Reidy – bass clarinet.

Paul's father, James, turned 64 on 2 July 1966. In response, Paul recalled and completed a song that had been kicking around for a few years. It was the first McCartney composition to be brought to the *Sgt. Pepper* sessions and, as with many of Paul's songs, seems effortless.

The basic track comprises John (guitar), Paul (bass) and Ringo (drums) performing together. Paul added piano and vocals in the same session, and Ringo overdubbed snare drum. Paul would fix parts of his vocals two days later. A mixdown at this stage was released in 2017.

The track was completed across two days at the end of the month, with backing vocals, chimes and George Martin's distinctive clarinet score.

'Lovely Rita' (Lennon, McCartney)

Recorded 23-24 February, 7 and 21 March 1967. Paul McCartney – lead and backing vocals, piano, bass; John Lennon – backing vocals, acoustic guitar; George Harrison – backing vocals, acoustic guitar; Ringo Starr – drums; George Martin – piano.

After four tracks that really don't meet the 'rock' label, Paul brings us this tale of horny energy.

The basic track for 'Lovely Rita' was recorded on 23 February 1967, comprising all four Beatles playing together: Paul on piano, Ringo on drums and John and George on acoustic guitars. The guitars are very clear during the introduction – Paul's lead vocal, drums and backing vocals are added in sequence. The track at this point can be heard on the Super Deluxe edition of *Sgt. Pepper*.

Paul remained at the studio afterwards, overdubbing his bass part. The next day, Paul replaced his lead vocals. Some reports suggest that David Crosby, who visited the sessions, also sang with The Beatles on 'Lovely Rita'. Crosby is pictured at the studios singing with John, Paul and George. Mark Lewisohn, however, suggests that the backing vocals were added on 7 March. Either way, after recording their vocals – once again with the feel of The Beach Boys – the band added a kazoo sound using combs and tissue paper.

George Martin's piano solo was recorded at EMI on 21 March. 'I wanted a rippling honky-tonk piano sound,' he wrote later, 'and got this by slowing the tape speed down to 41¼ cycles, thereby reducing the pitch by three semitones. That way, I was able to play the notes I wanted at a reasonable speed. When we brought the solo back up to normal speed again, it sounded quite fast and pretty good. Even better, it still sounded like a piano and not like a harpsichord, as double-speed piano tends to do.'

The final 30 seconds descend into chaos before it reaches a climax. You'd better believe it.

'Good Morning Good Morning' (Lennon, McCartney)

Recorded 8 and 16 February, 13, 28 and 29 March 1967. John Lennon – vocals, rhythm guitar; Paul McCartney – bass, lead guitar, backing vocals, drums; George Harrison – backing vocals, lead guitar; Ringo Starr – drums, tambourine; Barrie Cameron, David Glyde and Alan Holmes – saxophone; John Lee – trombone; unknown trombone and French horn.

The inspiration for the very idiosyncratic song 'Good Morning Good Morning' comes from John's habit of watching TV. The title is taken from a commercial for Kellogg's Corn Flakes, and there is a reference to a contemporary BBC sitcom called *Meet The Wife*.

The shifting metre (counting beats within musical bars) can be broken down like this:

16 beats (4+4+4+4) – introduction
10 beats (5+5) – 'nothing to do to save his life, call his wife in'

12 beats (5+3+4) – 'Nothing to say but what a day, how's your boy been?'
9 beats (5+4) – 'Nothing to do, it's up to you, I've got...'
14 beats (3+3+4+4) – '...nothing to say but it's okay, good morning, good morning, good morning, good morning'

Take 1 was released in 2017. Ringo is incredible here until the changes in metre catch him out. Take 8 is complete and is available in slightly different mixes on both *Anthology 2* (where it runs noticeably slower) and the Super Deluxe version of *Sgt. Pepper*.

'Sgt. Pepper's Lonely Hearts Club Band (reprise)' (Lennon, McCartney)
Recorded 2 April 1967. Paul McCartney – vocals, bass, Hammond organ; John Lennon – vocals, rhythm guitar; George Harrison – vocals, lead guitar; Ringo Starr – drums, tambourine, maracas.
This short reprise of the title track was recorded in a single session, with Paul on Hammond, George and John on guitars and Ringo on drums. The bass, lead and backing vocals and percussion were added before the end of the evening.

Lasting little more than a minute, it is over almost before it begins. The inclusion of audience applause neatly bridges the gap into the album's concluding track.

'A Day In The Life' (Lennon, McCartney)
Recorded 19-20 January and 3, 10 and 22 February 1967. John Lennon – vocals, acoustic guitar, piano; Paul McCartney – vocals, piano, bass; George Harrison – maracas; Ringo Starr – drums, congas, piano; Mal Evans – piano; George Martin – harmonium; Erich Gruenberg, Granville Jones, Bill Monro, Jurgen Hess, Hans Geiger, D. Bradley, Lionel Bentley, David McCallum, Donald Weekes, Henry Datyner, Sidney Sax, Ernest Scott and Carlos Villa – violin; John Underwood, Gwynne Edwards, Bernard Davis and John Meek – viola; Francisco Gabarro, Dennis Vigay, Alan Delziel and Alex Nifosi – cello; Cyril MacArther and Gordon Pearce – double bass; John Marson – harp; Roger Lord – oboe; Basil Tschaikov and Jack Brymer – clarinet; N. Fawcett and Alfred Waters – bassoon; Clifford Seville and David Sandeman – flute; Alan Civil and Neil Sanders – French horn; David Mason, Monty Montgomery and Harold Jackson – trumpet; Raymond Brown, Raymond Premru and T. Moore – trombone; Michael Barnes – tuba; Tristan Fry – timpani; Marijke Koger – tambourine.

Grab your coat and get your hat
Leave your worry on the doorstep
Just direct your feet
To the sunny side of the street
'On The Sunny Side Of The Street' (McHugh, Fields) 1930

If anyone suggests to you that The Beatles were 'overrated', or 'just a boy band', then play them 'A Day In The Life', preferably the remix from the 2023 reissue of *1967-1970*. It remains one of the most significant and celebrated songs in pop music history.

Why?

It's the perfect collaboration between John Lennon, Paul McCartney and George Martin, with kudos to Ringo Starr and Geoff Emerick. 'A Day In The Life' represents high-concept songwriting with classical and experimental techniques layered into a rock framework. This is prog rock *in utero*. One of your authors would argue that this is their finest song of all.

Its genesis can be tightly pinpointed. The lyrics of the first verse relate to the death of Paul's friend Tara Browne. John read a story in the 17 January 1967 edition of the *Daily Mail*, which reported the ruling on a custody action over Browne's two young children. The final verse also relates to a story in the *Daily Mail*. Under the headline 'The holes in our roads', the article reads: 'There are 4,000 holes in the road in Blackburn, Lancashire, or one 26th of a hole per person, according to a council survey. If Blackburn is typical, there are two million holes in Britain's roads and 300,000 in London.'

Two days later, on 19 January, The Beatles recorded four takes in a seven-hour session between 7.30 pm and 2.30 am. From take 1, the song's complex structure is already in place, with all of John's lyrics, the 'I love to turn you on' refrain, Paul's middle part (without vocals, as he is concentrating on his tricky piano runs) and the turnaround, which takes us back to the last verse. Let's just step back and repeat that. 'A Day In The Life', its structure, lyrics and awesome arrangement, was written in two-and-a-bit days. Take 1 will send chills down your spine.

'I was in awe', engineer Geoff Emerick would write later. 'I distinctly remember thinking, Christ, John's topped himself! As Lennon sang softly, strumming his acoustic guitar, Paul accompanied him on piano. A lot of thought must have gone into the piano part because it was providing a perfect counterpoint to John's vocal and guitar playing. The song was clearly unfinished, but it was so good nonetheless that it was decided to plough ahead and get it down on tape and then finish it later. In essence, the composition was going to be structured during the recording stage. Without any conscious forethought, we were in the process of creating not just a song, but a musical work of art.'

Overdubs added bass, drums, further vocals, that multiple orchestral crescendo and the massive slam of piano and organ.

And that's where the album should end. The quirky play-out gabble and the for-dogs-only high-pitched whistle are unnecessary add-ons.

'All You Need Is Love' b/w **'Baby, You're A Rich Man'** (Single)

UK: 7 July 1967. US: 17 July 1967.

Chart positions. UK: 1. US: 1.

Immediately following the completion of *Sgt. Pepper's Lonely Hearts Club Band*, which was finished on 21 April 1967, The Beatles continued to work on a variety of songs for the next few weeks. Most of these would be released on singles and EPs throughout the rest of the year, but a few were held back for other projects.

- Tuesday 25 April 1967: 'Magical Mystery Tour'
- Wednesday 26 April 1967: 'Magical Mystery Tour'
- Thursday 27 April 1967: 'Magical Mystery Tour'
- Wednesday 3 May 1967: 'Magical Mystery Tour'
- Thursday 11 May 1967: 'Baby, You're A Rich Man'
- Friday 12 May 1967: 'All Together Now'
- Wednesday 17 May 1967: 'You Know My Name (Look Up The Number)'
- Thursday 25 May 1967: 'It's All Too Much'
- Wednesday 31 May 1967: 'It's All Too Much'
- Friday 2 June 1967: 'It's All Too Much'
- Wednesday 7 June 1967: 'You Know My Name (Look Up The Number)'
- Thursday 8 June 1967: 'You Know My Name (Look Up The Number)'

This sporadic activity culminated in sessions for the band's next single, after which they took two months off to consider buying a Greek island and for George to visit Los Angeles and San Francisco.

'All You Need Is Love' (Lennon, McCartney)
Recorded 14, 19 and 23-26 June 1967. John Lennon – vocals, rhythm guitar, harpsichord, banjo; Paul McCartney – bass, double bass, backing vocals; George Harrison – lead guitar, backing vocals; Ringo Starr – drums; George Martin – piano; Sidney Sax, Patrick Halling, Eric Bowie and John Ronayne – violins; Lionel Ross, Jack Holmes – cellos; Rex Morris and Don Honeywill – tenor saxophones; David Mason – trumpet; Stanley Woods – trumpet, flugelhorn; Evan Watkins and Harry Spain – trombones; Jack Emblow – accordion; Keith Moon – hi-hat, background vocals; Mick Jagger, Keith Richards, Eric Clapton, Marianne Faithfull, Jane Asher, Pattie Boyd, Mike McGear, Graham Nash, Hunter Davies, Gary Walker and others – background vocals

The Beatles' 15th single, 'All You Need Is Love', would be high profile indeed: it would be debuted on 25 June 1967 (and released less than two weeks later) as Britain's contribution to the first live multinational multi-satellite television production. This was conceived by the BBC and titled *Our World*. Amid footage of an iron and steel works in Linz, a feature about the Spanish fishing industry, and rehearsals in Italy for the Franco Zeffirelli film *Romeo And Juliet*, we see what appears to be the most popular band in the world recording a new song. It was one of John's, of course; Paul's suggestion was 'Your Mother Should Know'.

Knowing that the stakes were high, they wisely performed to a pre-recorded backing track, adding lead and backing vocals, Paul's bass, George's guitar solo, Ringo's drums and the orchestra during the broadcast. John re-recorded his vocals the next day.

The final result is a song of two halves, very much in John's style of joining unrelated parts together to create a unified whole. His fondness for an irregular metre is evident in the verse, with bars of 7/4, 7/4, 8/4 and 7/4. The previous year's 'She Said She Said' and the recent 'Good Morning Good Morning' are obvious precedents. Here, John sings from his heart and doesn't worry at all about where the meter falls. The chorus is sing-along and catchy in straight 4/4 and universal in its message.

As with many of The Beatles' songs in 1967, the end result owes a great deal to George Martin's arrangement and production: elements of other musical works can be heard, including the French national anthem 'La Marseillaise', and as the song fades, quotations from 'Greensleeves', Bach's 'Invention No. 8 In F Major (BWV 779)', 'In The Mood', 'Prince Of Denmark's March' (more commonly known as 'The Trumpet Voluntary') and The Beatles' own songs 'She Loves You' and 'Yesterday'. The latter two were improvised by Lennon during rehearsals.

As with all Beatles songs, sometimes context is everything. One of your authors, as a teenager in Italy in the 1990s, closely associates 'All You Need Is Love' as the theme song of the TV series *Stranamore*, a very popular if sentimental reality show which attempted to reconcile couples in crisis. Love is all you need.

'Baby, You're A Rich Man' (Lennon, McCartney)

Recorded 11 May 1967. John Lennon – lead vocals, piano, clavioline; Paul McCartney – backing vocals, bass, piano; George Harrison – backing vocals, rhythm and lead guitar, handclaps; Ringo Starr – drums, tambourine, maracas, handclaps; Eddie Kramer – vibraphone; Mick Jagger – backing vocals.

The first B-side since 'Rain', and it's another banger. 'Baby, You're A Rich Man' combines John's verse with Paul's chorus and was recorded, start to finish, in a single session at Olympic Sound studios in Barnes, to the south-west of central London.

For all its quick gestation, the track is firmly of its time. The arrangement bristles with instruments and studio effects, while the lyric circles familiar late-1960s concerns: identity in flux, the hollowness of material comfort and a voice that can't quite decide whether it's offering reassurance or mockery. In The Beatles' catalogue, it feels like a midpoint between 'And Your Bird Can Sing' and 'Hey Bulldog'.

'Baby, You're A Rich Man' is full of interest and includes some novel musical ideas.

- From 0:07 to 0:21, and elsewhere in the song, John plays a clavioline, an early type of electronic analogue synthesiser used prominently on 'Runaway'

by Del Shannon (1961) and 'Telstar' by The Tornadoes (1962). Different performances are used in different mixes.
- Harrison's lead guitar doubles the vocal line (very clearly under the choruses at 1:15-1:23 and 2:11-2:18), mirroring the role of a sarangi in an Indian khyal vocal piece, as also heard in 'Lucy In The Sky With Diamonds'.
- Lennon plays piano on the basic track. McCartney overdubbed a second part, which enters at 1:45. The difference in their playing styles is noticeable.
- This piano is heard in reverse under the third verse (1:45 to 2:13), most clearly on the 1999 mix released on *Yellow Submarine Soundtrack*.

It was used on the soundtrack of David Fincher's 2010 film *The Social Network*, augmenting an award-winning score by Trent Reznor.

'Hello, Goodbye' b/w **'I Am The Walrus'** (Single)

UK: 24 November 1967. US: 27 November 1967.
Chart positions. UK: 1. US: 1.
In which the compositional tropes of McCartney and Lennon are obviously displayed on both sides of a very popular single, which was number one in the UK for seven weeks between 6 December 1967 and 23 January 1968. It also topped charts in the United States, France, West Germany, Canada, Australia and several other countries.

'Hello, Goodbye' (Lennon, McCartney)

Recorded 2, 19, 20 and 25 October, 2 November 1967. Paul McCartney – lead vocals, backing vocals, piano, bass, bongos, conga; John Lennon – backing vocals, lead guitar, Hammond organ; George Harrison – backing vocals, lead guitar; Ringo Starr – drums, maracas, tambourine, backing vocals; Kenneth Essex and Leo Birnbaum – viola.
If 'Day Tripper' and 'We Can Work It Out' were the yin and yang of Lennon and McCartney's songwriting traits, then 'Hello, Goodbye' and 'I Am The Walrus' are polar opposites, despite being recorded more or less contemporaneously.

The basic track for 'Hello, Goodbye', recorded on 2 October, comprises Paul (piano), John (organ), George (tambourine) and Ringo (drums). Additional percussion overdubs were completed on the first day of work. An instrumental outtake of take 1 has been available on bootlegs for many years.

Seventeen days later, Paul, John and George added their lead and backing vocals, followed by John and George's tightly arranged guitars. A mix at this stage, with guitar parts that would ultimately be unused, can be heard on *Anthology 2*.

Violas would be recorded on 20 October and, finally, Paul's sprightly bass on 25 October, which he replaced on 2 November. Just over a month later, 'Hello, Goodbye' would be number one in the UK.

'Hello, Goodbye' is undeniably classic pop, although lacking any great invention – then again, one cannot dispute its commercial appeal. It was the first of four consecutive A-sides written by Paul.

'I Am The Walrus' (Lennon, McCartney)
Recorded 5-6, 27 and 29 September 1967. John Lennon – lead vocals, Pianet, Mellotron; Paul McCartney – bass, tambourine; George Harrison – electric guitar; Ringo Starr – drums; session musicians – strings, brass, and woodwinds; Ray Thomas, Mike Pinder and the Mike Sammes singers – backing vocals. King Lear read by Mark Dignam (Gloucester), Philip Guard (Edgar) and John Bryning (Oswald).
'I Am The Walrus' sealed John Lennon's descent into glorious absurdity – dense, deranged and brilliant. It's a key song in The Beatles' catalogue – it was the first to be recorded with the piano as John's primary compositional tool. The many overdubs represent a kind of organised chaos. We wonder whether Paul told John about John Cage, the American avant-garde composer who pioneered non-standard use of musical instruments, especially in the serendipitous inclusion of some lines from a radio play in the closing seconds of the mix. This was added to the song on 29 September 1967 from a live broadcast of *King Lear* on the BBC Light Programme. During the fade of the song:

3:52 Oswald (played by John Bryning): Slave, thou hast slain me. Villain, take my purse. If ever thou wilt thrive, bury my body, And give the letters which thou find'st about me to Edmund, Earl of Gloucester; seek him out upon the British party. O, untimely Death!
4:23 Edgar (Philip Guard): I know thee well: a serviceable villain; as duteous to the vices of thy mistress as badness would desire.
4:30 Gloucester (Mark Dignam): What, is he dead?
4:31 Edgar: Sit you down, father, rest you.

The song's lyrics are nonsense, of course. We're not going to attempt to analyse them – they are deliberately impenetrable and open to subjective interpretation. Enjoy them for the sound they make, not any hidden meaning. If anything, they were penned intentionally to poke fun at scholarly analyses of The Beatles' lyrics. 'I Am The Walrus' was written, so the story goes, after John learned that the English master in his high school was making his class analyse lyrics from Beatles songs. In response, it is claimed, John wrote the most confusing lyrics he could, saying, 'Let the fuckers work that one out.'

'We write lyrics, and I write lyrics that you don't realise what they mean till after', Lennon said to Jonathan Cott in November 1968. 'Especially some of the better songs or some of the more flowing ones, like 'Walrus'. I had 'I am he as you are he as we are all together'. I had just these two lines on the typewriter, and then about two weeks later, I ran through and wrote another two lines, and then, when I saw something, after about four lines, I just knocked the rest of it off. Then I had the whole verse or verse and a half, and then sang it. I had this idea of doing a song that was a police siren, but it didn't work in the end (sings like a siren) 'I-am-he-as-you-are-he-as...' You couldn't really sing the police siren.'

Inspiration came from LSD trips and Lewis Carroll's 1871 poem 'The Walrus And The Carpenter'.

'The first line was written on one acid trip one weekend', Lennon told *Playboy* in 1980. 'The second line was written on the next acid trip the next weekend, and it was filled in after I met Yoko. Part of it was putting down Hare Krishna. All these people were going on about Hare Krishna, Allen Ginsberg in particular. The reference to 'Element'ry penguin' is the elementary, naive attitude of going around chanting, 'Hare Krishna', or putting all your faith in any one idol. I was writing obscurely, a la Dylan, in those days. It's from 'The Walrus And The Carpenter'. *Alice In Wonderland*. To me, it was a beautiful poem. It never dawned on me that Lewis Carroll was commenting on the capitalist and social system. I never went into that bit about what he really meant, like people are doing with The Beatles' work. Later, I went back and looked at it and realised that the walrus was the bad guy in the story and the carpenter was the good guy. I thought, 'Oh, shit, I picked the wrong guy.' I should have said, 'I am the carpenter.' But that wouldn't have been the same, would it? (singing) 'I am the carpenter ...''

According to Hunter Davies, George Harrison thought John's line about taking her knickers down in 'I Am The Walrus' was great. 'Why can't you have people fucking as well?' Davies reported George as saying. 'It's going on everywhere in the world, all the time. So why can't you mention it? It's just a word, made up by people. It's meaningless in itself. Keep saying it – fuck, fuck, fuck, fuck, fuck, fuck, fuck. See, it doesn't mean a thing, so why can't you use it in a song? We will eventually. We haven't started yet.'

Our advice: listen to 'Working Class Hero' from John's first solo album. Some claim that 'Hey Jude' at 2:38 includes the f-bomb (it doesn't, but listen anyway). We also recommend 'Piggy In The Middle' by The Rutles.

Magical Mystery Tour EP (UK)

8 December 1967.

Chart position. 1.

Magical Mystery Tour emerged from The Beatles' (well, Paul's) desire to keep innovating after *Sgt. Pepper*. Conceived in mid-1967 as both soundtrack and experiment, it was the product of a band convinced they could conjure magic from chaos. Paul McCartney, keen to sustain momentum, floated the idea of a television film built around a psychedelic bus trip – part holiday jaunt, part acid dream. The film floundered, but the music soared. Across six tracks, the EP captures the twilight of the 'Summer Of Love'.

What began as a whimsical side project became a bridge between the Technicolor optimism of *Pepper* and the fragmentation of the *White Album*. Typical Beatles: it's a half-failed experiment that still outclassed everyone else's triumphs.

'Magical Mystery Tour' (Lennon, McCartney)
Recorded 25-27 April, 3 May 1967. Paul McCartney – lead and backing vocals, piano, bass, percussion; John Lennon – lead and backing vocals, acoustic guitar, percussion; George Harrison – backing vocals, lead guitar, percussion; Ringo Starr – drums, percussion; Mal Evans and Neil Aspinall – percussion; David Mason, Elgar Howarth, Roy Copestake and John Wilbraham – trumpet.
The *Magical Mystery Tour* film was, in essence, a mad gamble born of overconfidence and curiosity. With manager Brian Epstein gone and no adult in the room, Paul McCartney pushed ahead with an idea for a film and a series of songs loosely inspired by the coach holidays of post-war Britain – ordinary folk packed onto a bus, headed nowhere in particular. Only this time, the passengers were The Beatles.

Ken Kesey's Merry Pranksters and their 1964 'Acid Tests' had etched the template for the psychedelic road trip – the idea that you could pile a bunch of free spirits onto a bus, dose them with mind-expanding chemicals and somehow find enlightenment. Their Day-Glo school bus, Furthur, and the film *Magic Trip* that documented it all, were circulating as an underground legend by the time The Beatles got the idea for their own mystery tour. McCartney, ever the magpie, absorbed this American countercultural energy. The Beatles were no strangers to LSD by 1967, and Kesey's experiments with spontaneity and 'happenings' fit perfectly with the era's faith in chaos as creativity.

Kesey's influence explains a lot of the tone of the *Magical Mystery Tour* film: the faith in improvisation, the sense that meaning might arise from nonsense and the belief that a journey – however directionless – could be a kind of art. The Beatles tried and failed to bottle that anarchic spirit for mainstream television.

Filmed over two chaotic weeks in September 1967, the production had no proper script, just a sketchy outline scrawled in McCartney's notebook. Scenes were improvised on the spot, stitched together later with crude editing and surreal flourishes: dream sequences, slapstick interludes and colour-saturated babble. The Beatles fancied it as a kind of cinematic happening – freeform, spontaneous, a mirror to the LSD experience. What they got was something that looked half-finished, part avant-garde, part amateur home movie. When the BBC aired it on Boxing Day, in black and white no less, the British public sat bewildered. Critics panned it as self-indulgent nonsense; McCartney took the brunt of the blame. Yet, over time, the film's failure has aged into a kind of mythic charm. Beneath the muddle lies a snapshot of The Beatles at a creative crossroads – still adventurous, still fearless and, for better or worse, convinced that anything they touched could be art.

This title song acts as a fanfare, just like, in its own way, the opening chord of 'A Hard Day's Night'.

'It employs all the circus and fairground barkers', Paul said in *Many Years From Now*. "Roll up! Roll up!'... is also a reference to rolling up a joint. We were always sticking those little things in that we knew our friends would get; veiled references to drugs and to trips. 'Magical Mystery Tour is waiting to take you away,' so that's a kind of drug, 'it's dying to take you away', so that's a Tibetan *Book Of The Dead* reference.'

Contemporary views of the song are polarised. For some, it's fun and lively. For others, it stretches a thin idea to the breaking point.

Listen closely in the right-hand channel from 0:20 of the 2023 mix for some previously-buried loud and lively electric guitar by George. This sounds like a Fender Stratocaster through a cranked-up Vox.

'Your Mother Should Know' (Lennon, McCartney)

Recorded 22-23 August and 29 September 1967. Paul McCartney – lead and backing vocals, piano, bass; John Lennon – backing vocals, Hammond organ; George Harrison – backing vocals, lead guitar; Ringo Starr – drums, tambourine.

'Your Mother Should Know' is a sort-of-sequel to 'When I'm 64', with a similar nostalgic nod to music hall and a generational call-back message. Once again, we hear the echoes of Paul's father's musical adventures. Paul, no doubt encouraged, would add 'Honey Pie' and 'Maxwell's Silver Hammer' to forthcoming Beatles albums. 'Teddy Boy', thankfully, didn't make the cut for *Let It Be.*

Interestingly, 'Your Mother Should Know' has distinct similarities to a much older McCartney song called 'Catswalk', which Paul had produced for the Chris Barber Band (as 'Catcall') at Chappell Recording Studios in London the month before sessions for 'Your Mother Should Know'. They would return to Chappell for 'Your Mother Should Know'. They would be joined there by their manager, Brian Epstein, their last confirmed meeting with him before his death on 27 August.

A 16 September session at EMI was a failed attempt at a remake. Take 27 of this abandoned version can be heard on *Anthology 2*.

The song was used at the end of the *Magical Mystery Tour* TV film as part of a very silly dance sequence as The Beatles walk down a grand staircase in white evening dress (and Paul has a black carnation, conspiracy fans). John and George's distaste is evident. This scene proves that the visuals for the individual songs were great fun, especially when extracted from the home movie nonsense that surrounds them. One of your authors places this song in his list of personal favourites due to the contrast between the upbeat arrangement and the almost melancholic tone of the lyrics. Paul McCartney was full of these contrasts in his music, as our chapter on *The Beatles* will attest.

'I Am The Walrus'

Previously released as the B-side of 'Hello, Goodbye'.

'The Fool On The Hill' (Lennon, McCartney)

Recorded 25-27 September and 20 October 1967. Paul McCartney – vocals, piano, acoustic guitar, recorder, bass, penny whistle; John Lennon – classical guitar, harmonica, Jew's harp; George Harrison – 12-string acoustic guitar, harmonica; Ringo Starr – drums, maracas, finger cymbals; Christopher Taylor, Richard Taylor and Jack Ellory – flutes.

Sheer class from Paul McCartney here, as he effortlessly takes a D major 6th chord and composes it out to fashion a complete and brilliant song. Its lyrical theme reflects both 'Eleanor Rigby' and 'She's Leaving Home': lonely, alienated isolation. Similarly, there are classical trimmings, this time flutes, recorder and penny whistle.

George Martin, in *Summer Of Love*: 'Paul ... never fell back upon the conventional clichés of songwriting. He would forever be coming up with a little musical twist that made a song or a phrase severely more interesting to listen to. 'The Fool On The Hill' has a basic melody, but at the end of what would, conventionally, have been the verse, the song does not stop to mark the transition into the chorus. The 'verse' section flows on, seamlessly, effortlessly, unnoticeably, into the next element:

> And he doesn't know the answer,
> But the fool on the hill,
> Sees the sun going down...

The song switches to D minor here ('the saddest of all the keys'), and as Alan W Pollock suggests, the text painting is 'quite chilling', like clouds covering the sun on an otherwise bright day.

John Lennon was also complimentary, saying in his 1980 interview with *Playboy* magazine, 'Now that's Paul. Another good lyric. Shows he's capable of writing complete songs.'

The 'fool' in the title possibly refers to the Dutch design collective who worked closely with The Beatles in this period, painting George Harrison's Mini, John Lennon's piano and a three-storey psychedelic mural on the outside of the Apple Boutique on Baker Street. The group was named in reference to the Fool tarot card. Or it might be Paul referring to himself as just a simple guy.

One cannot help but smile at the fact that The Beatles had just met Maharishi Mahesh Yogi and, within months, John would write 'Sexy Sadie', who 'made a fool of everyone'. 'I think I was writing about someone like Maharishi', Paul said in *Many Years From Now*. 'His detractors called him a fool. Because of his giggle, he wasn't taken too seriously. It was this idea of a fool on the hill, a guru in a cave, I was attracted to ... I was sitting at the piano at my father's house in Liverpool, hitting a D 6th chord, and I made up 'Fool On The Hill"

For a cover version with a difference, track down Björk's first solo album from 1977 (not a typo) in which she sings the song in Icelandic with the title 'Álfur ÚtÚr Hól'.

'Flying' (Harrison, Lennon, McCartney, Starkey)

Recorded 8 and 28 September 1967. John Lennon – vocals, Mellotron, Hammond organ; Paul McCartney – vocals, bass, guitar; George Harrison – vocals, guitar; Ringo Starr – vocals, drums, maracas.

'Flying' is surely the slightest of all Beatles tracks, but it's not without some period charm. Here we have a simple 12-bar blues. It consists of little more than four repeats of a very elementary 31-second musical phrase. This being The Beatles, of course, there is lots of invention to keep our attention.

It's the band's first-released instrumental for EMI, after 'Cry For A Shadow' (released by Polydor) and the then-unheard '12-Bar Original'.

Initially entitled 'Aerial Tour Instrumental', it was originally over nine minutes in length, extended by several minutes of tape loops.

'Blue Jay Way' (Harrison)

Recorded 6-7 September and 6 October 1967. George Harrison – vocals, Hammond organ; John Lennon – backing vocals, Hammond organ; Paul McCartney – backing vocals, bass; Ringo Starr – drums, tambourine; Peter Willison- cello.

Blue Jay Way is a street in the Hollywood Hills above Los Angeles. As the story goes, George Harrison had arrived from London and was struggling to stay awake as he waited for his friend, the music publicist Derek Taylor, to find his way to the house at 1567 Blue Jay Way.

These somnambulistic, almost hallucinatory, origins carry over into the song. It does sound like George is trying really hard to stay awake.

'Blue Jay Way' was written on Hammond organ, almost entirely on a single chord. It uses many traits of Indian music, including a later cello overdub that mimics an Indian sarod. The cellist Richard Willison is quoted as having completed the session directly after a performance at the Royal Albert Hall. That venue's archives show a concert by the Irish group The Dubliners on the night in question.

The production employs some of the favourite tricks of 1967: flanging, delay, Leslie wobble and reversed tapes. It's weird, but it's George, so we forgive anything.

Depending on your mood, 'Blue Jay Way' can be yearning and hypnotic, a colourful, exotic rush of sensation; or just boring and unfocused (sequencing it after 'Flying' doesn't help).

The performance clip from the *Magical Mystery Tour* film is marvellously unhinged.

Magical Mystery Tour (US album)

27 November 1967.
Chart position. 1.
'Magical Mystery Tour', 'Your Mother Should Know', 'I Am The Walrus', 'The Fool On The Hill', 'Flying', 'Blue Jay Way', 'Hello Goodbye', 'Strawberry Fields Forever', 'Penny Lane', 'Baby, You're A Rich Man', 'All You Need Is Love'

In the UK, the songs from *Magical Mystery Tour* were released as a double EP with just the six songs from the film. In the US, Capitol expanded it into a full-length LP by adding three A-sides and two B-sides from 1967 that had not yet appeared on a US album.

Here was perhaps the one time that Capitol got it right with the extracurricular Beatles albums. Because of its completeness and undoubted strength, the US version eventually became the canonical version adopted in CD reissues and later digital releases worldwide.

1968

'Lady Madonna' b/w **'The Inner Light'** (Single)

UK: 15 March 1968. US: 18 March 1968.
Chart positions. UK: 1. US: 4.

The Beatles recorded four songs during five days of sessions in February 1968. These sessions were expressly booked to produce a new single for release during a planned two-month stay in India.

- Saturday 3 February 1968: recording 'Lady Madonna' and 'Across The Universe'
- Sunday 4 February 1968: recording 'Across The Universe'
- Tuesday 6 February 1968: overdubs to 'The Inner Light' (backing track recorded in India in January 1968) and 'Lady Madonna'
- Thursday 8 February 1968: overdubs to 'The Inner Light' and 'Across The Universe'
- Sunday 11 February 1968: recording 'Hey Bulldog'

'Lady Madonna' and 'The Inner Light' got the nod as the A- and B-sides of the single. The other songs were put to one side, for now.

'Lady Madonna' (Lennon, McCartney)

Recorded 3 and 6 February 1968. Paul McCartney – lead vocals, piano, bass, handclaps; John Lennon – backing vocals, lead guitar, handclaps; George Harrison – backing vocals, lead guitar, handclaps; Ringo Starr – drums, handclaps; Ronnie Scott and Bill Povey – tenor saxophone; Harry Klein and Bill Jackman – baritone saxophone.

'Lady Madonna' was the first hint of the 'back to basics' approach that would drive the band's sessions over the next 12 months. It's pure piano-driven rock 'n' roll leaning heavily on Humphrey Littleton's 'Bad Penny Blues', a minor hit single from 1956. The piano playing is astounding: Paul must have been practicing a lot in the previous months.

We also have a saxophone solo by Ronnie Scott. Yes, that Ronnie Scott. Fellow saxophonist Harry Klein spoke to Beatles scholar Mark Lewisohn about the session for his book *The Complete Beatles Recording Sessions*. He said, 'I was in the bath at about 6:30 in the evening when Laurie [Gold, a session fixer employed by EMI] called and said, 'Are you working tonight?' 'No, I'm in the bath!' 'Well, get over to EMI as quick as you can' ... when I got to Abbey Road, Ronnie was there, along with Bill Jackman and Bill Povey. Paul didn't recognise Ronnie Scott until we told him who he was.'

Scott wasn't given an arrangement for his solo, which is perhaps why his playing (1:02-1:14) sounds so pissed off.

Paul's vocals are clearly influenced by Fats Domino (listen again to 'Ain't That A Shame'), and his lyrics might be a response to Domino's 'Blue Monday'. Compare:

> Here come Wednesday, I'm beat to my socks
> My gal calls, got to tell her that I'm out
> 'Cause Thursday is a hard workin' day
> And Friday I get my pay

With:

> Friday night arrives without a suitcase
> Sunday morning creeping like a nun
> Monday's child has learned to tie his bootlace
> See how they run

Paul later admitted that he'd forgotten to include Saturday. This being Paul McCartney, the music is effortlessly melodic, even when switching between just two chords in the verses. Macca's bass-playing here is superlative.

Dominic Pedler: "Lady Madonna' [is] The Beatles' Most Perfect Bridge. While there are arguably dozens of candidates for that title, the thinking was that, with the intricate mechanics of its modulation, which mixes simple textbook theory with breathtaking novelty, it neatly encapsulates exactly what a middle should be in a three-minute pop song.'

Actually, two minutes and 16 seconds.

'The Inner Light' (Harrison)

Recorded 13 January, 6 and 8 February 1968. George Harrison – lead vocals; John Lennon – backing vocals; Paul McCartney – backing vocals; Aashish Khan – sarod; Hanuman Jadev – shehnai; Hariprasad Chaurasia – bansuri; Mahapurush Misra – pakhavaj; Rijram Desad – harmonium; uncredited – tablatarang.

'The Inner Light', a magnificent B-side, combines a backing track recorded in Bombay (now Mumbai), India, as part of sessions for George's album *Wonderwall Music*, with instrumental and vocal overdubs in London.

The track utilises Indian instruments such as sarod (stringed cello-like instrument), shehnai (oboe), bansuri (wooden flute) and pakhavaj (hand drum). Lennon and McCartney appear as just a four-word overdub ('do all without doing'). It was the first George Harrison song to be selected for a single B-side, an important development in The Beatles' power shift in 1968-1969.

Fun fact: 'The Inner Light' is also the title of season 5, episode 25 of *Star Trek: The Next Generation*, first broadcast in June 1992. It uses some of the themes from chapter 47 of the *Tao Te Ching*, one of the inspirations for George Harrison's lyrics.

> Without going outside his door, one understands all that takes place under the sky; without looking out from his window, one sees the Tao of Heaven. The farther that one goes out from himself, the less he knows. Therefore, the

sages got their knowledge without travelling; gave their right names to things without seeing them; and accomplished their ends without any purpose of doing so.

'Hey Jude' b/w **'Revolution'** (Single)
UK: 30 August 1968. US: 26 August 1968.
Chart positions. UK: 1. US: 1.
The Beatles' return from India heralded a major sea change. They reconvened in late May at George's house, Kinfauns in Esher, to showcase their new compositions and prepare for their next album. One of these, 'Julia', includes the line 'Ocean child calls me', a reference to the Japanese artist Yoko Ono, whom John had first met in November 1966. They had consummated their relationship at the beginning of May 1968.

Sessions would stretch over the next four-and-a-half months, from 30 May to 14 October 1968. Ono would be present throughout, thus disturbing the equilibrium of The Beatles' first six years as a studio band.

Paul's 'Hey Jude' was the first song to be heard from these sessions, released on their own Apple label in August 1968.

'Hey Jude' (Lennon, McCartney)
Recorded 31 July, 1 August 1968. Paul McCartney – lead vocals, piano, bass, handclaps; John Lennon – backing vocals, guitar, handclaps; George Harrison – backing vocals, guitar, handclaps; Ringo Starr – backing vocals, drums, tambourine, handclaps; uncredited 36-piece orchestra.

> Powered by McCartney's genuinely soulful vocals, 'Hey Jude' embraced its listeners, supplying an object lesson in communal redemption and consolation that America desperately needed in the summer of '68.
> Simon Philo, ***British Invasion: The Crosscurrents Of Musical Influence*** (2014)

'Hey Jude' looms so large in The Beatles' canon that it's tempting to step back and say nothing.

It was composed for Lennon's son Julian, with whom Paul McCartney had developed a warm relationship. The song's original title was 'Hey Jules', and it was written to comfort Julian from the stress of his parents' separation. It didn't form part of the Kinfauns demos, therefore its composition can be pinpointed as June-July 1968 at around the same time that he started a relationship with Linda Eastman: he may well have been singing to himself as much as to Julian (or John, who assumed it was about him).

Keen to make the best-possible recording, the band booked Trident Studios in London. EMI was still using 4-track recording at that time, and Trident offered 8-track recording. They would return there for 'Dear Prudence' (28-30 August 1968), 'Honey Pie' (1-4 October 1968), 'Savoy Truffle' (3-5 October 1968) and 'Martha My Dear' (4-5 October 1968), and also initial sessions for 'I Want You (She's So Heavy)' (22 February 1969). Apple artists such as Jackie Lomax, Mary Hopkin, Billy Preston and Badfinger recorded there in 1968-1969.

The lineup on the basic track, recorded on 31 July 1968, was Paul McCartney on piano and lead vocals, John Lennon on acoustic guitar, George Harrison on electric guitar and Ringo Starr on drums. Overdubs took place the following day: bass guitar, backing vocals and a 36-piece orchestra.

The song offers a sharp lesson in how to stretch simple materials across a vast canvas and how harmony, bass and orchestration can be used to shape contrast and structure. Rather than the usual verse-chorus cycle, The Beatles build the track as a binary form: first, a fully realised, hymn-like song; then an extended mantra set over a static chord sequence. The second half alone runs through 19 repetitions of the same line, ebbing away mid-phrase as the record fades. The lyric here is little more than 'na-na' sung straight on the beat, but over it Paul throws in improvised cries – half-sung, half-screamed – that push the mantra into something closer to incantation. And yet, despite its excessive length, the song never outstays its welcome.

'Hey Jude' was a massive hit: number one in the US for nine weeks, number one for 13 weeks in Australia and a chart-topper all over the world. It was also the band's 15th number one in their home country (or 16th if you add 'Please Please Me', which you should). By the end of 1968, the music weekly *NME* reported that sales had reached nearly six million copies worldwide.

Its communal message and sing-along finale mean that 'Hey Jude' remains one of The Beatles' most popular and enduring songs.

Some suggest that The Beatles drop an f-bomb at 2.58. We think it's Paul saying, 'coming up now', or similar, to indicate the start of the coda.

'Revolution' (Lennon, McCartney)

Recorded 9, 11 and 13 July 1968. John Lennon – vocals, lead guitar, handclaps; Paul McCartney – bass, Hammond organ, handclaps; George Harrison – lead guitar, handclaps; Ringo Starr – drums, handclaps; Nicky Hopkins – electric piano

Boom. John Lennon's loud and dirty guitar kicks off this basic rocker, a faster, more urgent version of the first song recorded for *The Beatles* (later released as 'Revolution 1'). The lyrics eschew the abstract of the previous year's psychedelia for something much more direct, although expressing doubt about the methods and tactics of a number of protests in the UK, Poland, France and elsewhere.

> You say you got a real solution. Well, you know. We'd all love to see the plan.
> You ask me for a contribution. Well, you know. We're all doin' what we can.

The Beatles play their traditional instrumentation, with the guitars compressed, limited, red hot and plugged directly into the mixing console.

John is playing his Epiphone Casino, George has chosen his Gibson SG and Paul is playing a Fender Jazz bass. There is added electric piano by session maestro Nicky Hopkins.

The song is based on the familiar blues progression in B, but with a neat switch to a minor key at 'But when you talk about destruction/Don't you know that you can count me out?'

Originally available only in mono, it was remixed for stereo in December 1969 for the *Hey Jude* album and is easily available on *1967-1970* and *Past Masters*. John Lennon preferred the mono mix, as do we.

In 1987, 'Revolution' made history of sorts as the first Beatles recording to be licensed for use in a television commercial. The sports equipment manufacturer Nike paid $500,000 for the right to use the song, but the surviving Beatles objected, and the dispute was settled out of court in 1989.

The Beatles (The White Album)

UK: 22 November 1968. US: 25 November 1968.
Chart positions. UK: 1. US: 1.

By the end of 1968, rock music dominated the *Billboard* album listings. Rock albums spent a total of 44 weeks at number one that year: only three acts would buck the trend: jazz trumpeter Herb Alpert, French orchestra leader Paul Mauriat and the peerless Glen Campbell.

The Beatles includes not only lots of loud rock music but nearly every other style of contemporary popular music: blues, country & western, heavy metal, folk, soul, vaudeville and baroque. Despite this, it has a distinct rawness throughout, a dryer and simpler sound which contrasts deeply with the band's music from 1967 and points towards the stripped-back sounds of the *Get Back* sessions.

It might be raw, but it's not ragged. The Fab Four were arguably at the peak of their creativity here: whether it's Paul's complex storytelling ('Ob-La-Di, Ob-La-Da', 'Honey Pie' and 'Rocky Racoon') and off-the-cuff minimalism ('Wild Honey Pie' and 'Why Don't We Do It In The Road?'), or George's two-sided spiritualism, applying human emotions to his guitar with the one hand ('While My Guitar Gently Weeps') and pigs with the other ('Piggies'), whilst dropping arguably his best-ever Beatles song half-hidden at the end of side three ('Long, Long, Long'), or John's mixed messages of a soul in turmoil from the brutal ('Happiness Is A Warm Gun') to the tender ('Julia') via self-introspection ('I'm So Tired') to the world's most widely owned avant-garde artwork ('Revolution 9'), *The Beatles* has it all. Even Ringo's first-ever song, the charming 'Don't Pass Me By'.

They started with a series of demos, recorded at George's house in May 1968. Twenty-eight songs were recorded, mostly written in India on acoustic guitars. Paul later claimed to have penned 15 songs during his five-week stay. These demos, released in 2018, are therefore very basic and the antithesis of the band's psychedelic music from 1966 and 1967. Of these, 21 would be recorded for *The Beatles*, two were held over for *Abbey Road* and a couple more appeared on solo albums. The Beatles, of course, continued to write new songs as the album sessions progressed.

All of this new material required a double album. *The Beatles* wasn't the first double album in rock music – both Bob Dylan and The Mothers Of Invention preceded it – but, at that time, it was the longest and most successful. A flurry of others followed over the next year or so: *Love Is* By The Animals; The Bee Gees' *Odessa*; Donovan's *A Gift From A Flower To A Garden*; *Sweet Child* By Pentangle; *Electric Ladyland* By The Jimi Hendrix Experience; The Incredible String Band's *Wee Tam And The Big Huge*; The Rascals' *Freedom Suite*; *Trout Mask Replica* By Captain Beefheart And His Magic Band; *Out Here* By Love; Golden Earring's *On The Double*; The Small Faces' *Autumn Stone*; Chicago's *The Chicago Transit Authority*; The Who's *Tommy*. The following decade brought major statements such as *Exile On Main Street*, *Quadrophenia*, *Goodbye Yellow Brick Road*, *Tales From Topographic Oceans*, *The Lamb Lies Down On Broadway* and *The Wall*.

One can argue whether all of these maintain interest across four sides of vinyl. There have been many debates about whether you can make a coherent single album from each of these releases, some of them justified. But do *you* think you can edit *The Beatles* into a single album? We tried ... three times.

An obvious approach to selecting the 'best' songs. Here's a 51-minute playlist.

Side One: 'Back In The USSR', 'Dear Prudence', 'While My Guitar Gently Weeps', 'Martha My Dear', 'I'm So Tired', 'Blackbird', 'Happiness Is A Warm Gun', 'Long, Long, Long'
Side Two: 'Birthday', 'Yer Blues', 'Mother Nature's Son', 'Everybody's Got Something To Hide...', 'Sexy Sadie', 'Helter Skelter', 'Cry Baby Cry', 'I Will', 'Julia'

Plus EP (12 minutes)

'Ob-La-Di, Ob-La-Da', 'The Continuing Story Of Bungalow Bill', 'Don't Pass Me By', 'Piggies'

Or, to tackle the sometimes bewildering diversity of styles, we can split the album into two: a pop/acoustic album and a rock album.

The Pop/Acoustic Album (45 minutes)
Side One: 'Dear Prudence', 'Ob-La-Di, Ob-La-Da', 'Wild Honey Pie', 'The Continuing Story of Bungalow Bill', 'Martha My Dear', 'Blackbird', 'Piggies', 'Rocky Raccoon'
Side Two: 'Don't Pass Me By', 'I Will', 'Julia', 'Mother Nature's Son', 'Sexy Sadie', 'Long, Long, Long', 'Honey Pie', 'Good Night'

The Rock Album (48 minutes)
Side One: 'Revolution 1', 'Glass Onion', 'While My Guitar Gently Weeps', 'Happiness Is A Warm Gun', 'I'm So Tired', 'Why Don't We Do It In The Road?', 'Birthday', 'Yer Blues', 'Everybody's Got Something To Hide Except Me And My Monkey'
Side Two: 'Back In The USSR', 'Cry Baby Cry', 'Savoy Truffle', 'Revolution 9', 'Helter Skelter'

There's no doubt that a collection of The Beatles' loud songs from 1968 would have been one of the best-ever rock 'n' roll albums.

Or, we could add 'A Beginning', 'Not Guilty', 'Sour Milk Sea', 'Hey Jude', 'Revolution' and 'What's The New Mary Jane?' to the existing track list to have a triple album.

Side One: 'Back In The USSR', 'Dear Prudence', 'Glass Onion', 'Ob-La-Di, Ob-La-Da', 'Wild Honey Pie', 'The Continuing Story Of Bungalow Bill', 'While My Guitar Gently Weeps' (21 minutes)
Side Two: 'Martha My Dear', 'I'm So Tired', 'Blackbird', 'Piggies', 'Rocky Racoon', 'Happiness Is A Warm Gun', 'Long, Long, Long' (18 minutes)
Side Three: 'A Beginning', 'Don't Pass Me By', 'Not Guilty', 'Revolution', 'Why Don't We Do It In The Road?', 'I Will', 'Julia' (19 minutes)
Side Four: 'Birthday', 'Yer Blues', 'Mother Nature's Son', 'Sour Milk Sea', 'Everybody's Got Something To Hide...', 'Hey Jude' (23 minutes)
Side Five: 'Revolution 1 (full-length take)', 'Revolution 9', 'What's The New Mary Jane?' (19 minutes)
Side Six: 'Sexy Sadie', 'Helter Skelter', 'Honey Pie', 'Savoy Truffle', 'Cry Baby Cry', 'Good Night' (21 minutes)

I'm sure all readers have their own ideas on how (or whether) to condense a sprawling 30-track album into a more cohesive statement. Then again, as Paul said, 'it's the bloody *White Album*! Shut up!'

The Beatles took almost five months to record. The band worked for 77 days between May and October 1968, with several more for mixing and editing. During this time, their personal relationships were starting to unravel along with the chaos of their business dealings. The connections that had bound them together for so long were broken, and this can be heard in both the songwriting (no collaborations at all) and the recording process. We note that John appears on only 22 of the songs on the album and Ringo on only 21. Less than half of the 30 tracks feature all four of The Beatles: 'Glass Onion', 'The Continuing Story Of Bungalow Bill', 'While My Guitar Gently Weeps', 'Happiness Is A Warm Gun', 'I'm So Tired', 'Birthday', 'Yer Blues', 'Everybody's Got Something To Hide Except Me And My Monkey', 'Sexy Sadie', 'Helter Skelter', 'Long, Long, Long', 'Revolution 1', 'Cry Baby Cry'. There's another possible track list for a single *White Album*.

The Beatles' final photo shoot, 22 August 1969, at John Lennon's Tittenhurst Park estate. This occurred just two days after their last recording session together, marking the final time all four members gathered for band-related activities.

Left: 'Strawberry Fields Forever'/'Penny Lane' single, released on the Odeon Records label in several European markets in 1967. (*EMI*)

Right: The iconic front cover of *Sgt. Pepper's Lonely Hearts Club Band*, designed by Peter Blake and Jann Haworth. The elaborate collage features The Beatles in colourful band uniforms surrounded by dozens of cultural figures. (*EMI*)

Left: Cardboard cut-outs included with early pressings of *Sgt. Pepper's Lonely Hearts Club Band*, designed by Peter Blake. Fans could punch out the moustache, badges and stand-up figures. (*EMI*)

Right: The American LP edition of *Magical Mystery Tour*, issued by Capitol Records in late 1967. It expanded the group's British double EP into a full album. (*EMI*)

Left: The British single of 'All You Need Is Love', backed with 'Baby, You're A Rich Man' and released on Parlophone in July 1967. (*EMI*)

Right: The British single of 'Hey Jude', the first release on the group's own Apple Records label. Backed with 'Revolution', it became one of the band's biggest international hits. (*EMI/Apple*)

Above: The interior gatefold photograph of *Sgt. Pepper's Lonely Hearts Club Band*, showing The Beatles posed against a vivid yellow backdrop. (*EMI*)

Right: 19 May 1967, the launch of *Sgt. Pepper's Lonely Hearts Club Band* at Brian Epstein's house, 24 Chapel Street, London. (*Alamy*)

Left: George, Ringo and John recording *Sgt. Pepper's Lonely Hearts Club Band* at EMI Studios in spring 1967. (*Henry Grossman/Govinda Gallery/Washington Post*)

Right: Paul McCartney conducts the orchestra during the recording of 'A Day In The Life', while Mick Jagger watches from the studio floor, 10 February 1967. (*Alamy*)

Below: The Beatles and their partners in India during the spring of 1968, where much of their next album would be written. (*Paul Saltzman*)

Right: Paul McCartney at the mixing desk during sessions for the *White Album* as George Martin and Ringo Starr look on. (*Linda McCartney*)

Left: The stark minimalist sleeve of *The Beatles* – commonly known as the *White Album*. Designed by Richard Hamilton, the cover intentionally contrasted the elaborate artwork of *Sgt. Pepper*. (*EMI/Apple*)

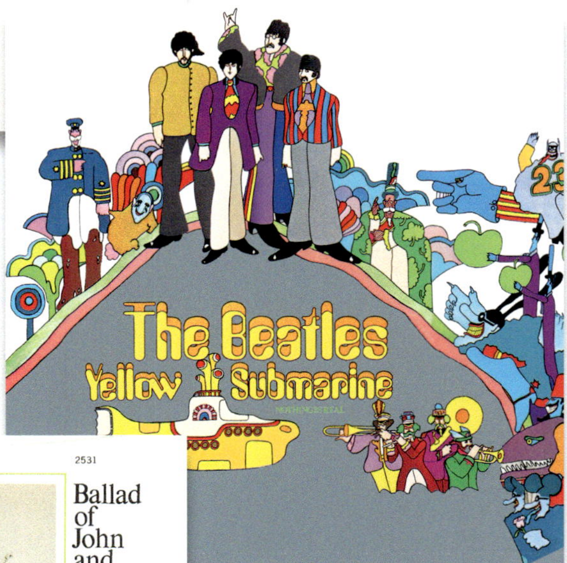

Right: The soundtrack album to the animated film *Yellow Submarine*, released in 1969 as *Yellow Submarine*. One side featured new songs by The Beatles, while the other contained orchestral score pieces by George Martin. (*EMI/Apple*)

Left: The single of 'The Ballad Of John And Yoko', a chronicle of the marriage and media attention surrounding John Lennon and Yoko Ono. (*EMI/Apple*)

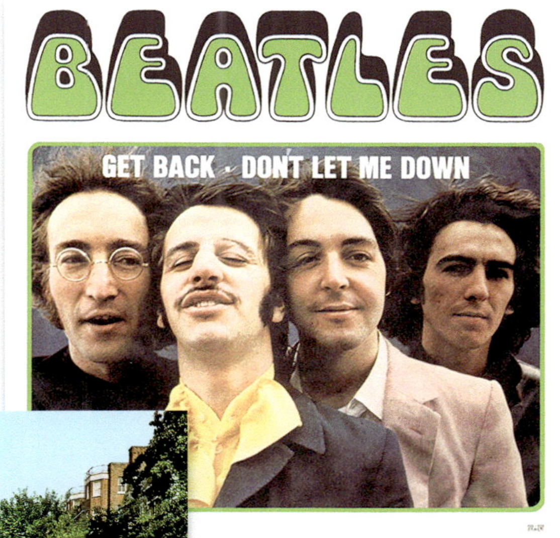

Right: The British single of 'Get Back', issued on Apple Records. Credited to 'The Beatles with Billy Preston', it was recorded during the band's January 1969 sessions. (*EMI/Apple*)

Left: The famous cover of *Abbey Road* shows the band stepping onto the zebra crossing outside Abbey Road Studios. The photograph became one of the most recognisable images in popular music. (*EMI/Apple*)

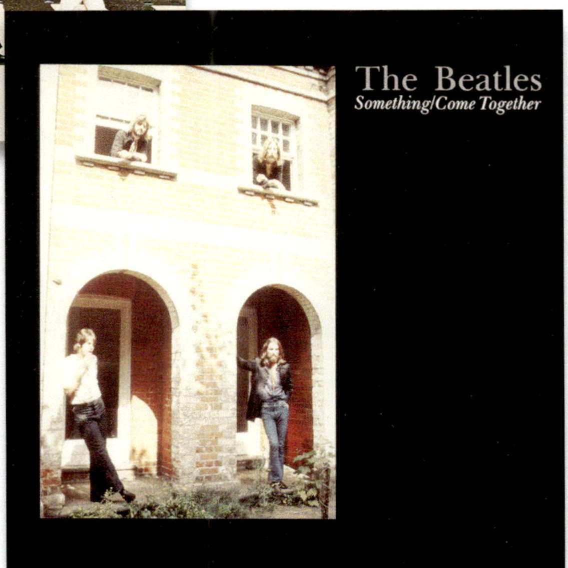

Right: The British single of 'Something', issued as a double A-side with 'Come Together'. It became the first song written by George Harrison to be released as a single A-side. (*EMI/Apple*)

Above: Paul McCartney with his longtime friend and assistant Mal Evans in India, early 1968. (*Bettmann/Bettmann Archive*)

Right: Paul meets Linda Eastman for the second time, 19 May 1967, at the press launch for *Sgt. Pepper's Lonely Hearts Club Band*. (*John Pratt/ Getty Images*)

Left: John with Eric Clapton at the recording of *Rock and Roll Circus* in December 1968. (*Chris Walter/ Wireimage*)

Right: The *Get Back* sessions in Apple Studios, January 1969. The beginning of a traumatic year. (*Ethan A Russell*)

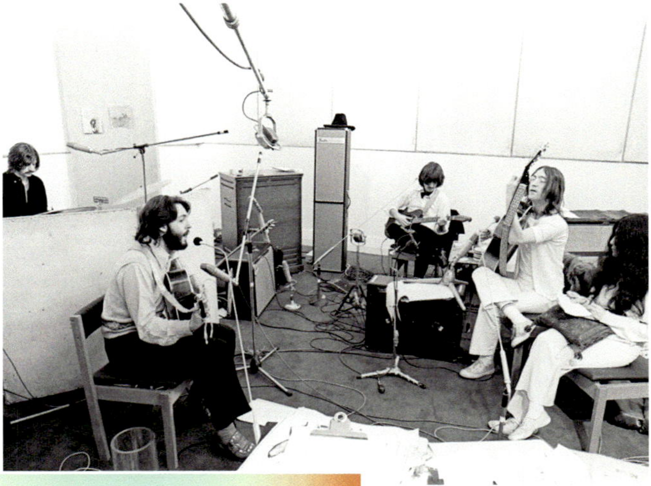

Left: The Beatles during the *Get Back* rehearsals at Twickenham Film Studios, January 1969. (*Linda McCartney*)

Right: Mixing *Get Back* at Apple Studios. L-R: Ringo Starr, George Martin, Paul McCartney, George Harrison, Yoko Ono and John Lennon. (*Apple Corps*)

Left: The American compilation album *Hey Jude*, released by Capitol Records to gather non-album singles and B-sides for the US market. (*EMI/Apple*)

Right: *Let It Be*, the final album released by The Beatles. Mostly compiled from the group's 1969 recording sessions, it accompanied the documentary film of the same name. (*EMI/Apple*)

Left: The US single of 'The Long And Winding Road', produced with orchestral overdubs by Phil Spector. It became the band's final number-one single in the United States. (*EMI/Apple*)

Right: The compilation *1962-1966* – often called the *Red* album – collects highlights from the band's early career. (*EMI/Apple*)

Left: Companion compilation *1967-1970* – known as the *Blue* album – covers the group's later recordings. (*EMI/Apple*)

Right: *Rarities*, issued to gather previously hard-to-find tracks and alternate versions. (*EMI*)

Right: Billy Preston's arrival helped ease tensions during the *Get Back* sessions.

Left: The Beatles' rooftop concert atop Apple headquarters, 30 January 1969 – the group's final public performance. They passed the audition. (*Express/Getty Images*)

Right: 22 August 1969. George cannot force a smile. (*Apple Corps*)

Right: Abbey Road sessions, 8 August 1969, adding Moog synthesiser overdubs to several tracks. (*Apple Corps*)

Left: The Amsterdam bed-in, March 1969, later described in *The Ballad Of John & Yoko*. (*Eric Koch/ National Archives of the Netherlands*)

Right: An outtake from the famous photo session on 8 August 1969. (*Apple Corps*)

This page: The three double-album sets – *Anthology 1*, *Anthology 2* and *Anthology 3* – issued as part of the multimedia The Beatles Anthology project. (*EMI/Apple*)

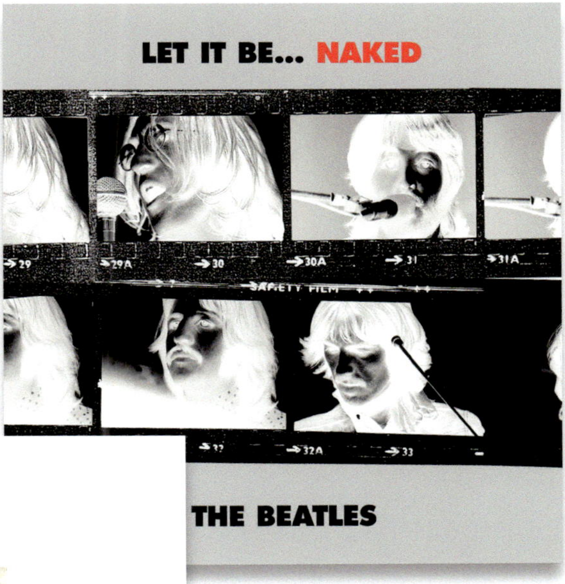

Right: *Let It Be ... Naked* presents the original 1969 recordings without the orchestral overdubs added for the 1970 release. (*EMI/Apple*)

Left: 'Now And Then', completed using modern audio technology from a demo recorded by John Lennon. The track reunited the voices and performances of all four Beatles. (*EMI/Apple*)

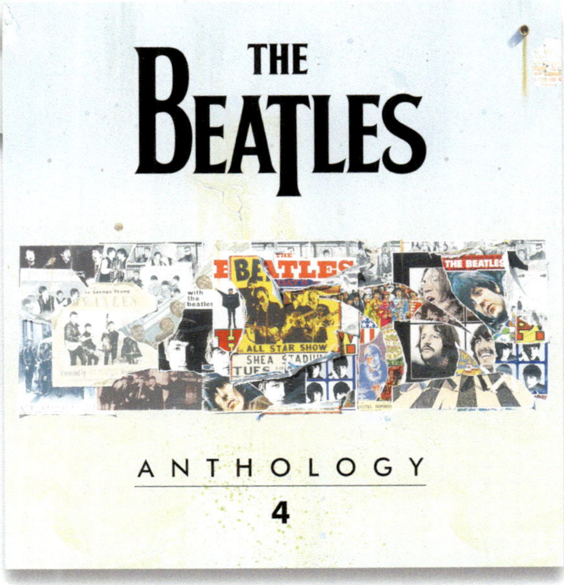

Right: The fourth volume of the Anthology project, a continuation of the archival series. (*EMI/Apple*)

Above: Paul, George and Ringo recording 'Now And Then' at Paul's studio in Sussex on 23 June 1994.

Below: Ringo and Paul, 2023. 'Now and then, I miss you. Oh, now and then. I want you to be there for me. Always to return to me.'

Hidden amongst the remaining tracks are songs which hint at the individual members' future solo careers: 'Wild Honey Pie' and 'Why Don't We Do It In The Road' would sit happily on *McCartney*, 'Julia' could easily grace *John Lennon/Plastic Ono Band*, 'Savoy Truffle' would not be out of place on *All Things Must Pass* and 'Don't Pass Me By' and 'Good Night' would slot into *Beaucoups Of Blues* and *Sentimental Journey*.

The Beatles is perhaps the band's most beguiling, intriguing, frustrating, uneven and brilliant collection of songs. It's chaotic yet meticulously constructed. Yes, the album's diversity is its strength, but it's also what makes it, at times, a maddening listen. For every iconic track, there's a lesser-known, often underwhelming moment. 'Wild Honey Pie' is a curiously maddening snippet of nonsense; 'The Continuing Story Of Bungalow Bill' seems to exist purely as a strange experiment in whimsy. Even within the greatest tracks, there's a feeling that The Beatles are pushing the boundaries of their sound without always knowing where they'll land. But it is remarkable in its fearlessness. It's a snapshot of four men throwing everything they can into the creative cauldron. There's a sense of spontaneity here, an urgency to capture everything that was in their minds before it vanished. The result is a work that resonates with raw energy and an unmistakable sense of ambition. Perhaps what makes *The Beatles* so endlessly fascinating is its imperfections. It feels like a true representation of The Beatles at their most human: their brilliance on full display, but so too their contradictions, their fragility and their occasional missteps. It's not an album designed for easy listening, but rather an invitation into the strange, often tumultuous universe of a band at the height of their powers.

For all its eccentricities, *The Beatles* remains one of the most compelling and complex works of popular music.

Early UK copies of The Beatles were individually numbered on the front sleeve. Ringo Starr's copy, 0000001, was auctioned in 2015 for $790,000.

'Back In The USSR' (Lennon, McCartney)

Recorded 22-23 August 1968. Paul McCartney – lead and backing vocals, piano, bass, drums, lead guitar, handclaps, percussion; John Lennon – backing vocals, rhythm guitar, six-string bass, handclaps, drums, percussion; George Harrison – backing vocals, rhythm and lead guitars, bass, drums, handclaps, percussion.

'Back In The USSR' adds the music of Chuck Berry – 'Back In The USA' (1959) is the obvious starting point – to the vocal and lyrical traits of The Beach Boys ... 'Surfin' USA', indeed.

That Beach Boys connection is no accident. Mike Love, one of the band's singers, was present in India and claims to have suggested that Paul should write a bridge section that mirrored 'California Girls' (1965). Macca added 'Ukraine girls' and 'Moscow girls'. Love has been claiming royalty payments ever since.

Is it a political song? Was Paul McCartney sympathetic to socialism? Does it provide evidence of The Beatles' pro-Soviet sentiment? No. It's fun with a hint of sarcasm: just one of Paul's little story-songs along with 'Ob-La-Di, Ob-La-Da', 'Rocky Racoon' and 'Honey Pie' (each of which also employs pastiche arrangements). It might be the first of several McCartney takeoffs on *The Beatles*, but it certainly rocks.

'Back In The USSR' was recorded during a short period when Ringo Starr had left The Beatles. Paul took over on drums for the basic track, with John on bass and George on guitar. Subsequent overdubs replaced John's bass playing and added vocals, more guitars, piano and handclaps. An instrumental backing track, which sounds like the final version with vocals removed, is available on the 50th anniversary re-issue.

The song opens side three of the immensely popular *1967-1970* compilation album and was issued as a single in 1976 to promote the album *Rock 'N' Roll Music*, reaching number 19 in the UK. It was The Beatles' second top 20 hit that year and their last until 1995. The 2018 remix is particularly good, jumping out of the speakers as though the band were performing live right in front of you. We very much enjoy lively cover versions by Chubby Checker and Motorhead.

'Dear Prudence' (Lennon, McCartney)

Recorded 28-30 August 1968. John Lennon – lead and backing vocals, rhythm guitars; Paul McCartney – backing vocals, drums, bass, piano, tambourine; George Harrison – backing vocals, rhythm guitar, lead guitars, tambourine, handclaps; Mal Evans, Jackie Lomax and John McCartney – backing vocals, handclaps, percussion.

We wrote in our previous book that 'I Saw Her Standing There' opens *Please Please Me* like 'a slap in the face'. Five-and-a-half years later, 'Back In The USSR' and 'Dear Prudence' hit you with a jab and cross.

'Dear Prudence' originates in a very simple guitar figure – a D chord with a descending bassline, which can be learned in seconds. For the full effect, the low E string is detuned to D (very audible in the Esher demo released in 2018). The song has its origins in finger-picking sessions in India, and the lyrics directly address Prudence Farrow, who was present in Rishikesh with The Beatles and chose to spend many hours meditating.

'A song about Mia Farrow's sister,' Lennon told David Sheffin in 1980, 'who seemed to go slightly barmy, meditating too long, and couldn't come out of the little hut that we were living in.'

The original demo, which is much lighter in tone than the studio version, has a voice-over from John, which says, 'No one was to know that sooner or later she was to go completely berserk, under the care of Maharishi Mahesh Yogi. All the people around were very worried about the girl because she was going insane. So, we sang to her.'

'Dear Prudence' remains an unqualified masterpiece. Lennon's singing is magnificent, with thrilling dynamics and a palpable tension and release in the perfectly layered musical arrangement. The finished version – which is impeccably recorded (at Trident) and beautifully clear – is as much McCartney's performance as Lennon's. With Ringo still absent, Paul again sits at the drum kit. His tight playing – very different to Ringo's – has a ten-bar fill which just makes it back onto the beat for the final refrain and is matched by wide-stanced, thumpingly loud bass guitar playing. He also plays flugelhorn. Harrison adds beautiful Indian-influenced lead guitar. Backing vocalists include Apple singer Jackie Lomax and Paul's cousin, John.

Note that the marvellous mix used on the 2023 re-release of *1967-1970* has a clean introduction, without the cross-fade from 'Back In The USSR'. For three further examples of The Beatles' pervasive influence, seek out Siouxsie and the Banshees' cover version, a top five hit in the UK in 1983, a brittle instrumental by Hungarian jazz guitarist Gábor Szabó (from the album *1969*) and the many extended in-concert versions by The Grateful Dead's Jerry Garcia.

Prudence Farrow titled her 2015 autobiography after the track. 'George was the one who told me about it. At the end of the course, just as they were leaving, he mentioned that they had written a song about me, but I didn't hear it until it came out on the album. I was flattered. It was a beautiful thing to have done.'

'Glass Onion' (Lennon, McCartney)

Recorded 11-13 September and 10 October 1968. John Lennon – vocals, acoustic guitar; Paul McCartney – bass, piano, recorder; George Harrison – lead guitar; Ringo Starr – drums, tambourine; Chris Thomas – recorder (possibly); Henry Datyner, Eric Bowie, Norman Lederman and Ronald Thomas – violin; John Underwood and Keith Cummings – viola; Eldon Fox and Reginald Kilby – cello.

'Glass Onion' is a wry comment on the over-analysis of song lyrics. So we will tread carefully. 'There'd been so much gobbledygook about *Pepper*', John Lennon is quoted as saying in *Anthology*. 'Play it backwards and you stand on your head and all that.'

In 'Glass Onion', nothing is quite as it seems, which makes Rian Johnson's choice of that title for his spoof murder mystery film of 2023 all the more apt.

There are, we think, seven direct references to earlier Beatles songs:

1. 'I told you about Strawberry Fields/You know the place where nothing is real'
2. 'Well here's another place you can go/Where everything flows' (possibly a call back to the opening line of 'There's A Place')
3. 'Looking through a glass onion' links, obliquely, to 'I'm Looking Through You'
4. 'I told you about the walrus and me, man/You know that we're as close as can be, man' (with a deliberate misdirection, 'the walrus was Paul')
5. 'Lady Madonna trying to make ends meet, yeah'
6. 'I told you about the fool on the hill/I tell you, man, he's living there still'
7. 'Fixing a hole in the ocean'

There are also *non-sequiter* mentions of part of the Mersey shoreline (the Cast Iron Shore, now redeveloped as Liverpool Festival Gardens) and a woodworking technique (a dovetail joint).

Of course, it's John Lennon, so the lyrics are as important as a musical statement: the impact is in the way he sings as much as for the words' meaning.

'Glass Onion' would be remixed for *Love* (2006). An 80-second extract features elements from 'Hello, Goodbye' (two snippets of McCartney's vocals), 'Things We Said Today' (acoustic rhythm guitar), 'Magical Mystery Tour' (trumpets), 'Eleanor Rigby' (vocals) and 'Penny Lane' (trumpet).

'Ob-La-Di, Ob-La-Da' (Lennon, McCartney)

Recorded 8, 9, 11 and 15 July 1968. Paul McCartney – vocals, electric and acoustic bass, handclaps; John Lennon – piano, backing vocals, handclaps; George Harrison – acoustic guitar, backing vocals, handclaps; Ringo Starr – drums, bongos, maracas, other percussion, handclaps, backing vocals; unnamed session players – saxophones.

'Ob-La-Di, Ob-La-Da' is undeniably commercial and fun, with an infectious reggae groove. But it's also trite and shallow. On its own merits, it's a fine song, but it sits uneasily on *The Beatles*. The happy vibes stick out on this mostly dark, fractured album.

The apparent spontaneity hides four days of sessions and three different versions. By the end, everyone was thoroughly fed up. As with the rest of the album, the production is phenomenal: powerful and punchy. Paul's vocal is towards the top of his range and, with no respite for any instrumental solos, it's always *there*. The song is difficult to sing, and it's not surprising that after Paul messed up the names in the last verse, he didn't bother to fix his error.

'Ob-La-Di, Ob-La-Da' has a chorus that can be sung in any language. It was released in several countries as a single in 1969 (but not the UK or US) and was a number one in Switzerland (six weeks, January-March 1969), Australia (six weeks, March-April 1969), New Zealand (one week, March 1969), West Germany (four weeks, March 1969), Japan (four weeks, April 1969). It reached number 15 in Finland. A copycat recording by the Scottish band Marmalade reached number one in the UK singles chart in January 1969.

Its influence persevered. Happy Mondays heavily borrowed parts of the song for their track 'Desmond' on their debut album *Squirrel And G-Man Twenty Four Hour Party People Plastic Face Carnt Smile (White Out)*. This was replaced on later pressings of the album.

Life goes on, bra.

'Wild Honey Pie' (Lennon, McCartney)

Recorded 20 August 1968. Paul McCartney – lead and backing vocals, acoustic guitars, bass drum, percussion.

Fifty-three seconds of 'Wild Honey Pie' is about 43 seconds too much. There are several sound experiments on *The Beatles*, and this is one of them. It might have fitted better on side two of *McCartney*, but here it's corny, discordant and out of place. It's the first song on the album that we'd skip.

'The Continuing Story Of Bungalow Bill' (Lennon, McCartney)
Recorded 8 October 1968. John Lennon – lead vocals, acoustic guitar, Hammond organ, Mellotron; Paul McCartney – backing vocals, bass; George Harrison – backing vocals, acoustic guitar; Ringo Starr – backing vocals, drums, tambourine; Chris Thomas – Mellotron; Yoko Ono – vocals; Maureen Starkey (and others) – backing vocals.
What at first seems a Lennon invention has, like 'Sexy Sadie', its origins in a real person and an actual event during The Beatles' stay in India. "[The Continuing Story Of] Bungalow Bill' was written about a guy in Maharishi's meditation camp who took a short break to go shoot a few poor tigers,' Lennon said in 1980, 'and then came back to commune with God. There used to be a character called Jungle Jim, and I combined him with Buffalo Bill. It's sort of a teenage social-comment song and a bit of a joke.'

'The Continuing Story Of Bungalow Bill' was one of the 28 songs recorded during the band's demo sessions in May. It would be almost five months after that pre-production session that they would turn their attention to a formal recording. The song was recorded on 8 October 1968 during the last batch of sessions for *The Beatles* and was one of two completed from start to finish that day; the other was 'I'm So Tired'. Three more were recorded that same week as they pushed to complete the album: 'Long Long Long', 'Why Don't We Do It In The Road?' and 'Julia'.

The verses include Lennon's usual droll, sometimes ambiguous wordplay, some odd chord choices and the occasional dropped beat. The chorus is campfire simple.

'The Continuing Story Of Bungalow Bill' contains vocals by Yoko Ono ('not when he looked so fierce'); the only time the group featured lead vocals by someone who was not a member. There are also two interesting voicings for the Mellotron, played by engineer Chris Thomas. The Spanish guitar flourish at the start and the bubbling trombone-sound at the end (heard most clearly at 3:00) both originated as Mellotron tapes.

'While My Guitar Gently Weeps' (Harrison)
Recorded 5-6 September 1968. George Harrison – lead and backing vocals, acoustic guitar, Hammond organ; John Lennon – electric guitar; Paul McCartney – backing vocals, piano, bass; Ringo Starr – drums, tambourine, castanets; Eric Clapton – lead guitar.
In which George Harrison invents stadium rock.

The perennial 'While My Guitar Gently Weeps' was the second song he brought to the formal sessions for *The Beatles*. The first, 'Not Guilty', had taken over 100 takes to perfect on 7-9 August, and even then George wasn't happy. The others demoed in May, 'Circles' and 'Sour Milk Sea', were not taken any further by The Beatles. 'While My Guitar Gently Weeps' was most probably written sometime in June or July. The beautiful solo demo, dating from 25 July, was released on *Anthology 3*, one of the highlights of that collection. Another take emerged in 2018. The first band session commenced on 16 August with 14 unsatisfactory takes. George Harrison spent an entire session on 3 September recording a backwards guitar solo.

> George particularly wanted to get the sound of a crying guitar, but he didn't want to use a wah-wah pedal, so he was experimenting with a backwards guitar solo. This meant a lot of time-consuming shuttling back and forth from the studio to the control room. We spent a long night trying to get it to work, but in the end, the whole thing was scrapped, and it was around that time that Eric Clapton started to get involved with the song.
> Brian Gibson, technical engineer, quoted in *The Complete Beatles Recording Sessions*

As George told *Guitar Player* in 1987, 'I worked on that song with John, Paul and Ringo one day, and they were not interested in it at all. And I knew inside of me that it was a nice song. The next day [5 September], I was with Eric, and I was going into the session and I said, 'We're going to do this song. Come on and play on it.' He said, 'Oh, no. I can't do that. Nobody ever plays on The Beatles records.' I said, 'Look, it's my song, and I want you to play on it.' So Eric came in, and the other guys were as good as gold because he was there. Also, it left me free to just play the rhythm and do the vocal. So Eric played that, and I thought it was really good.'

Legend has it that Clapton recorded his contribution in a single take. This story was put to bed in 2018 with the release of take 27, which breaks down when George 'tried to do a Smokey [Robinson]' falsetto. Eric's playing is very evident on the outtake.

In fact, 28 takes were recorded on 5 September. Further overdubs on 6 September completed the song. The bass sound is fat, almost distorted, as though it was directly plugged into the mixing desk. Ringo's groove is perfect, very simple: almost a country beat on such a rocky song. For the first 30 seconds, he sticks to just bass drum and hi-hat. His characteristic rolls around the tom-toms at the end of each section are glorious. Our favourite is the one at 3:00. The bass and drums together are yet another example of Paul and Ringo's work as a world-class unit.

The song's perennial popularity would ensure that it would be rolled out for George's high-profile live performances, including the Concert For Bangladesh (August 1971; with Clapton), his solo tour of the US (November-December 1974), The Prince's Trust Rock Gala (June 1987; with Clapton and Starr) and his solo tour of Japan (December 1991; again with Clapton). Clapton himself sang the song, with Ringo on drums and Paul on piano, at the Concert for George in November 2002. Topping all of these is the performance from the 2004 Rock and Roll Hall of Fame induction ceremonies, when George was inducted as a solo artist. On that night, Tom Petty and Jeff Lynne sang 'While My Guitar Gently Weeps' with a powerfully moving solo by Prince.

'Happiness Is A Warm Gun' (Lennon, McCartney)
Recorded 23-26 September 1968. John Lennon – lead and backing vocals, electric guitar, Hammond organ; Paul McCartney – bass, backing vocals, piano; George Harrison – lead guitar, backing vocals; Ringo Starr – drums, tambourine.
Both of your authors' favourite-ever songs were released in 1968. For one, it's 'Wichita Lineman'; for the other, it's 'Happiness Is A Warm Gun', the eighth and final song on the original side one of *The Beatles*.

It's funny. It's heavy. It's dark. Its title is hugely ironic considering what happened 12 years later.

Here, John Lennon uses his well-documented method of stitching together small parts of several songs, resulting in significant rhythmic challenges and many changes of time signature.

00:00 – 00:15 finger-picked guitar introduction, 'She's not a girl who misses much'.
00:15 – 00:45 the full band enter, with a marked increase in dynamics. It's easy to imagine Radiohead singing this part of the song.
00:45 – 01:14 blues-based, 'I need a fix' section.
01:14 – 01:36 the 'Mother Superior' refrain. The knotty rhythm reminds us of 'America' from *West Side Story*, but with a bit more volume, it is pure heavy metal.
01:36 – 2:41 doo wop-style section exploring the 'warm gun' theme. The chords use the familiar I – vi – IV – V turnaround (here it's C – Am – F – G) used from the 1930s onwards. Listen to 'Earth Angel' by The Penguins (1954), 'Unchained Melody' by The Righteous Brothers (1956), 'Angel Baby' by Rosie and the Originals (1960), 'Please Mr Postman' by The Marvelettes (1961), or The Beatles' own 'This Boy' (1963). In 'Happiness Is A Warm Gun', a beat is dropped in the 'when I hold you in my arms/and I feel my finger on your trigger' section. Ringo is uncharacteristically uncertain here (1:49-2:02) as he sticks to a 4/4 beat under a ¾ rhythm.

This highlights not only John's remarkable and idiosyncratic approach to composition, but also a band deft enough to play them. Or at least open to playing them, because in the end, it took 70 takes to get it right. The final master was an edit of two takes, both recorded on 24 September 1968. An early take from 23 September released in 2018 has the final structure in place and is gloriously ragged.

John's original demo, which includes only sections three and four above, was released on *Anthology 3* in 1996. An edited version, with a fluffed chord and an expletive removed, can be heard on the super deluxe edition of *The Beatles*.

Alberto Bravin: 'This was one of the first lesser-known Beatles songs that we decided to play with my band, Marshmallow Pies. Of course, you have to play the famous hits, 'Please Please Me and 'All My Loving' and that kind of stuff. And I said, 'Why are we not playing weird stuff that nobody else is playing?' 'Happiness Is A Warm Gun' was one of the first of the more obscure songs that we did, and it was really challenging. It's not an easy song to play.'

'Martha My Dear' (Lennon, McCartney)

Recorded 4-5 October 1968. Paul McCartney – vocals, piano, bass, drums, handclaps; George Harrison – electric guitar; Bernard Mille, Dennis McConnell, Lou Sofier and Les Maddox – violins; Leo Birnbaum and Henry Myerscough – violas; Reginald Kilby, Frederick Alexander and Peter Halling – cellos; Leon Calvert – trumpet, flugelhorn; Stan Reynolds and Ronnie Hughes – trumpets; Tony Tunstall – French horn; Ted Barker – trombone; Alf Reece – tuba.

Paul McCartney's innate musicianship is on display on this sprightly tune with syncopated piano and a bright vocal. It opens side two of *The Beatles* and could have come from one of Paul's 1970s albums with Wings.

This marvellous, positive song was recorded over two days at Trident Studios. On 4 October, Paul recorded piano (magnificent, naturally), drums and vocals. Brass and strings were overdubbed later that day, which can only mean that musical parts for these were written in advance; therefore, an unheard demo (or take) must exist. The following evening, Paul re-recorded his vocals, added handclaps, bass and guitar parts. The sharp guitar stabs from 1:02 to 2:02 are possibly Paul, possibly George (he was at Trident that day to add guitar to 'Savoy Truffle'). If the former, then Paul plays and sings everything on 'Martha My Dear' except the brass and strings. You can hear a Macca-only mix without these second-session overdubs on the 50th anniversary edition of *The Beatles*.

'I'm So Tired' (Lennon, McCartney)

Recorded 8 October 1968. John Lennon – lead vocals, acoustic guitar, lead guitar, Hammond organ; Paul McCartney – bass, electric piano, backing vocals; George Harrison – lead guitar; Ringo Starr – drums.

Just as only Paul could have written 'Martha My Dear', then 'I'm So Tired' is 100% John. The song dates from Rishikesh (in a longer and less tense arrangement). It's a typically direct song with seemingly no hidden meaning: a simple paean to a frustrating bout of insomnia. Or just being simply fed up with India ('you know it's three weeks, I'm going insane'), with being married to Cynthia, with being low on supply of recreational medication, with being a Beatle.

After some fine-tuning, 'I'm So Tired' was laid down, start to finish, with two other songs in a long, 16-hour session in the last week of production of *The Beatles*. Despite being recorded at 3 am, the dynamics are impressive. John's vocals are lethargic and weary in the verses, but in the refrain, he sings in a raging, full-throttle style. It's a sharp, almost tangible portrait of turmoil, swinging in short bursts between weary resignation and uneasy tension.

There is some Lennon wordplay when Lennon calls Sir Walter Raleigh 'a stupid get' (good Northern English slang, there) for introducing tobacco to England in the 17th century.

Takes 7 and 14 are available. On both, John is totally committed. Take 7 is a decent run-through of the basic track. 'It's so complicated,' John bemoans, 'if you think it was good, keep it. If you don't scrap it.' Take 14, the released take, has many overdubs; in particular, some startling vocal harmonies and additional guitar playing that were mixed out before release.

'Blackbird' (Lennon, McCartney)

Recorded 11 June 1968. Paul McCartney – vocals, acoustic guitar.

This is not just one of Paul's best songs, but one of the best Beatles songs (which, therefore, makes it one of the greatest songs of all time).

Paul's starting point is Johan Sebastian Bach's *Bourrée In E minor*, which he and George Harrison tried to learn as teenagers. Paul was recorded playing the piece in New Zealand in June 1964. Inspired by a bird call in Rishikesh and completed at his farm in Scotland, the track was fully developed for the band's demo session at George's house in May 1968. Three or so weeks later, he took 32 attempts to record the song in a single session in Studio 2, as John compiled 'Revolution 9' in Studio Three.

George Martin later remarked that, for the first time, he had to 'split myself three ways' because different Beatles were effectively working in different studios at once.

'Blackbird' is tricky to play, full of wide-open chord changes that are fully exposed in the acoustic setting. To our ears, it's definitely a metronome that provides the tip-tap accompaniment, despite engineer Geoff Emerick's insistence that it's Paul's feet. This sound is especially clear on take 28.

> Well, [the song is] simple in concept because you couldn't think of anything else to put on it. Maybe on *Pepper*, we would have sort of worked on it until we could find some way to put violins or trumpets in there. But I don't think it needs it, this one. There's nothing to the song. It is just one of those 'pick it and sing it' and that's it. The only point where we were thinking of putting anything on it is where it comes back in the end ... sort of stops and comes back in ... but instead of putting any backing on it, we put a blackbird on it. So there's a blackbird singing at the very end. And somebody said it was a thrush, but I think it's a blackbird!
>
> Paul McCartney from an interview with Radio Luxembourg, 1968

McCartney is fond of the song. It's been included in his solo sets consistently since 1975. He also recorded a sort-of follow-up, 'Jenny Wren', on his 2005 album *Chaos And Creation In The Back Yard*.

'Blackbird' remains simple, timeless and beautiful. Is it really about the civil rights movement in the Southern United States, or is this just clever revisionism by Paul, who often seems keen to rewrite his own history?

As if to underline The Beatles' continuing wide reach, Beyoncé recorded a cover of 'Blackbird' for her 2024 album *Cowboy Carter*. It's simply gorgeous, with Paul's original guitar track enhanced by stunning harmony vocals by Beyoncé, Brittney Spencer, Reyna Roberts, Tanner Adell and Tiera Kennedy. The strings are also pure George Martin. It peaked at number 27 on the *Billboard* Hot 100.

Previously, in 2019, with McCartney's permission, Rachel Fuller took the original Beatles track and added lush new parts by the Royal Philharmonic Orchestra and Chamber Choir of London. This can be heard on the album *Animal Requiem* and gives a suggestion of how *The Beatles* might have sounded if produced by Phil Spector. For something completely different, try Rick Wakeman's gentle prog rock arrangement on 1997's *Tribute To The Beatles*.

'Blackbird' was sung by one of the characters in the finale of *Gavin & Stacey*, a popular UK sitcom, first broadcast on 25 December 2024. Subsequent downloads of The Beatles' 1968 original pushed the song to number 96 on the UK's Official Singles Downloads chart the following week.

'Piggies' (Harrison)

Recorded 19-20 September and 10 October 1968. George Harrison – lead and backing vocals, acoustic guitar; John Lennon – backing vocals; Paul McCartney – bass, backing vocals; Ringo Starr – tambourine, bass drum; Chris Thomas – harpsichord; Henry Datyner, Eric Bowie, Norman Lederman and Ronald Thomas – violin; John Underwood and Keith Cummings – viola; Eldon Fox and Reginald Kilby – cello.

The second of three animal-related songs on *The Beatles*, George's 'Piggies' is a dry, anti-establishment social commentary, nine years before Pink Floyd covered similar territory on 'Pigs (Three Different Ones)'. Harrison's lyrics are sharp and sardonic, influenced by George Orwell's biting satire, *Animal Farm* (1945). Wealth and class divisions are picked apart. These are set against a fastidious mock-baroque music arrangement, with harpsichord played by engineer Chris Thomas and overdubbed cello, viola and violin. There's also a mock-operatic chorus. Of course there is.

The May 1968 demo has an unused fourth verse, which Harrison reinstated for live shows in 1992.

> Everywhere there's lots of piggies/playing piggy pranks
> You can see them on their trotters/at the piggy banks
> Paying piggy thanks/to thee pig brother

'Piggies' is one of six Harrison songs considered for *The Beatles*. Typically, none of them is remotely alike. This one might not be a top-flight Beatles track, but it's difficult to imagine *The Beatles* without it.

'Rocky Raccoon' (Lennon, McCartney)
Recorded 15 August 1968. Paul McCartney – lead vocals, acoustic guitar; John Lennon – backing vocals, harmonium, six-string bass, harmonica; George Harrison – backing vocals, bass; Ringo Starr – drums; George Martin – piano; Yoko Ono – backing vocals.
Another pastiche story-in-a-song from Paul McCartney, this time telling a vivid if silly tale of a love triangle, presented in a folk-country ballad style with hints of bluegrass and campfire sing-along.

The titular hero, Rocky, has a girlfriend, Lil (but 'everyone knew her as Nancy'), who leaves him for another, Dan, who punches Rocky in the eye. Rocky lodges at the local saloon, vowing revenge. Here, he finds a Gideon Bible. Rocky confronts Dan and Nancy, but Dan shoots him. A drunken doctor attends to Rocky ('the doctor came in, stinking of gin', a call back to Paul's moped accident in 1965), who advised that Rocky's gunshot wound is minor. Rocky goes back to his room, where he sees the Gideon Bible once more and interprets it as a sign that he will recover. There are smart double-meanings here on 'Gideon checked out' (as in 'was worthwhile' and 'left a hotel') and 'Rocky's revival' (both physical and spiritual).

McCartney's choice of names was possibly influenced by the Robert W. Service poem, 'The Shooting Of Dan McGrew' (1907).

> Back of the bar, in a solo game, sat Dangerous Dan McGrew,
> And watching his luck was his light-o'-love, the lady that's known as Lou.

The looped 5-chord composition is almost childishly simple. What makes the song shine, though, is the arrangement, a definite case of style over substance. There is fabulous honky-tonk piano from George Martin, a rare late-period outing for John's harmonica, an early example of the Fender VI, some polka-beat scat singing and brilliant backing vocals. The shoot-out – exactly halfway through the song – is coloured by a sharp snare from Ringo (at 1:49).

For another way to approach this song, with menace rather than tongue-in-cheek, seek out Richie Havens' 1969 cover version. The vocal melody of the verses of Queen's 'Spread Your Wings' has more than a passing resemblance to 'Rocky Racoon' (with the chord progression to 'Eight Days A Week' underneath). We can also thank this song for the name of the procyonid superhero Rocket Raccoon from the *Guardians Of The Galaxy* comics and films.

'Don't Pass Me By' (Starkey)
Recorded 5-6 June, 12 and 22 July 1968. Ringo Starr – vocals, piano, sleigh bells, cowbell, maracas, congas; Paul McCartney – piano, bass, drums; Jack Fallon – violin.

From Macca country to Ringo country. Here's Ringo's first-ever solo composition, and it's as simple as you like, sticking resolutely to the blues trio of I, IV and V (in this case, C, F and G). Ringo had the chorus, at least, for several years; it was mentioned – and Paul sang part of it – in one of the band's 1964 radio sessions (*Top Gear*, broadcast on 16 July 1964).

The basic track is Ringo (drums) and Paul (piano). All overdubs were performed by just these two musicians, with one exception. We should call out the out-of-tune fiddling by Jack Fallon, an experienced jazz bassist who had played with the likes of Duke Ellington, Django Reinhardt, Count Basie, Stéphane Grappelli, Sarah Vaughan, Lena Horne, Humphrey Lyttelton and Big Bill Broonzy. It's ironic that his biggest-selling performance is busking the violin – not even his primary instrument – on a minor song by The Beatles.

Ringo's placement of his vocal lines is idiosyncratic: not in the way that John's songs would deliberately cross the meter, but the mark of an inexperienced songwriter. It was the best that he had to offer and would surely have been dismissed for any other Beatles album.

The released mono and stereo versions are quite different. The former is sped-up and half-a-step higher than the latter. The closing fiddling is unique in each. These are both also edited from the unmixed version that Ringo gave to his friend Peter Sellers, where an unwelcome reprise of the first verse appears after the breakdown section between the final two refrains. The edit is at 2:54 on the released version; the full-length take can be heard on the 50th anniversary box set of *The Beatles*, should you have trouble sleeping.

'Don't Pass Me By' was released as a single in Denmark in 1969, reaching number one there for a week in April ahead of The Hollies ('Sorry Suzanne', top five in the UK that same week) and Dave Dee, Dozy, Beaky, Mick & Tich ('Don Juan', a minor British hit earlier that year). The Georgia Satellites go full boogie on their 1988 version, heard on their album *Open All Night*.

'Why Don't We Do It In The Road?' (Lennon, McCartney)
Recorded 9-10 October 1968. Paul McCartney – vocals, acoustic guitar, piano, electric guitar, bass, handclaps; Ringo Starr – drums, handclaps.

'Why Don't We Do It In The Road?' sounds like a John Lennon song in structure and attack, but it's Paul all the way. Paul said later that it was inspired by the sight of two monkeys enjoying conjugal rights in India. There is a total of 13 words: the word 'throwaway' might have been invented for it.

After *Sgt. Pepper*, The Beatles insisted upon, and were given, total artistic control. It's inconceivable that a song such as this would have been suggested for *Rubber Soul* or *Revolver*, never mind recorded and released.

The basic track was recorded on John's 28th birthday during the last week of sessions for *The Beatles*. Whilst John remixed 'The Continuing Story Of Bungalow Bill' in the control room of EMI's Studio Two, Paul nipped to the vast Studio One to play five takes comprising only acoustic guitar and vocals, then adding piano to the last of these.

Overdubs were finalised the following evening in Studio Three (vocals, handclaps, electric slide guitar, bass and Ringo's drums). At the same time, John and George were supervising strings for 'Glass Onion' and 'Piggies' in Studio Two. Paul's singing is in his full-blast chest register. The following year's 'Golden Slumbers' uses a similar timbre (compare 'smiles awake you when you rise' from that song with 'no one will be watching us' here).

'Why Don't We Do It In The Road?' gets a passing mention in Blake Edwards' 1979 film, *10*, in which George Webber, played by Dudley Moore, grumbles to Don, a bartender played by Brian Dennehy.

> George: If you were dancing with your wife, or girlfriend you knew in high school, and you said to her, 'Darling, they're playing our song', do you know what they'd be playing?
> Don: What?
> George Webber: 'Why Don't We Do It In The Road?' Fuckin' hell kind of era is that?

'I Will' (Lennon, McCartney)

Recorded 16-17 September 1968. Paul McCartney – vocals, acoustic guitars; John Lennon – percussion, maracas; Ringo Starr – bongos, cymbals.

Side two ends with two beautiful songs. Paul's 'I Will' and John's 'Julia' are both acoustic, but each is utterly different from the other. They are both amongst the very best songs by these world-class writers.

It took 68 takes to lay down a perfect performance of the astoundingly melodic 'I Will', with Paul on vocals and guitar, and John and Ringo tapping various types of percussion.

The song was most likely written around the time of the end of Paul's relationship with Jane Asher. Their engagement had officially ended on 20 July, just over three weeks before this recording session.

Is it Jane he's singing to, or to an unknown future lover?

> And when at last, I find you
> Your song will fill the air

He'd already met Linda by this time, and they would become a couple soon afterwards. There's something spiritual about 'I Will', as though the clouds have parted and the sun is shining.

There are several official outtakes from the 16 September session: *Anthology 3* provided an alternative take of 'I Will' (take 1). Twenty-two years later, two more (takes 13 and 29) appeared on the deluxe edition of *The Beatles*.

In between formal attempts to record 'I Will', Paul broke into 'Step Inside Love' and 'Blue Moon' (both on *The Beatles* box) and extemporisations 'Los Paranoias' (different excerpts on *Anthology 3* and *The Beatles* box), 'The Way You Look Tonight' and 'Down In Havana' (both released on bootlegs) and a two-minute ditty later titled 'Can You Take Me Back?'. Twenty-seven seconds of this can be heard, uncredited, on side four of *The Beatles* between 'Cry Baby Cry' and 'Revolution 9'. These are all very good-humoured and relaxed.

'Julia' (Lennon, McCartney)
Recorded 13 October 1968. John Lennon – vocals, acoustic guitar.
Placing 'Julia' immediately after 'I Will' is a stroke of sequencing genius. If 'I Will' is relaxed, peaceful and bright, 'Julia' has a rarefied atmosphere: nostalgic, pleading and dark.

Of the six acoustic songs on *The Beatles*, only 'Julia' is written by John Lennon – he chose to use predominantly electric, full band versions of his other songs from that period, such as 'Dear Prudence', 'Revolution 1' and 'Happiness Is A Warm Gun'. The acoustic arrangement of 'Julia' certainly exposes John's emotions, which was, we assume, his objective.

'Julia', which was the last song recorded for *The Beatles*, pays tribute to Lennon's mother, who died in 1958. It also acknowledges Yoko Ono in the lyrics: 'ocean child, calls me' is a direct translation of Yoko from Japanese: 'child of the sea'. A couple of lines are borrowed from *Sand And Foam* (1926) by Lebanese poet Kahlil Gibran (1883-1931).

> Half of what I say is meaningless, but I say it so that the other half may reach you
> When life does not find a singer to sing her heart she produces a philosopher to speak her mind

The performance is restrained, tender even. Yearning, certainly. Knowing that Julia was John's mum layers your appreciation of the song with some unavoidable, sentimental heft. But here's the real question: strip away that little nugget of trivia, and tell us – how much less does the song actually tug at your heart?

'Birthday' (Lennon, McCartney)
Recorded 18 September 1968. Paul McCartney – lead vocals, bass, piano; John Lennon – vocals, guitar; George Harrison – guitar, tambourine; Ringo Starr – drums, handclaps; Pattie Harrison – backing vocals; Yoko Ono – backing vocals; Mal Evans – handclaps.
Side three of *The Beatles* has four of the band's hardest, most unpretentious rockers. Each of these sees the band return to their two guitar/bass/drums format with, in the case of 'Birthday', only a phased piano addition to break up the dense sound.

'Birthday' was written, recorded and mixed in a single 11-and-a-half-hour session. Paul says that it's a true 50-50 collaboration between him and John, but engineer Chris Thomas says that Paul had the bluesy riff written and ready to roll before the others arrived. John later uncharitably called it 'a piece of garbage'. Even John cannot deny the brilliance of Ringo's drumming. Enjoy the sharp snare fills at 0:59, 1:09, 1:27, 2:01, with terrific, breathtaking variations at 2:07-2:09 and 2:25. It sounds like a loud, energetic live performance with Paul and John singing together.

Midway through the session, they all decamped to Paul's house to watch the 1956 rock 'n' roll film *The Girl Can't Help It,* which was being shown for the first time on British television.

'Yer Blues' (Lennon, McCartney)

Recorded 13, 14, 20 August 1968. John Lennon – vocals, guitar; Paul McCartney – backing vocals, bass; George Harrison – guitar; Ringo Starr – drums.

If Paul's 'Honey Pie', 'Back In The USSR' and 'Rocky Racoon' can be classed as pastiches, then we should pop this loud, overwrought blues song in that same bucket. It's another return to guitar/guitar/bass/drums, a nice balance between self-mocking and absolute sincerity. The song's format pokes fun at the British blues bands of 1966-1967, including Cream, Fleetwood Mac, Ten Years After and Savoy Brown. And yet the lyrics seem to be absolutely straight, including a sly reference to Bob Dylan's 'Ballad Of A Thin Man'.

The song was recorded 'as live' in a tiny room at EMI: it's very loud, and you can almost smell the sweat. Paul's Fender Jazz Bass has a terrific thump. An early take, dirty and mean, can be heard on the 50th anniversary box set of *The Beatles*. In the end, two takes were edited together, rather obviously, at 3:17. The guitar solos are by John (2:29-2:54) and George (2:54-3:17). John re-recorded his lead vocals the following day. His original guide vocal can be heard, picked up by the microphones in the room, as the song fades.

Alan W Pollack: 'The rough edit for the outro has a visceral effect similar to that of accidentally, unexpectedly smacking your forehead against a hard surface, a brief seconds-worth of fainting spell, or if you like, a small but critical few frames of celluloid cut out of a film.'

Even when taking the mick, The Beatles could play as hard and loud as anyone.

'Mother Nature's Son' (Lennon, McCartney)

Recorded 9 and 20 August 1968. Paul McCartney – vocals, acoustic guitars, timpani, bass drum; Unknown session musicians – two trumpets, two trombones.

In complete contrast to 'Yer Blues', 'Mother Nature's Son' is delicate and acoustic and an early hint at Paul's eco-friendly lifestyle.

Another Rishikesh song demoed in May, Paul recorded 25 takes of 'Mother Nature's Son' after the rest of the band had left the studio following a series of overdubs to 'Not Guilty'. It's delightful.

A brass arrangement and some percussion overdubs completed the recording.

Takes 2 and 15 have been released on *Anthology* and *The Beatles* 50th Anniversary Edition, respectively. They're cute, but don't match the appeal of the familiar version.

'Everybody's Got Something To Hide Except For Me And My Monkey' (Lennon, McCartney)

Recorded 26 and 27 June, 1 and 23 July 1968. John Lennon – lead vocals, rhythm guitar, handclaps; Paul McCartney – backing vocals, bass, hand bell, chocalho, handclaps; George Harrison – backing vocals, lead guitar, handclaps; Ringo Starr – drums, handclaps.

The fifth song started for *The Beatles*, the energetic, punkish 'Everybody's Got Something To Hide Except For Me And My Monkey' quotes directly from the teachings of Maharishi Mahesh Yogi, who would declare, 'Come on. It's such a joy. Take it easy.'

John explained the meaning of 'Everybody's Got Something To Hide Except For Me And My Monkey' in his final interview, recorded the day he died. '[The song] means really that one cannot be absolutely oneself in public because the fact that you're in public makes you ... you have to have some kind of defence, or whatever it is.'

Even though they sound like they're having fun, the track is urgent, almost desperate. Again, we have the classic two guitars/bass/drums lineup, one of four songs that use this on the rocking side three of *The Beatles*. George Harrison's guitar-playing is spiky, angry and very loud.

'The song is a Lennon salute to the joys of 1950s rock 'n' roll animalism,' David Fricke wrote in *Rolling Stone* (2001), 'but its locomotive heart is Harrison's whirl-around guitar figure, played with ferocious attitude against Lennon's crisp strum.'

A handbell clangs relentlessly through the first and third verses. There's also a fun breakdown as John gabbers 'c'mon, c'mon' and Paul drops an astounding bass riff (2:03-2:05).

John will have been delighted that one of his heroes, Fats Domino, recorded a funky cover in 1972. American indie pioneers The Feelies' cover, on their 1980 debut album *Crazy Rhythms*, sounds like The Beatles performed by The Velvet Underground.

'Sexy Sadie' (Lennon, McCartney)

Recorded 19 and 24 July, 13 and 21 August 1968. John Lennon – lead and backing vocals, rhythm guitar; Paul McCartney – backing vocals, piano, bass, Hammond organ, guitar; George Harrison – backing vocals, lead guitar, tambourine; Ringo Starr – drums.

With so many of the songs on *The Beatles* reflecting positively about their time in India, it somehow feels odd to have this kiss-off. 'That was inspired by Maharishi', John told David Scheff in 1980. 'I wrote it when we had our bags packed and were leaving. It was the last piece I wrote before I left India. I just called him 'Sexy Sadie' instead of (sings) 'Maharishi what have you done, you made a fool...' I was just using the situation to write a song, rather calculatingly, but also to express what I felt. I was leaving the Maharishi with a bad taste. You know, it seems that my partings are always not as nice as I'd like them to be.'

It took three attempts to record the song. Twenty-one takes on 19 July and another 23 five days later were scrapped. Two from the first session are officially available.

The band's final arrangement is sweetened by John's marvellous singing, Paul's bright piano playing, Ringo's pin-sharp drumming and lush, intricate doo-wop backing vocals. It's one of the album's sleeper classics.

'Helter Skelter' (Lennon, McCartney)

Recorded 18 July, 9-10 September 1968. Paul McCartney – lead and backing vocals, lead and rhythm guitar; John Lennon – backing vocals, six-string bass, piano, saxophone; George Harrison – backing vocals, lead, rhythm and slide guitar; Ringo Starr – drums, vocals; Mal Evans – trumpet.

There is nothing delicate or soft about the explosive, almost sinister 'Helter Skelter', which is supposedly a direct response to The Who's Pete Townshend claiming that 'I Can See For Miles' was the loudest-ever rock song. As Paul McCartney told Radio Luxembourg in 1968, 'I'd read a review of a record ['I Can See For Miles'], which said, 'and this group really got us wild, there's echo on everything, they're screaming their heads off.' And I just remember thinking, 'Oh, it'd be great to do one. Pity they've done it. Must be great – really screaming record.' And then I heard their record, and it was quite straight, and it was very sort of sophisticated. It wasn't rough and screaming and tape echo at all. So I thought, 'Oh well, we'll do one like that, then."

And so they did with three very long, loud, raucous versions on 18 July. A 4:27 edit of the second take from 18 July was released on *Anthology 3*. The unedited take was released in 2018. It's slow and menacing, but little more than a jam.

Seven weeks later, they laid down another 18 takes, numbered 4 to 21. By take 17 and the fifth or sixth hour of the session, producer Chris Thomas sounds decidedly weary. Paul is chemically stimulated, but his voice is impeccable. 'Keep that one,' he says, 'mark it Fab.'

The final take was kept as 'best'. Backing vocals, lead vocals, more electric guitars and a cacophony of saxophone and trumpet comprised overdubs the next day (the latter most obvious between 3:23 and 3:50). The stereo and mono mixes are startlingly different, mastered loud and with enormous headache-inducing impact. It can be thrilling or tiresome, depending on your mood.

Was 'Helter Skelter' the first heavy metal song? There's no doubt that Black Sabbath, who came together in the early part of 1969, used 'Helter Skelter' as a spark for some of the songs that formed their debut album and created a new genre. Covers by Aerosmith (1975), Siouxsie and the Banshees (1978), Motley Crue (1983), U2 (1988) and, perhaps predictably, Oasis (2002) fade into irrelevance when compared to Soundgarden's stunning live arrangement from 1996. Paul McCartney himself recognises that the song has a unique, rough energy and has performed it as an encore at many of his shows since 2004.

And perhaps the legendary 28-minute Beatles version remains unreleased because – gasp! – it might not be any good?

'Long, Long, Long' (Harrison)

Recorded 7-9 October 1968. George Harrison – lead vocals, acoustic guitars; Paul McCartney – backing vocals, Hammond organ, bass; Ringo Starr – drums; Chris Thomas – piano.

If George Harrison's three other songs on *The Beatles* are, in turn, spiritual ('While My Guitar Gently Weeps'), ironic ('Piggies') and frivolous ('Savoy Truffle'), then perhaps the serene, dreamy, often-overlooked 'Long, Long, Long' is closest to the genuine man. It shows a strong influence of both Bob Dylan ('Sad Eyed Lady Of The Lowlands' in particular) and his musical compadres The Band, whose seminal *Music From Big Pink* was released around five weeks into the recording sessions for *The Beatles*.

The song is, on the face of it, a straightforward love song. And yet George's deep, intelligent worldview is evident in the understated, meditative arrangement, in the bursts of frustration ('so many tears I was wasting') and in lyrics, which address a reconsolidation both with a loved one and with God.

The basic take comprises George on acoustic guitar and ghostly, almost whispered vocals, Paul playing Hammond organ, and Ringo on devastating, perfect drum fills. Overdubs include George's second lead vocal and a distorted acoustic guitar (sounding like a sitar at 0:00, 0:16 and elsewhere), plus Paul's backing vocals and deeply resonant bass and Chris Thomas' distinctive piano in the bridge. The 'found sound' of a vibrating wine bottle adds a spooky element to the closing seconds: it's a sound you don't expect and that could easily have been removed.

As with many of George's late-period Beatles songs, John Lennon makes no contributions whatsoever. Ringo's and Paul's outstanding playing make up for his absence. The 2009 stereo re-master is particularly gorgeous.

David Quantick of *Uncut* described 'Long, Long, Long' as 'an oasis of calm and faith in the clattering chaos of the *White Album*'.

He's right. Go and listen to it again.

'Revolution 1' (Lennon, McCartney)

Recorded 30-31 May, 4 and 21 June 1968. John Lennon – lead vocals, acoustic guitar, lead guitar; Paul McCartney – bass, piano, Hammond organ, backing vocals; George Harrison – lead guitar, backing vocals; Ringo Starr – drums; Derek Watkins and Freddy Clayton – trumpets; Don Lang, Rex Morris, J. Power and Bill Povey – trombones.

This first version of 'Revolution', but the second to be released, has a slower tempo and a more laid back mood in comparison to the powerful remake used as the B-side of 'Hey Jude'. It's acoustic, in a lower key, adds brass and doo-wop backing vocals. It has a slightly different arrangement, lacking the guitar/piano solo and a fade-out ending.

The 50th anniversary box set includes an extended take 18, which reveals how the final part of 'Revolution 1' – the last six minutes of this take – was the progenitor of 'Revolution 9'.

We should make reference here to John's mention of Mao Zedong (1893-1976), Chairman of the Chinese Communist Party from 1943 until his death. Mao was personally responsible for the mass repressions of the Chinese people through policies that promoted extensive public executions and 'reform through labour', a criminal justice system that sent dissidents to prison camps where many died.

As the 1960s progressed, Lennon became increasingly vocal in his political views, and many of his songs started to carry more overtly political messages. The themes of war, peace, love and social justice became central in his songwriting. His Beatles work, especially after 'Revolution 1', shows a growing shift toward activism and protest, setting the stage for the more politically engaged solo work that came later in songs such as 'Working Class Hero', 'Power To The People', 'New York City' and many others.

'Honey Pie' (Lennon, McCartney)

Recorded 1, 2 and 4 October 1968. Paul McCartney – vocals, piano; John Lennon – lead and rhythm guitar; George Harrison – six-string bass; Ringo Starr – drums; Harry Klein, Dennis Walton, Ronald Chamberlain, Jim Chester and Rex Morris – saxophone; Raymond Newman and David Smith – clarinet.

Hmm. That *The Beatles* includes both 'Ob-La-Di, Ob-La-Da' and 'Honey Pie' is perhaps over-egging the pudding with the 'granny music'. Either, possibly. Both, perhaps not. Whereas 'Ob-La-Di, Ob-La-Da' was commercially successful for both The Beatles (a hit single outside the UK and US) and Marmalade, 'Honey Pie' does little more than prove the band's enormous range. Which other band could write and record both 'Helter Skelter' and 'Honey Pie' on the same album?

We can admire the craft, even if it's eminently skippable.

John Lennon is on top form here. 'John played a brilliant solo on 'Honey Pie'', George told *Guitar Player* in 1987. 'Sounded like Django Reinhardt or something. It was one of those where you just close your eyes and happen to hit all the right notes. Sounded like a little jazz solo.' This occurs from 1:33 to 1:41.

Much as we enjoy Paul's vocal range and delivery, the instrumental backing track released in 2018 on the 50th anniversary edition of *The Beatles* sounds like a soundtrack to a 1940s movie. John's banjo-like guitar is mixed to the fore and is utterly charming. George Martin's saxophone and clarinet arrangement is authentic and beautiful.

'Savoy Truffle' (Harrison)

Recorded 3, 5, 11 and 14 October 1968. George Harrison – vocals, acoustic, lead and rhythm guitars, Hammond organ; Paul McCartney – backing vocals, bass;

Ringo Starr – drums; Chris Thomas – electric piano; Art Ellefson, Danny Moss and Derek Collins – tenor saxophone; Ronnie Ross, Harry Klein and Bernard George – baritone saxophone; uncredited – tambourine.

This rocking shuffle is a lot of fun, but would surely have been chopped from a single album version of *The Beatles*. Even as filler, though, it's very good indeed. Everyone plays brilliantly: the jazzy, hotly recorded horns, Chris Thomas' electric piano and, in particular, the peerless Starr-McCartney rhythm section. There's also a piercing, tight guitar solo from The Quiet One, who is playing his Gibson Les Paul. These elements are heard very clearly in the backing track released in 2018.

The title and many of the lyrics are taken from the contents of the Good News brand of chocolates by confectioners Mackintosh, much loved by George's pal Eric Clapton: crème tangerine, Montelimart (a type of French nougat, named after the town but with an incorrect spelling on the box), ginger sling, pineapple treat (renamed to rhyme better), coffee dessert, Savoy truffle.

Coconut fudge, cherry cream and 'nice apple tart' are George's own additions. He also drops a hint to one of the other songs on *The Beatles* recorded three months earlier.

Astoundingly, Ella Fitzgerald recorded a faithful cover in 1969.

'Cry Baby Cry' (Lennon, McCartney)

Recorded 15, 16 and 18 July 1968. John Lennon – vocals, acoustic guitar, piano, organ; Paul McCartney – bass, backing vocals; George Harrison – lead guitar; Ringo Starr – drums, tambourine; George Martin – harmonium.

'Cry Baby Cry' is something of a throwback, dating to late 1967, with nursery rhyme lyrics that hark back to the end of the band's psychedelic period mixed with references to 'Sing A Song Of Sixpence'. The arrangement is very 1968, though. The lyrics might tell a silly children's story, but the music has a dark undertone. This is underlined by the use of the flat-seventh, adding a tension to the chorus ('Cry baby cry, *make your mother* sigh).

The arrangement starts as an acoustic strum, and various instruments are added in turn: harmonium (0:06), very busy bass (from 0:16, listen to the left channel in the 2018 mix), piano (0:17), drums (0:20, but more prominent from 0:28), organ (0:41), sound effects (1:11), electric guitar (from 1:16) and falsetto backing vocals (from 2:04).

The *Anthology 3* version is a basic take before any of the overdubs were added. The bass and drums are phenomenal, and John's vocal is exceptional. It might be even better than the final version on *The Beatles*. A rehearsal version with John playing organ sounds like *Meddle*-period Pink Floyd. This can be heard on the 50th anniversary box set.

We should mention here the uncredited 'Can You Take Me Back', recorded during a 16 September 1968 session for 'I Will', which segues from 'Cry Baby Cry' into 'Revolution 9'.

'Revolution 9' (Lennon, McCartney)

Recorded June 1968. John Lennon – spoken vocals, tape loops, sound effects, piano, Mellotron, cymbals; George Harrison – spoken vocals, tape loops, sound effects, electric guitar; Yoko Ono – spoken vocals, tape loops, sound effects; George Martin – spoken vocals; Alistair Taylor – spoken vocals.

We'll leave the reader to make their own conclusions about 'Revolution 9'. Self-indulgent, yes, but also ground-breaking, using over 40 different sources to create an eight-minute sound collage. Other creative media, *The Sixth Sense*, *Yeesus* and *Guernica*, to take three examples, rely on novelty, shock value, or experimental nature to make an initial impact. One wonders how hearing 'Revolution 9' for the first time, perhaps late at night after imbibing recreational chemicals, would have similarly affected the listener.

Although credited to Lennon-McCartney, 'Revolution 9' is a three-way collaboration between John Lennon, Yoko Ono and George Harrison. George's 'Dream Scene' from *Wonderwall Music* (November 1967 – February 1968) is a clear blueprint for 'Revolution 9'. It includes a similar cut-and-paste approach, with different sounds being manipulated with echo, distortion and stereo panning. Everything was done by hand.

While divisive, 'Revolution 9' marks The Beatles abandoning pop altogether to experiment with *musique concrète*. Nothing like this existed in commercial music at the time, and for that alone, 'Revolution 9' deserves your attention. Is it a piece of art? Undoubtedly. Difficult to hum? Certainly. Like all art, 'Revolution 9' is designed to invoke an emotional response. Does it matter whether you like it? Not really. Does it make you think? Absolutely.

In 1994 and 2014, the American band Phish performed the entire *White Album*, including 'Revolution 9', as part of their celebrated New Year's Eve concerts. In other years, they would tackle *Quadrophenia*, *Abbey Road*, *Exile On Main Street*, *Tommy*, *Let It Bleed* and *Sticky Fingers*.

We also shout out to The Alarm Will Sound, who arranged 'Revolution 9' for strings, horns and percussion. It sounds like a lost Schoenberg.

'Good Night' (Lennon, McCartney)

Recorded 28 June, 2 and 22 July 1968. Ringo Starr – vocals; George Martin – celesta; The Mike Sammes Singers – backing vocals; unnamed session musicians – 12 violins, three violas, three cellos, three flutes, clarinet, horn, vibraphone, double bass, harp.

As 'Revolution 9' finally withers away, a syrupy orchestra fades in. The lush woodwind, strings and brass, along with George Martin's celesta (a bell-piano), sound very incongruous after eight minutes of random sound bites.

To understand why *The Beatles* closes with 'Good Night', you first have to look at what comes just before it. Where else could 'Revolution 9' possibly go? Put it too early and the rest of the record collapses under its shadow – everything that follows risks sounding diminished. Save it for the very end, and you give it a weight it doesn't deserve, a grand finale it was never built to be. Stick it on the close of one of the earlier sides, and most listeners won't bother to flip the disc again. This leaves the penultimate slot: exactly where it sits.

But then comes the problem. What on earth could follow 'Revolution 9'? The piece demands contrast – stark, decisive contrast. Almost any other track would sound like a misstep: too slight, too similar, too strange. 'Good Night', though, solves the puzzle neatly. It anchors the sprawl with something musically conservative, almost old-fashioned, and in doing so becomes every bit as surprising as the avant-garde chaos that precedes it. And, of course, it serves the obvious function: a lullaby that tells you the record is finished and the curtain has fallen.

The band worked hard on the arrangement. An early outtake recorded on 28 June sounds like The Band. There are just two fingerpicked guitars and perfect four-part harmonies. This was one of the highlights of the 50th Anniversary box set of *The Beatles*. A different arrangement has John on piano, George playing percussion and a wonderfully sincere vocal from Ringo. This can be heard on *Anthology 3,* skilfully mixed into the orchestral overdub.

1969

Yellow Submarine

UK: 17 January 1969. US: 13 January 1969.
Chart positions. UK: 3. US: 2.

The *Yellow Submarine* album smacks of 'contractual obligation'. Three of the four songs for the animated film were written and recorded for the project in spring 1967, with one more in early 1968. By early 1969, The Beatles and the wider world had changed.

An EP containing the four new songs used in the film had been considered, along with the then-unreleased 'Across The Universe'. This was mastered for potential release in March 1969, but was left on the shelf, presumably because there was no obvious lead track.

Side one of *Yellow Submarine* may have been pulled together to satisfy lawyers rather than muses, but it still crackles with The Beatles' instinctive charm and melodic generosity. Even their offcuts have wit, invention and that peculiar knack for making minor throwaways feel like essential fragments of a much larger story.

The second side of *Yellow Submarine* is often relegated to a footnote, containing seven beautiful instrumental pieces composed and arranged by George Martin for the film's score. While frequently overlooked in favour of the rock tracks on side one, a critical, non-hyperbolic assessment reveals that this orchestral material possesses significant artistic and functional merit. The score allows George Martin to operate fully within his orchestral comfort zone. He produced a focused suite of music that employs techniques familiar from 20th-century classical and film music, giving the album depth beyond the band's tracks. The score incorporates several musical devices that align with the era's broader experimentation in popular music and film, mirroring The Beatles' own *Sgt. Pepper* and *Magical Mystery Tour* periods. Tracks like 'Sea Of Holes' utilise tape manipulation and less conventional harmonies (often associated with *musique concrète*) to depict the surreal, non-linear qualities of the storyline.

Martin also weaves Beatles themes into the orchestral fabric, most notably in the track 'Yellow Submarine In Pepperland', which reinterprets the iconic tune with a rich, cinematic arrangement. Side two of *Yellow Submarine* functions as a well-executed, contextually relevant and musically sophisticated film score that deserves recognition both for its technical merits and for its crucial role in the overall artistic success of the *Yellow Submarine* project. The recordings took place with a 41-piece orchestra over two three-hour sessions on 22 and 23 October 1968; these are not the same versions as heard in the film, which date from Olympic Sound Studios in London earlier in 1968.

1999's *Yellow Submarine Songtrack* includes the six Beatles songs from the original album together with nine others heard in the film, all newly remixed. It's a great listen.

'Yellow Submarine'

Released on Revolver [UK: 5 August 1966. US: 5 August 1966] and as a single [UK: 5 August 1966. US: 8 August 1966]

In the context of the film, 'Yellow Submarine' functions as a ritual of togetherness. Ringo's voice, with its unhurried warmth and genial naivety, is a friendly guide inviting us into a world that might otherwise feel dizzying or chaotic. His charm makes the impossible – talking fish, floating landscapes, colour explosions – immediately approachable. If Ringo can inhabit this universe with comfort and cheer, so can we.

'Only A Northern Song' (Harrison)

Recorded 13-14 February and 20 April 1967. George Harrison – vocals, Hammond organ; John Lennon – glockenspiel, piano; Paul McCartney – bass, trumpet; Ringo Starr – drums, noises. Uncredited – timpani, Mellotron, percussion.

George Harrison has an unwarranted reputation for being grumpy, and some of his songs bear this out: 'Don't Bother Me', 'Taxman', 'Blue Jay Way', 'Piggies'. Of course, he was a much more complex character than this simple reading suggests.

'Only A Northern Song' has a distinct contrast between the ill-tempered lyrics and the composer's penchant for mediation and Zen philosophy. They read like a petty gripe about publishing and pennies, but that's precisely the joke: Harrison dresses a very real contractual frustration in the clothes of wilful nonsense and psychedelia. The lyrics might moan about ownership and indifference, but the music itself embodies his broader philosophy ... that meaning, beauty and even spirituality can survive perfectly well inside systems that are arbitrary, unfair and faintly absurd. George would have been entirely aware that the shareholders of Northern Songs, in which he was a very junior partner, would earn more from his music publishing than he did.

The music has levels of dissonance that would have been out of place on *Sgt. Pepper*. The unusual instrumentation has no guitars at all: only 'Blue Jay Way' and 'Being For The Benefit Of Mr Kite!' also follow this pattern of a rock ensemble without guitars.

George plays a simple Hammond organ part (as he would on two of his other songs in this period, 'Blue Jay Way' and 'Savoy Truffle'), John is credited with piano and haphazard glockenspiel (most audible at 2:17-2:18 and 2:55) and Paul is on bass and parps a trumpet (from 0:41-0:50, 2:18-2:21 and elsewhere).

The song was not mixed into stereo on first release – buyers were treated to a horrendous mock stereo mix with most of the music panned far right. The first true stereo mix of the song was made as late as 1999. We prefer the 1967 mono mix, as you might expect.

A different edit of 'Only A Northern Song' was included on *Anthology 2*. This comprises the basic track without most of the later overdubs. A different vocal take contains some changes to the lyrics and it runs slightly faster.

'All Together Now' (Lennon, McCartney)

Recorded 12 May 1967. Paul McCartney – vocals, bass, acoustic guitar, handclaps, percussion; John Lennon – vocals, ukulele, harmonica, handclaps; George Harrison – backing vocals, acoustic guitar, handclaps; Ringo Starr – backing vocals, drums, finger cymbals, handclaps.

'All Together Now' was recorded in the post-*Sgt. Pepper* sessions in May and June 1967, which also included 'Magical Mystery Tour', 'Baby, You're A Rich Man', 'You Know My Name (Look Up The Number)', 'It's All Too Much' and 'All You Need Is Love'.

That these were released across two singles, an EP and a film soundtrack perhaps indicates a degree of restlessness and lack of direction once *Sgt. Pepper* had been put to bed.

'All Together Now' suits *Yellow Submarine* admirably and was used as its finale, as introduced by The Beatles themselves: 'Newer and bluer meanies have been spotted within the vicinity of this theatre. There's only one way to go out! Singing!'

Its delivery might sound simple, but there's a sly, artful balance at play – childlike at heart, yet stuffed with just enough clever detail to keep the grown-ups' attention. There is sharp syncopation, jagged phrasing, wordplay that sneaks up on you and a form that refuses to be pinned down.

The song was recorded, produced and mixed in a single session by engineer Geoff Emerick. It breaks down thus:

0:00-0:10 introduction, acoustic guitar.
0:10-0:21 first verse: Paul sings, single-tracked.
0:21-0:30 second verse with added ukulele (or capo'ed acoustic guitar).
0:30-0:42 bridge, with John on lead vocals, bass guitar, drums and backing vocals.
0:42-0:53 chorus, with fuller backing vocals, harmonica, finger cymbals and percussion.
0:53-1:02 third verse sung by Paul with full instrumental backing.
1:02-1:35 two more choruses and a repeat of the bridge.
1:35-1:59 two more choruses, getting more raucous, adding handclaps.
1:59-2:11 huge closing chorus, with a final honking bulb horn in the final seconds.

McCartney's detractors suggest that this is an example of his 'granny music'. We say that this is a finely executed and very clever song, perfectly judged for the *Yellow Submarine* project, but perhaps on a 'proper' Beatles album it would have been read as filler rather than relief. By 1967-68, the group's standards had shifted toward cohesion, depth and a sense of forward motion, and this little burst of communal bonhomie belonged to a parallel Beatles universe where charm was still allowed to be the whole point. It does, however, sound particularly fine on the 1999 remix.

We also enjoy The Muppets' version on the album *Kermit Unpigged* (1995). They censor one of the original lyrics. You'll need to listen for yourself to find out which one.

'Hey Bulldog' (Lennon, McCartney)

Recorded 11 February 1968. John Lennon – vocals, piano; Paul McCartney – backing vocals, bass, tambourine, lead guitar (?); George Harrison – guitar; Ringo Starr – drums.

'Hey Bulldog' dates from the same series of sessions that gave us 'Lady Madonna' and 'Across The Universe'. It was arranged and recorded in a single day and is by far the most substantial new song on the *Yellow Submarine* album. It is simple and effective, comprising a backing track of piano, bass, guitar and drums. It's driven by a thrilling piano riff, sharing DNA with 'Lady Madonna', which had been recorded the previous weekend. It's entirely possible that John wrote 'Hey Bulldog' in direct response to Paul's upbeat piano rocker.

John's singing and Paul's bass-playing are simply incredible: two very fine musicians working in total concord. We also have extremely rare footage of the band in Abbey Road during the recording sessions. It's a joy to watch John and Paul interacting, laughing and smiling. You can hear and feel their pleasure listening to the finished recording.

The performer of the growling guitar solo from 1:13 to 1:32 is open to question. Writers Walter Everett, Ian MacDonald and John C. Winn attribute it to Paul McCartney. Engineer Geoff Emerick, however, says that George Harrison performed the solo, writing: 'Harrison's solo was sparkling ... one of the few times that he nailed it right away. His amp was turned up really loud, and he used one of his new fuzz boxes, which made his guitar absolutely scream.'

Listen for yourself. It sounds like George's pumped-up Gibson SG, but could it be Paul, playing the SG upside down? The guitar solo closely follows the flow and rhythm of Paul's phenomenal bass guitar line, especially in the musicality of the descending lines and the *sound* of the notes, which suggest the attack of an upside-down guitar. Some commentators think that it's John, with his aggressive, bluesy and jagged playing. He's shown playing the SG in the promo film. Either way, it's definitely not George.

Hidden on the *Yellow Submarine* soundtrack, the rock-solid 'Hey Bulldog' was overlooked for years. It was rightly added to the expanded *1967-1970* compilation in 2023, and this latest mix jumps out of the speakers.

'It's All Too Much' (Harrison)

Recorded 25-26 May and 2 June 1967. George Harrison – lead and backing vocals, Hammond organ, lead guitar, handclaps; John Lennon – backing vocals, lead guitar, handclaps; Paul McCartney – backing vocals, bass, cowbell, handclaps; Ringo Starr – drums, tambourine; David Mason and three uncredited session players – trumpets; Paul Harvey – bass clarinet.

George's LSD song. By 1969, 'It's All Too Much' was well over its sell-by date: 1967 seemed a long way in the past when *Yellow Submarine* was released. But the ability to appreciate 'It's All Too Much' from a distance of almost 60 years reveals an incredibly dense soundscape.

There is the Indian-influenced drone, a burst of howling Jimi Hendrix guitar feedback, Hammond organ (played by George), parping brass and a closing passage that lasts longer than 'She Loves You'. The sustained organ chords create a hypnotic, mantra-like quality reminiscent of tambura drones. The vocal lines and instrumental riffs lean on Mixolydian and Phrygian modes, which are common in Indian ragas, giving it that slightly 'Eastern' flavour. And while it's mostly Western rock drums and percussion, the layered tambourine, hand percussion and organ accents evoke the rhythmic complexity of Indian music. The Indian influence isn't strict or authentic; it's blended with Western orchestration, brass and fuzz guitar to create a kind of 'psychedelic India'.

We have George's mix of grumbling and teasing lyrics ('Show me that I'm everywhere and get me home for tea'), loud lead guitar from John Lennon, particularly striking from 2:13-2:30, and more brass (trumpeter David Mason gets his fifth credit). Bands such as Mercury Rev and Flaming Lips have based entire careers on the sound of this song.

The track was used as the marvellous climax of the *Yellow Submarine* film, heavily edited to 2:22. The album version is one of The Beatles' longest, at 6:26. An even longer mix, 8:14 in length, is in circulation.

The 1999 mix for *Yellow Submarine Songtrack* brings out Ringo's incredible drumming.

But taken out of context of the *Yellow Submarine* project, this song can be a drag. If this wasn't by The Beatles, would anyone still be listening?

'All You Need Is Love'

Previously released as a single [UK: 7 July 1967, US: 17 July 1967] and on Magical Mystery Tour [US: 27 November 1967]

'All You Need Is Love' works in the *Yellow Submarine* film because it's presented as the emotional apex of the plot rather than a standalone pop song. Placed amid the story's chaos and colour, it transforms from a chart-topping slogan into a unifier, a basis for joy and absurdity.

'Get Back' b/w **'Don't Let Me Down'** (Single)

UK: 11 April 1969. US: 5 May 1969.
Chart positions. UK: 1. US: 1.
Credited to The Beatles with Billy Preston.

Issued in April 1969, 'Get Back'/'Don't Let Me Down' captured The Beatles at a pivotal moment: a band attempting to rediscover the immediacy of live performance while quietly unravelling behind the scenes. Although conceived as part of the ambitious Get Back project, the single stands apart from the later Let It Be album, pairing one of Paul McCartney's most exuberant rockers with one of John Lennon's most emotionally direct love songs. Together, they offered a reminder of the extraordinary creative balance that still existed between the group's two principal songwriters, even as their partnership approached its end.

'Get Back' (Lennon, McCartney)

Recorded 27-28 January 1969. Paul McCartney – lead vocals, bass; John Lennon – lead guitar, backing vocals; George Harrison – rhythm guitar; Ringo Starr – drums; Billy Preston – electric piano.

The period from 2 to 31 January 1969 is particularly well-documented, with hundreds of hours of audio and, eventually, an 8-hour documentary. Almost every moment of the composition, arrangement, recording and mixing of *Get Back* is available.

'We were sitting in the studio,' Paul wrote in the press release accompanying the single, 'and we made it up out of thin air ... we started to write words there and then ... when we finished it, we recorded it at Apple Studios and made it into a song to roller-coast by.'

In one heart-stopping moment in Peter Jackson's *Get Back* series, we see Paul and John working on the lyrics of 'Get Back'. John's look of 'this guy is good' when Paul nails down 'Tucson, Arizona' is a joy. George and Ringo also realise that Paul is onto something, and once they move to Apple Studios and are joined by Billy Preston, the collective musicians develop the song into a tight, punchy rocker.

'Get Back' is, in effect, a variation on an eight-bar blues, mostly on the I (A or A7) and IV (D), with a quick turnaround to flat-VII (the G-D at the end of each line), which is usually accented dynamically by the band. The simplicity of the composition is enhanced by the band's wonderful, entertaining, on-point performance. Ringo shuffles, John plays upstroke rhythm and bluesy lead guitar, and Billy Preston adds a thrilling electric piano solo (1:13-1:28), which earned him a co-performance credit. This was the only Beatles single released with a featured artist credit at their request.

The single mix patches the majority of take 11 from 27 January with the coda from 28 January. This mix is the first example of Ringo's drums being presented in true stereo, mixed across the left and right channels. The only other Beatles tracks to employ this technique were 'Don't Let Me Down' and 'The End'.

'Get Back' was released as a single in the UK in April 1969. It was a huge hit, entering the charts at number one and staying there for the first six of its 17-week chart run. It was a number one for five weeks in the US in May and June 1969.

As the final song performed at the rooftop gig on 30 January 1969, 'Get Back' holds the honour as the last-ever song played by The Beatles in public, only halting when the police arrive to shut down the show. Boo.

'Don't Let Me Down' (Lennon, McCartney)
Recorded 28 January 1969. John Lennon – lead vocals, rhythm guitar; Paul McCartney – bass, backing vocals; George Harrison – lead guitar, backing vocals; Ringo Starr – drums; Billy Preston – electric piano.
'Don't Let Me Down' is another classic B-side by The Beatles. You can say what you like about Yoko Ono's musical attributes, but as a muse she inspired many of John Lennon's late-period classics, including this edgy, powerful, almost desperate love song. It utilises a simple chord change from F#m7 to E, borrowed from 'Albatross' by Fleetwood Mac, resident in the UK top five throughout January 1969. John's 'Sun King', written and rehearsed in the same period, uses the same change.

This is a true band performance: George's descending guitar counterpoint is delicious (1:23 to 1:45); Paul's scintillating bass and harmony vocals are peerless (with a trademark 'whoo!' at 1:58); there is another solo for Billy Preston (3:05-3:28); and Ringo is perfect as always.

The recording has a very live feel, and the muddy 1969 mix sounds like a band who have rehearsed *just enough*. The slightly more ragged Glyn Johns mix for the rejected *Get Back* album was recorded on 22 January and released in 2021 on *Let It Be: Special Edition*.

'The Ballad Of John And Yoko' b/w **'Old Brown Shoe'** (Single)
UK: 30 May 1969. US: 4 June 1969.
Chart positions. UK: 1. US: 8.
The pairing of 'The Ballad Of John And Yoko' and 'Old Brown Shoe' presents two very different perspectives on The Beatles' final year. Recorded while John Lennon and Paul McCartney briefly worked without George Harrison and Ringo Starr on the A-side, the single juxtaposes Lennon's witty autobiographical account of his marriage to Yoko Ono with Harrison's increasingly confident songwriting on the B-side. Together, the two songs underline how The Beatles remained artistically vibrant even as their internal relationships became ever more fragile.

'The Ballad Of John And Yoko' (Lennon, McCartney)
Recorded 14 April 1969. John Lennon – lead vocals, lead guitars, acoustic guitar, percussion; Paul McCartney – bass, drums, piano, maracas, backing vocals.
A minor Beatles song, and yet it was a number-one single in the UK. 'The Ballad Of John And Yoko' chronicles the events surrounding the wedding of John Lennon and Yoko Ono. Their marriage took place in Gibraltar on 20 March 1969, where they flew in for a couple of hours from Paris. John wrote this reportage song over the next few days during a stay in Amsterdam for the first of their 'bed-in' events and 'a lightning trip to Vienna'.

They returned to the UK on 1 April and 'The Ballad Of John And Yoko' was recorded two weeks later in a single seven-hour session. With George unavailable and Ringo filming *The Magic Christian*, all of the instruments and vocals are by

John Lennon and Paul McCartney. Precisely for this reason, it holds a uniquely magical spot in The Beatles' story: 'The Ballad Of John And Yoko' is entirely a Lennon-McCartney duet in the purest sense. It is stripped of The Beatles' usual ensemble feel: every note, rhythm and texture comes directly from them.

The basic take has Paul on drums and John on acoustic guitar and vocals. Paul overdubbed bass guitar, then John added two different electric guitar parts (panned hard left and right). The second of these guitar overdubs features Paul's piano, recorded simultaneously. Paul's backing vocals and then percussion by both musicians, John hitting the back of his guitar and Paul shaking a pair of maracas, completed the recording, which was mixed immediately afterwards.

You can hear Paul's basslines and drums locking perfectly with John's guitar and vocals, like two halves of a single mind in the studio. That intimacy gives the track a raw immediacy and some personal charm: it's a Beatles song, but it's also just two old friends telling a story together. There's no crowd of instruments to hide behind, no orchestration to soften the edges – just Lennon and McCartney, John and Paul.

With its literal and episodic lyrics, the song reads like a diary set to music. It chronicles events with almost journalistic precision but lacks the poetic depth or metaphorical richness of other Lennon/McCartney lyrics. Lines like 'Made a lightning trip to Vienna/Eating chocolate cake in a bag' are whimsical and fun but arguably clunky or even banal in conventional lyrical terms.

The song, however, is both impulsive and economical. It's a rock 'n' roll postcard where every note serves the story. It would be their last number one in the UK for 54 years.

'Old Brown Shoe' (Harrison)

Recorded 16 and 18 April 1969. George Harrison – lead vocals, guitars, organ; John Lennon – piano, organ, backing vocals; Paul McCartney – drums, bass, backing vocals.

'Old Brown Shoe' is a weird little gem in The Beatles' catalogue because, beneath its rollicking shuffle and seemingly light-hearted groove, it hints at metaphysical reflection. It's a tightly-arranged and focused up-tempo rocker, first brought forward during the *Get Back* sessions. There is a good-humoured rehearsal performance seen in Peter Jackson's *Get Back* series (recorded on 28 January 1969), with George on piano ('pianos are very difficult, aren't they?', he says), Paul on guitar, Ringo on drums and Billy Preston on six-string bass.

A month later, at EMI, George celebrated his 26th birthday by recording demos of three new songs. 'Old Brown Shoe', in retrospect, pales in comparison to two of his best-ever compositions: 'Something' and 'All Things Must Pass'.

Nevertheless, when needing a B-side for 'The Ballad Of John And Yoko', three of The Beatles convened to formally record 'Old Brown Shoe'. It was their first session at Abbey Road for six months. The lineup for the basic track is George on lead vocals and acoustic guitar, John on piano and Paul on drums. George's electric guitar was overdubbed that same day, along with Paul's thrumming and intricate bass. New lead vocals and Paul and John's backing vocals completed that day's work. George's fabulous solo (from 1:38 to 1:52) would be added later that week – presumably after giving George a couple of days to work it out. George also added organ, with John's help, most prominent in the second half of the song.

In his 1980 autobiography, *I, Me, Mine*, Harrison states that the lyrical content started as a study in the metaphysical theme of opposites and addresses 'the duality of things'. George juxtaposes light and dark, right and wrong. 'Old Brown Shoe' asks questions without offering resolutions.

Abbey Road

UK: 26 September 1969. US: 1 October 1969.
Chart positions. UK: 1. US: 1.

Abbey Road is undoubtedly one of the greatest artistic statements of the 20th century. It's one of your authors' favourite albums by anyone, ever.

Alberto Bravin: 'I'm very connected to this album. All of my beloved music starts with *Abbey Road*: progressive rock, heavy metal, piano ballads, everything. It's a perfect album for me. It has two of George's most beautiful songs, you have Ringo's best-ever song and three great tracks by John: 'Come Together', 'I Want You (She's So Heavy)' and 'Because'. But then we see who's in charge, and that's Paul. Not only do we have 'Maxwell's Silver Hammer', which I love, and 'Oh! Darling', but also the side two medley, which Paul conceived and executed with George Martin. The Beatles recorded *Abbey Road* knowing it would likely be their last. It's full of universal, magical moments. Finishing with 'The End', with lyrics literally about love being returned, doesn't feel accidental: *Abbey Road* is a goodbye in everything but name. And that makes it special, too.'

But first, some well-documented history. The band's difficult *Get Back* sessions in January 1969 generated just enough material for a new album. Their engineer, Glyn Johns, was tasked with creating a running order, but with post-production on the accompanying documentary film likely to take up the rest of 1969, and with the band wanting to continue recording, they commenced their 11th album only three weeks after their rooftop concert with 'I Want You (She's So Heavy)'.

Seven sessions in April and May yielded 'Oh! Darling', 'Octopus's Garden', 'Something' and the first element of the long medley, 'You Never Give Me Your Money'. The remainder would be laid down in a busy set of recording sessions between 1 July and 1 August, followed by a further three weeks of overdubs and mixes.

The mellow sound of the album owes much to EMI Studio's new 8-track recording technology, a solid-state mixing desk, and to the return of engineer Geoff Emerick, who had manned the console for the majority of the band's recordings in 1966 and 1967. The tape operator was 20-year-old Alan Parsons. Three years later, in the same studio, he would engineer *Dark Side Of The Moon* on the same mixing desk. The production choices, essentially made by The Beatles with George Martin, Geoff Emerick and fellow engineer Phil McDonald, are perfect. The band themselves are at their performance peak. Witness Ringo's in-the-pocket drumming (famously damped by tea towels), the complex vocal harmonies, Paul's perfect bass playing, George's outstandingly melodic lead guitar ... these elements define 'The Beatles' sound' to listeners in the 21st century.

Was *Abbey Road* a valediction? By mid-1969, their personal relationships were shot, Apple was a mess and John had privately said he wanted out. The tensions in the *Get Back* sessions were real. But The Beatles were also aware of their important collective status as artists. Paul explicitly pushed for a 'real' final statement from the most successful band of all time. They surely felt the weight of their impact, culturally and musically, between 1963 and 1969. So, after the chaos of the *Get Back* sessions, they said, essentially: Let's do one more album the right way ... tight, produced, polished.

'Come Together' (Lennon, McCartney)

Recorded 21-30 July 1969. John Lennon – lead and backing vocals, guitar, handclaps, tambourine; Paul McCartney – backing vocals, bass, electric piano; George Harrison – lead and rhythm guitars; Ringo Starr – drums, maracas.

The swampy, inscrutable 'Come Together' marks out the territory of *Abbey Road*. The title comes from John Lennon's promise to write a campaign song for Timothy Leary, an American psychologist who had met the Lennons during their Montreal 'Bed-in for Peace' in late May and early June 1969. Leary intended to run for Governor of California, and Lennon's springboard for his song was based on the campaign's slogan, 'Come Together – Join the Party!'. This was a strong symbol of unity in a time of political and cultural fragmentation.

The lyrics of 'Come Together' – a long song at 4:20 – are typically cryptic. A sample:

He bag production.
He got walrus gumboot.
He got Ono sideboard.
He one spinal cracker.
He got feet down below his knee.

The meaning of the words doesn't really matter: they fit together musically. The opening line, 'Here come old flat-top', was borrowed from Chuck Berry's 'You Can't Catch Me'. That song's publisher, Morris Levy of Big Seven Music, sued Lennon for copyright infringement. Following the settlement in 1973, Lennon agreed to record three songs from Big Seven's publishing catalogue for his next album.

The chorus is very short, only eight bars, but powerfully dark. It's also saucy enough to make a 1969 radio producer clear his throat and decide not to think too hard about it.

Takes 1 and 5 from 21 July 1969 reveal the basic lineup of John singing lead vocal and clapping, Paul on bass, George on guitar and Ringo on drums. Take 5 is *phenomenal*. The groove pushes bass and rhythm as primary musical drivers. The band are incredibly tight, and John sings like a demon, even when his voice cracks at 2:06. By take 9, the backing track was in place. The overdubs recorded in the coming days included percussion, a new lead vocal (and handclaps), Paul's very funky Rhodes electric piano (audible from 2:03, presumably the same instrument played by Billy Preston on 'Get Back'), George's harmony guitars (from 2:15) and John's heavily distorted guitar during the choruses (all recorded 22 July); Paul's harmony vocals from the second verse (25 July); unused guitar from John (29 July); and George's expressive lead guitar solo with the fat, tough sound of his Gibson Les Paul from 3:14 (30 July).

'Come Together' is vibrant, smouldering, sexy and utterly fabulous. It sounds like it was recorded last week.

There are some high-profile cover versions. Ike and Tina Turner started performing the song immediately after *Abbey Road*'s release in 1969. A stirring studio version followed before the end of the year. Aerosmith released their cover as a single in July 1978, reaching number 23 on the *Billboard* Hot 100. Michael Jackson recorded the song in 1986 for his album *Bad*, later released as a B-side and more easily available on *HIStory: Past, Present And Future, Book I* (1995). It was a big hit for The Smokin' Mojo Filters (1995, Macca on bass), Arctic Monkeys (2012) and Gary Clark Jr. and Junkie XL (2017). We also enjoy Godsmack's very loud, bad-ass 2012 version.

'Something' (Harrison)

Recorded 2 May, 5 May, 16 July and 15 August 1969. George Harrison – lead vocals, lead and rhythm guitars; John Lennon – piano; Paul McCartney – bass, backing vocals; Ringo Starr – drums; Billy Preston – Hammond organ; unidentified session musicians – twelve violins, four violas, four cellos, string bass.

The beautiful, timeless, quietly triumphant 'Something' was started in 1968. George worked on it for several months. In Peter Jackson's *Get Back* series, George asks for his bandmates' songwriting advice.

> 'What could it be, Paul?' George says. 'Something in the way she moves ... what attracted me?'
> 'Just say whatever comes into your head each time', John suggests. 'Attracts me like a cauliflower, until you get the word.'
> 'Yeah, but I've been through this one, like, for about six months', George replies. 'Attracts me like a pomegranate ... We could have that.'

George, of course, eventually comes up with the poetic 'attracts me like no other lover'.

George's songwriting naturally reflects the different sides of his complex personality. There is the mystic: the songs that reveal his spiritual yearning, introspection and fascination with the transcendent ('Within You Without You', 'Long, Long, Long', 'The Inner Light', 'While My Guitar Gently Weeps', 'Old Brown Shoe' and the forthcoming 'My Sweet Lord', 'Awaiting On You All', 'Isn't It A Pity' and 'All Things Must Pass'). We have his wry sense of humour, which is cheeky, flippant, ironic, or playfully absurd (viz: 'Piggies', 'Savoy Truffle', 'Only A Northern Song' and the later 'Crackerbox Palace' and 'I Dig Love'). Occasionally, his frustration floats to the surface ('Taxman', 'Only A Northern Song', the solo 'Wah-Wah' and 'Beware Of Darkness'). And, from time to time, the optimism of love breaks through: warm, affectionate, sometimes playful. George didn't write as many love songs as Lennon or McCartney, but a few shine with understated, deeply felt and tender devotion. 'Something', of course, but also 'Here Comes The Sun', 'I Need You' and 'If I Needed Someone'.

Musically, 'Something' is cheerful on the surface but quietly devastating underneath. On first listen, it drifts by with the untroubled grace of a love song that seems to know exactly where it's going. The melody is so fluid and polite that it barely asks to be questioned. Yet that surface ease is precisely the disguise. Harrison's lyric circles rather than declares, hedging its devotion with doubt. The 'I don't know' section presumably reflects on George's inability to express himself: he also wrote 'I Want To Tell You' three years earlier, in which his lack of articulation is similarly documented. This is reinforced by the simple but uplifting guitar lick, which goes against the tone of tongue-tied frustration. That upbeat, optimistic hook that kicks off and wraps up the song and crops up in every verse feels almost heroic ... until the amazing bassline, especially under the guitar solo, drags you under with a constant, nagging undertow.

It took a few attempts to get the recording just right. George recorded a demo on 25 February 1969.

Engineer Glyn Johns recalls in his memoirs *Sound Man* (2014): 'One morning before the others arrived at the studio, George asked me if I would stay behind at the end of the day to cut a demo with him of a song he had written, as he didn't want to play it in front of the others. So we waited for everyone to leave, and he went out into the empty studio and played 'Something In The Way She Moves', which might just be the greatest song he ever wrote. He came into the control room, and after having it played back to him, he asked what I thought of it, as he seemed unsure. I told him it was brilliant and that he must play it to the others. I can only assume that his confidence had been dented as a result of living in the shadow of John and Paul.'

Rather than presenting 'Something' to The Beatles (at least for now), the demo was first offered to Jackie Lomax, then passed to Joe Cocker, whose version was recorded in Los Angeles that summer for his album *Joe Cocker!*

After completing recording work on 'Old Brown Shoe' on 16 April, The Beatles recorded thirteen takes of 'Something' in a late-night session. One presumes that, with Paul on drums in Ringo's absence and John covering on bass, George was dissatisfied. They returned to Studio 3 on 2 May, now with Ringo in place. Across 36 takes, they laid down a backing track comprising guitar (George), piano (John), bass (Paul) and drums (Ringo). We should note that even at this stage, Ringo hits the right groove straight away: he was indispensable. An overdub of Billy Preston's organ completed the day's work.

If George cannot express himself verbally, then the emotional impact comes from his instrument. His perfect guitar solo would be added on 5 May at Olympic. It is impeccable, with a light touch and a gorgeous melody. On the same day, John added new piano and Paul re-worked his masterful bass part (one of his very best, listen to it in isolation on YouTube, it has a rhythm and melody all of its own). Lead and backing vocals were added on 11 July and redone five days later. Finally, orchestral strings would complete the track on 15 August.

The arrangement and production of 'Something' are undeniably sumptuous: those lush strings, the gentle layering of instruments, the subtle dynamics that make it feel alive. But they are, in many ways, icing on the cake. At its core, the song thrives because of its composition. George Harrison's original demo, stripped down to a single guitar, reveals a melody and harmonic structure so compelling that it stands on its own, intimate and complete. The song's enduring appeal is further illustrated by Paul McCartney's ukulele performances, delivered with nothing more than a tiny instrument and his voice, yet still resonating with profound emotional clarity in concert over 500 times. Composition dictates this resilience: the shape of the melody, the way the chords wind and resolve, the phrasing of the lyric ... all of these elements ensure the song survives any arrangement, any instrumentation, any decade. Frank Sinatra's version from 1972 proves this theory. Production can enhance, highlight, or even reinterpret, but it cannot create the kind of fundamental, structural brilliance that makes a song timeless.

All of this definitively realised George's potential as the songwriting equal of Paul and John. As the second most covered Beatles song after 'Yesterday', 'Something' won the prestigious Ivor Novello award for 'Best Song Musically And Lyrically' in 1971, the band's fourteenth.

George has said that Ray Charles was a key influence. It seems appropriate that Charles himself would record the song, although it's given a schmaltzy arrangement. Its composer was more fond of Joe Cocker's and James Brown's versions: 'The best [cover] I ever heard was [from] James Brown, and he did it in 1972, but ... only as the B-side of a re-recorded version of 'Think', which is a very old song of his. I sent him a postcard and said: 'You should make it the A-side, it's a killer! It's really good."

It is. But not as good as the original, which is our favourite track on *Abbey Road* and remains one of the best songs of the 20th century. It's perfect. John Lennon later said that 'Something' was the best song on *Abbey Road*. There's just something about it, right?

'Maxwell's Silver Hammer' (Lennon, McCartney)

Recorded 9-11 July, 6 August 1969. Paul McCartney – lead and backing vocals, piano, acoustic guitar, Moog synthesiser; George Harrison – backing vocals, bass, electric guitars; Ringo Starr – backing vocals, drums, anvil; George Martin – Hammond organ

'If any single recording shows why The Beatles broke up, it's 'Maxwell's Silver Hammer", writes music historian Ian MacDonald in the impeccable *Revolution In The Head: The Beatles' Records And The Sixties*.

Your authors are not in agreement in their views about 'Maxwell's Silver Hammer'. One of us loves it; the other wouldn't worry if he never heard it again. The world would be very boring if we all thought the same way.

The song is, according to Paul McCartney in *Many Years From Now*, 'my analogy for when something goes wrong out of the blue, as it so often does, as I was beginning to find out at that time in my life. I wanted something symbolic of that, so to me it was some fictitious character called Maxwell with a silver hammer. I don't know why it was silver; it just sounded better than Maxwell's hammer. It was needed for scanning. 'Joan was quizzical, studied pataphysical science in the home' – nobody knows what it means. I am the only person who ever put the name of pataphysics into the record charts, c'mon – it was great. I love those surreal little touches.'

For his part, John Lennon disliked 'Maxwell's Silver Hammer', claiming it was more of Paul's 'granny music'. He doesn't contribute to the *Abbey Road* version. 'That's Paul's. I hate it', John said in 1980, 'He made us do it a hundred million times [in the *Get Back* sessions]. He did everything to make it into a single, and it never was, and it never could've been, but he put guitar licks on it, and he had somebody hitting iron pieces, and we spent more money on that song than any of them in the whole album. I think.'

'Sometimes Paul would make us do these really fruity songs', George said to *Crawdaddy* in 1977. 'I mean, my god, 'Maxwell's Silver Hammer' was so fruity. After a while, we did a good job on it, but when Paul got an idea or an arrangement in his head ...'

'The worst session ever was 'Maxwell's Silver Hammer", Ringo told *Rolling Stone* in 2008. 'It was the worst track we ever had to record. It went on for fucking weeks. I thought it was mad.'

'They got annoyed because 'Maxwell's Silver Hammer' took three days to record', Paul said in *Anthology*. 'Big deal.'

Yes, Paul had a fondness for 'granny music'. But 'Maxwell's Silver Hammer' has not only experimentation in its musical elements (hammer, anvil and Moog synthesiser in the same song?) but also a strangely sinister lyric.

Whereas 'All Together Now', 'Honey Pie', 'Your Mother Should Know', 'Ob-La-Di, Ob-La-Da' and 'When I'm 64' are chirpy and thumbs-aloft, 'Maxwell's Silver Hammer' is seriously dark:

Bang, bang, Maxwell's silver hammer
Came down upon her head
Bang, bang, Maxwell's silver hammer
Made sure that she was dead

Perhaps John Lennon was jealous that the lovable Beatle had written one of the blackest popular songs as a light-hearted joke?

Listening again, one cannot deny the craft; this is *Abbey Road* after all. The production is immaculate, the musicianship peerless. It might not be one of the greatest Beatles songs, but it's an integral part of *Abbey Road* and therefore demands to be heard.

Perhaps programming it after two of the greatest songs ever written was, in retrospect, a mistake? Try swapping tracks three and four in your *Abbey Road* playlist ...

'Oh! Darling' (Lennon, McCartney)
Recorded 20 April – 11 August 1969. Paul McCartney – lead and backing vocals, piano, guitar, tambourine; John Lennon – backing vocals, guitar; George Harrison – backing vocals, bass; Ringo Starr – drums.

From the ridiculous to the sublime? Paul surely channels Otis Redding on this outstanding, loud and passionate 12/8 soulful rocker. Listen to Redding's 'These Arms Of Mine' (1962), 'I've Been Loving You Too Long (To Stop Now)' (1965) and 'Try A Little Tenderness' (1966). Paul, for all his attributes as a musician, can surely only pay lip service to songs such as these?

'Oh! Darling' was first recorded on 27 January 1969 as part of the *Get Back* sessions. This version can be heard (in different edits) on both *Anthology 3* and the deluxe box set of *Let It Be*. Returning to the song for *Abbey Road*, it took ten sessions and five months of work to complete it to Paul's satisfaction.

The first, 20 April, comprised 26 takes of the backing track by Paul (on piano and vocals), John (on guitar, whose aggressive off-beat chops in the verses are twinned with an arpeggiated pattern in the bridges), George (playing bass with some minor flubs at 0:49, 1:25 and 3:02 that you wouldn't hear from Macca), Ringo (on drums, genius, especially 1:02 to 1:08) and Billy Preston (organ). Preston had taken part in the earlier *Get Back* version of the song. Take 4 can be heard on the extended re-release of *Abbey Road*, where it is already sounding awesome, if rough-and-ready. Paul, singing at something like 60% of his capacity, manages some incredible vocalising.

Paul re-recorded his vocals on 26 April, and there the song rested until 17 July, when he spent several days re-recording his lead part. As Paul said in *Anthology*: 'I came into the studios early every day for a week to sing it by myself because at first my voice was too clear. I wanted it to sound as though I'd been performing it on stage all week.' When he gives it his all from 1:08 (on 'when you told me'), his vocal range and expression are untouchable. He simply roars in his full chest voice: it's also there in 'Golden Slumbers' (30-31 July). There's a groovy flattened chord under 'you didn't *need* me any more' and the song goes into orbit with his extemporised 'ooh!' at 2:16.

The final version is a deft combination of three separate vocal tracks. This process removed Billy Preston's organ from the mix (it's audible on take 4, if you want to hear it). Final overdubs in August added a guitar part from Paul (the introductory chord), tambourine and doo-wop backing vocals, which enter at different points in each verse.

'Donna' by 10cc is a very obvious callback. Robin Gibbs' version from the shockingly awful 1978 film *Sgt. Pepper's Lonely Hearts Club Band* is, perhaps surprisingly, given the context, rather marvellous.

'Octopus's Garden' (Starkey)

Recorded 26 and 29 April, 17-18 July 1969. Ringo Starr – lead vocals, drums, percussion, piano; John Lennon – backing vocals, rhythm guitar; Paul McCartney – backing vocals, bass, piano; George Harrison – backing vocals, lead guitar.

'Octopus's Garden' is the perfect 'Ringo' song, his second and last original composition for The Beatles. He's seen tinkering on the piano in Peter Jackson's *Get Back* documentary, where he has a basic tune and the first verse. The final version on *Abbey Road* is much more sophisticated, and although the sole songwriting credit is given to Ringo, George helped considerably with the arrangement. It's a very basic I, vi, IV, V sequence used in hundreds of songs such as 'All I Have To Do Is Dream', 'Blue Moon', 'Please Mr Postman', 'Stand By Me' and The Beatles' own 'Tell Me Why' and 'Happiness Is A Warm Gun'.

For take 2 of the basic track, recorded on 26 April, Ringo drums and provides a guide vocal, using the same set of lyrics for all three verses. John and George play guitar and Paul is on bass. Three days later, with the lyrics now finished, Ringo re-recorded his lead vocals (later redone) and Paul added piano. Final overdubs in mid-July added that *Abbey Road* polish. The arrangement is very cool, from George's opening guitar runs to the silly-but-fun backing vocals, sound effects and the sound of Ringo blowing bubbles into a glass of water.

George Harrison was fond of the song, perhaps offering solidarity to a bandmate who also had to push to get his compositions taken seriously. 'I think it's a really great song,' he said in 1969, 'because on the surface, it's just like a daft kids' song, but the lyrics are great. For me, you know, I find very deep meaning in the lyrics, which Ringo probably doesn't see, but all the things like 'resting our head on the sea bed' and 'We'll be warm beneath the storm', which is really great, you know. Because it's like this level is a storm, and if you get sort of deep in your consciousness, it's very peaceful. So Ringo's writing his cosmic songs without noticing.'

'Octopus's Garden' is charming and unpretentious – much like its composer.

'I Want You (She's So Heavy)' (Lennon, McCartney)

Recorded 22 February, 18 and 20 April, 8 and 11 August 1969. John Lennon – lead and backing vocals, lead guitars, Moog synthesiser; Paul McCartney – backing vocals, bass; George Harrison – backing vocals, lead guitars; Ringo Starr – drums, congas, wind machine; Billy Preston – Hammond organ.

The Beatles play progressive rock? Maybe, although that term hadn't even been invented yet. The ground-breaking *In The Court Of The Crimson King* was recorded at Wessex Studios, about five miles east of Abbey Road, in July and August 1969. This is serendipity rather than any cross-fertilisation. Either way, this is a devastating song, eight minutes, 11 words, utterly original, intense, still modern-sounding.

> I want you so bad it's driving me mad she's so heavy.

If we argue that progressive rock boils down to dynamics, changes of metre, repeated motifs and taking your time to make a point, then 'I Want You (She's So Heavy)' has all of this.

It also has a monster guitar riff starting at 4:37 that predicts the first Black Sabbath album, recorded on 16 October 1969 – three weeks after *Abbey Road* went on sale – at Regent Sound on Denmark Street, just across Regent's Park from EMI's studios in St. John's Wood. We're not suggesting that The Beatles invented Black Sabbath, but the chaos and volume of 'I Want You (She's So Heavy)', and the earlier 'Helter Skelter', must have provided a degree of validation. Dream Theater's song 'Finally Free' from *Metropolis Pt. 2: Scenes From A Memory* (1999) has clear musical allusions to 'I Want You (She's So Heavy)', including an abrupt ending. Listen from 7:23 to 9:50.

Harmonically, 'I Want You (She's So Heavy)' has a yin and yang: a mix of darkness and light. The introduction and coda are ominous, almost Wagnerian, or with overtones of Mussorgsky's 'Night On A Bare Mountain'. The verses are straight, heavy minor-key blues. So, progressive rock, heavy metal, blues and classical bombast in one song ...

It breaks down thus:

0:00-0:13 five bars of 6/8 using a distinctive arpeggiated set of chords, namely Dm, Dm/F, $E9^{-7}$, Bb7 and Aaug.

0:13-1:04 first verse, Paul's bass is already very lively. It concludes with a short syncopated major section with bubbling bass and a sizzling hi-hat from Ringo.

1:04-1:55 second verse, a slightly more relaxed repeat of the first.

1:55-2:24 the first 'she's so heavy' chorus, using the same arpeggiated chords from the intro and swirling organ.

2:24-3:16 instrumental verse, loose and dirty, with variation on the second bass riff.

3:16-3:45 the second 'she's so heavy' chorus, with Paul wailing at full power.

3:45-4:35 a faster, funkier verse – 70 seconds of musical bliss. John's scream at 4:27 will make your hair curl.

4:35-7:45 a three-minute crescendo, 14 repeats of the five-bar introduction, gaining in intensity and white noise. At 7:45, an abrupt, jarring silence signals the end of side one of *Abbey Road*. This harsh edit took place during a mixing session on 20 August 1969, the last day on which all four Beatles were together in the studio.

Ten mixes were made and John, being John, liked bits of different ones and these were spliced together. An obvious cross-fade at 3:43 has been smoothed out on the 2019 remix.

Each musician's performance is consummate. Paul's bass is exceptional, but also the massed guitars, Ringo's groove and, of course, John's singing. Everybody shines and the song does not outstay its excessive length.

Consider this: from 'Love Me Do' through 'Yesterday', 'She Said She Said', 'Within You Without You', 'Strawberry Fields Forever' and 'Blackbird to 'I Want You (She's So Heavy)' in just six-and-a-half years!

'Here Comes The Sun' (Harrison)

Recorded 7 July – 19 August 1969.George Harrison – lead and backing vocals, acoustic and electric guitars, harmonium, Moog synthesiser, handclaps; Paul McCartney – backing vocals, bass, handclaps; Ringo Starr – drums, handclaps; uncredited session musicians – four violas, four cellos, double bass, two piccolos, two flutes, two alto flutes, two clarinets.

As side one ends with the dark chaos of 'I Want You (She's So Heavy)', side two opens with the hopeful, fresh 'Here Comes The Sun', George's second masterpiece on *Abbey Road*. It was composed in April 1969, and although it employs a vastly different musical style from 'I Want You (She's So Heavy)', there remains a consistency of production and sound palette that seems wholly natural. Those knee-jerk genre switches in the *White Album* are smoothed out on *Abbey Road*. This entire album sounds like it's by the same band.

"Here Comes The Sun' was written at the time when Apple was getting like school', George wrote in his memoirs. 'We had to go and be businessmen: 'Sign this' and 'sign that'. Anyway, it seems as if winter in England goes on forever; by the time spring comes, you really deserve it. So one day, I decided I was going to sack off Apple and I went over to Eric Clapton's house [Hurtwood Edge in Ewhurst, Surrey]. The relief of not having to go see all those dopey accountants was wonderful, and I walked around the garden with one of Eric's acoustic guitars and wrote 'Here Comes The Sun'.'

The opening riff is based around a basic D chord (in this case, with a capo on the seventh fret). 'If I Needed Someone' uses a similar approach, as does 'Norwegian Wood (This Bird Has Flown)' at a different position on the fretboard.

'Any guitar player knows,' George told *Guitar World* in 1992, 'that with that open-position D chord, you just move your fingers around and you get all these little maladies ... I mean melodies! ... And that became a thrill, to see how many more tunes you could write around that open D, like 'Here Comes The Sun'.'

Noel Gallagher, for one, learned a great deal about songwriting by employing this very technique.

The lyrics were completed in June during a holiday in Sardinia. 'Here Comes The Sun' is acoustic in foundation and is extremely tricky to play well. Multiple changes of time signatures hint at the influence of Indian music. The song features straight 4/4 in the verse, and the bridge ('sun, sun sun, here it comes') has a sequence of 11/8 + 4/4 + 7/8 (or 11/8 + 15/8 if you wish, take your pick – trying counting along!). One wonders whether George worked hard on this section or whether, like John, he just wrote what felt right and ignored the 'rules' of pop song composition. It certainly has the feel of an Indian raga.

The basic track was recorded on 7 July, comprising George, Paul and Ringo. Take 9 from that day was included on the deluxe reissue of *Abbey Road* in 2019. Ringo is finding his way around the tricky changes in the bridge. You can hear him listening as the bridge progresses and adding some lovely fills with building confidence. The section from 2:34 to 2:40 is delicious. Paul's thrumming bass drives the track along wonderfully.

With take 36 kept as 'best', George added lead vocals the following day, along with backing vocals. Further overdubs included a harmonium and handclaps (16 July), electric guitar (6 August, doubling the acoustic guitar in certain places throughout the song, audible at 0:23, 0:44, 0:52, 1:14-1:25 and elsewhere), George Martin's orchestral arrangement (15 August – four violas, four cellos, double bass, two piccolos, two flutes, two alto flutes and two clarinets), further acoustic guitar (6 and 11 August) and Moog synthesiser (19 August, with a woody clarinet sound at 0:08, 0:59-1:13, 1:23-1:29; a fuzzier distorted setting at 1:47-2:04; and a delicious counter-melody from 2:12 to 3:02). None of this additional instrumentation overwhelms the basic core of George's guitar and vocals.

'Here Comes The Sun' bridges folk-pop accessibility with mathematical precision – it's subtle but deeply innovative and yet still fresh-sounding and commercial. As of 2026, it is the most-streamed Beatles song of all time.

It was a classic in 1969, it's a classic now, and will remain so for all time.

'Because' (Lennon, McCartney)

Recorded 1, 4 and 5 August 1969. John Lennon – vocals, guitar; Paul McCartney – vocals, bass; George Harrison – vocals, Moog synthesiser; George Martin – electric harpsichord.

'Because' was supposedly inspired by John Lennon listening to Yoko Ono playing Ludwig van Beethoven's 'Moonlight Sonata'. 'I was lying on the sofa in our house, listening to Yoko play 'Moonlight Sonata' on the piano', he told *Playboy* in 1980. 'Suddenly, I said, 'Can you play those chords backward?' She did, and I wrote 'Because' around them. The song sounds like 'Moonlight Sonata', too.'

Although some commentators have found similarities – mood, home key, 7th notes and triplet arpeggiation – we call this out as revisionist nonsense: if you listen to a song played backwards when you are stoned, then anything can spring to mind.

The vocal melodies and underlying chord changes are so interlinked that it's impossible to tell which came first. What we so observe is that the first four chord intervals in 'Because' are close enough to the main riff in 'I Want You (She's So Heavy)' that, despite being in different keys and with 'Because' having a couple of extra measures, they must spring from the same well of inspiration. The arpeggiated arrangements of both are surely no coincidence, either.

'I Want You (She's So Heavy)' – Dm, E9-7, Bb7 and Aaug (or I-II-VI-V)
'Because' – C#m, D#m7, G#7 and A (or I-II-V-VI)

George Harrison was effusive about the song. 'Paul usually writes the sweeter tunes,' he said in 1969, 'and John writes the sort of more raving-up things, or the freakier things. But John's getting to where he doesn't want to. He just wants to write twelve bars. But you can't deny it, I think this is possibly my favourite one on the album. The lyrics are so simple. The harmony was pretty difficult to sing. We had to really learn it. But I think that's one of the tunes that will impress most people. It's really good.'

The three-part harmonies were triple-tracked to give nine voices in the final mix. These drape the song in a kind of wide-eyed, unblinking reverie. You can't really tell who is singing what, but there's no autotune here. Sure, the technique nods to early Beatles – 'This Boy', 'Yes It Is' – but there's a transcendent lift here that feels more like Bach's 'Air' from the *Third Suite*. It's another classical allusion then, which is heightened by the use of harpsichord, underpinned by electric guitar and synthesiser.

'The lyrics are clear,' Lennon said, however, 'no bullshit, no imagery, no obscure references.'

Paul McCartney has suggested that Yoko might have lent a hand. 'I wouldn't mind betting Yoko was in on the writing of that', he says in *Many Years From Now*. 'It's rather her kind of writing: wind, sky and earth are recurring, it's straight out of *Grapefruit* and John was heavily influenced by her at the time.'

The harmonies, isolated from their instrumental backing, were available on bootlegs for years and can be heard on both *Anthology 3* and *Love*.

'Because' was the first song on *Abbey Road* to receive a Moog overdub. George had ordered a Moog, with George Harrison playing the part twice, and Mike Vickers, formerly of Manfred Mann, helping with programming.

Vickers was one of the few musicians in the UK to own a Moog – he charged £30 for his services. 'They were playing 'Because' as I walked into the control room,' Vickers told Reverb.com in 2020, 'and it just sounded so utterly beautiful. I couldn't believe it. They were so calm and relaxed, adding a couple more harmonies down in the studio. They told me vaguely what they might want [for the Moog overdubs] – something tinkly, something like horns, big brass, whatever, and then ... I'd set the sounds up and then they'd play their part. They all seemed to know exactly what they wanted to do ... so it all went very quickly. It was all done in about three hours [for overdubs on 'Because' and three others]. I thought the way they worked was amazing. Nobody seemed to say anything, but it all happened. Extraordinary.'

'You Never Give Me Your Money' (Lennon, McCartney)
Recorded 6 May, 1, 15, 30 and 31 July, 5 August 1969. Paul McCartney – lead and backing vocals, piano, bass, wind chimes; John Lennon – guitar, backing vocals; George Harrison – guitar, backing vocals; Ringo Starr – drums, tambourine.
We're 30 minutes into *Abbey Road*. The remainder of the album consists of a 16-minute medley of eight tracks. This comprises mostly older songs and fragments, some dating back to the beginning of 1968. These were kicked off with 'You Never Give Me Your Money' in May, with the remainder recorded during the July and August sessions. It was worked into a cohesive suite by Paul McCartney and George Martin with only two parts specifically written for the medley, McCartney's opening 'You Never Give Me Your Money' and conclusive 'The End'.

These break down thus:

- 'You Never Give Me Your Money', written in March 1969
- 'Sun King', written in late 1968 and rehearsed on the first day of *Get Back* sessions, 1 January 1969
- 'Mean Mr. Mustard', written between February and April 1968, demoed for *The Beatles* in May 1968 and rehearsed several times during the *Get Back* sessions in January 1969
- 'Polythene Pam', written between February and April 1968, demoed for *The Beatles* in May 1968 and rehearsed at least once during the *Get Back* sessions in January 1969
- 'She Came In Through The Bathroom Window' was rehearsed several times during the *Get Back* sessions, January 1969
- 'Golden Slumbers' was rehearsed at least once during the *Get Back* sessions, January 1969
- 'Carry That Weight' was rehearsed at least once during the *Get Back* sessions, January 1969
- 'The End' was most likely written in mid-1969, once recording of the medley had commenced

McCartney and Martin were able to draw these together into a cohesive suite of varying styles: from the piano ballad of 'You Never Give Me Your Money' to the three-guitar wig-out of 'The End'.

The backing track for 'You Never Give Me Your Money' was recorded at Olympic Sound Studios on 6 May 1969. Thus, it was the first part of the medley to be recorded, and comprised Paul on piano and vocals, John and George on electric guitars (George is particularly good here) and Ringo on drums.

Take 30 was taken forward for future overdubs in July, including bass guitar, backing vocals (multi-part harmonies and the closing '1-2-3-4-5-6-7'), percussion, organ and new lead vocals from Paul.

The song itself has a structure similar to 'Happiness Is A Warm Gun' in that it comprises several different sections, all written by Paul:

0:00-1:07 'You never give me your money', solo piano and lead guitar.
1:07-1:31 'Out of college, money spent', harder, faster and in a new key, boogie-woogie piano and a gruff vocal from Paul, sounding a lot like Ringo.
1:31:2:08 The uplifting 'Oh that magic feeling' plus guitar solo.
2:08-2:29 An exquisite transition between two sections where, according to Dominic Pedler, 'McCartney set about conjuring what is arguably the most technically adept of all Beatles modulations. And that's saying something. [It] is one of McCartney's most accomplished musical moments.'
2:29-2:48 'One sweet dream'. Urgent, with dropped bars and loud guitars.
2:48-4:02 Repeating arpeggios which recall 'I Want You (She's So Heavy)', 'Here Comes The Sun' and 'Because', to fade.

The recording originally extended into a three-minute jam. This remains unreleased, but you can get the idea from take 36, which can be heard on the deluxe edition of *Abbey Road*.

'Sun King' (Lennon, McCartney)

Recorded 24-25 July 1969. John Lennon – lead and backing vocals, electric guitar; Paul McCartney – backing vocals, bass; George Harrison – backing vocals, electric guitar; Ringo Starr – drums, bongos, tambourine, maracas; George Martin – Lowrey organ.

Tape loops and sound effects gently ease us into the moody 'Sun King', which was recorded with 'Mean Mr. Mustard' as a continuous performance.

It owes an obvious debt in both musical texture and the underlying chords to 'Albatross' by Fleetwood Mac. 'Don't Let Me Down' comes from the same motherlode.

'Sun King' is another showcase of John's genius with form. The track grows from a handful of short phrases, repeated and shuffled, until it takes on a satisfying cohesion.

0:00-0:52 Introduction. Instrumental, using a variant of the 'Albratross' riff and chords from 'Don't Let Me Down'.
0:52-1:24 Wordless vocal harmonies and a G11 chord change the mood for the verse, which develops the musical themes of the introduction.
1:24-1:37 Refrain. 'Everybody's happy'.
1:37-1:47 Abbreviated second verse.
1:47-2:26 An illogical muddle of English, Italian and Spanish words, set to the introduction chords.

The whole thing feels like a tiny, self-contained song (1:24-1:37) surrounded by hefty layers of verse-like sections that, on their own, wouldn't quite add up to a song at all. 'Sun King' is meticulous and mischievously incomplete.

'Mean Mr. Mustard' (Lennon, McCartney)
Recorded 24-29 July 1969. John Lennon – lead and backing vocals, rhythm guitar, piano; Paul McCartney – backing vocals, fuzz bass; George Harrison – lead guitar; Ringo Starr – drums, tambourine, maracas.
This piece of fluff comes and goes in just over a minute. It's a minor piece in its own right, but it fits well inside the context of the medley. Lennon later dismissed it as 'a bit of crap I wrote in India', so it had been bubbling under for 18 months. A demo from May 1968 and some half-hearted rehearsals from January 1969 also exist.

It seems that the titular character was a real person. A newspaper article from the 7 June 1967 edition of the Scottish newspaper *Daily Record* has the headline 'A Mean Husband Shaved In The Dark'. This describes a man called John Mustard, who lived in Enfield, Middlesex. In his 1980 *Playboy* interview, Lennon said: 'I'd read somewhere in the paper about this mean guy who was hiding £5 notes, not up his nose but somewhere else, and so I wrote about him.'

'Polythene Pam' (Lennon, McCartney)
Recorded 25-30 July 1969. John Lennon – lead vocals, 12-string acoustic guitar; Paul McCartney – backing vocals, bass; George Harrison – backing vocals, lead guitars; Ringo Starr – drums; uncredited – tambourine, maracas, cowbell, percussion.
'Mean Mr. Mustard' segues sharply into 'Polythene Pam'. Originally, of course, 'Her Majesty' was slotted in between these two songs. That the last chord of 'Mean Mr. Mustard' is the same as the first of 'Polythene Pam' (a simple D major) is either perfect serendipity or very clever musical arranging.

'She Came In Through The Bathroom Window' (Lennon, McCartney)
Recorded 25-30 July 1969. John Lennon – lead vocals, 12-string acoustic guitar; Paul McCartney – backing vocals, bass; George Harrison – backing vocals, lead guitars; Ringo Starr – drums; uncredited – tambourine, maracas, cowbell, percussion.
'Polythene Pam' moves directly into 'She Came In Through The Bathroom Window'. They were recorded as one piece.

The song was inspired by the many fans who loitered outside Paul's house in St. John's Wood, one of whom broke in and stole some artefacts.

It segues from 'Polythene Pam' with a thrilling downward swoop in the opening seconds. The land on the home key (at 0:06) brings to mind a similar climactic moment in 'Day Tripper', as the rave-up section settles back to the verse (at 1:41 on that song).

The production is immaculate: acoustic guitar, tambourine, perfect layered harmony vocals, George's stinging lead guitar, Ringo's characteristic tom fills and Paul's fat bass.

Although it feels longer, 'She Came In Through The Bathroom Window' clocks in at under two minutes. To our ears, this song points to the ***Band On The Run*** album, especially 'Mamunia'.

Outside The Beatles' back catalogue, we recommend cover versions by Joe Cocker (1970) and Ike & Tina Turner (1972), both of which take the song and blast it full of soul.

'Golden Slumbers' (Lennon, McCartney)

Recorded 2-4, 30-31 July and 15 August 1969. Paul McCartney – vocals, piano; George Harrison – 6-string bass; Ringo Starr – drums, timpani; uncredited session musicians – twelve violins, four violas, four cellos, double bass, four horns, three trumpets, trombone, bass trombone.

Another piano-led ballad, with lyrics, erm, 'borrowed' from a poem credited to the Elizabethan poet Thomas Dekker (c.1572 – 1632).

Golden slumbers kiss your eyes,
Smiles awake you when you rise;
Sleep, pretty wantons, do not cry,
And I will sing a lullaby,

Care is heavy, therefore sleep you,
You are care, and care must keep you;
Sleep, pretty wantons, do not cry,
And I will sing a lullaby,

A bit cheeky of Paul, we think. Nevertheless, this is classic McCartney, one of his greatest songs. The vocals and dynamics are first-class. It's a super-sweet song with a superb arrangement, introducing horns to the texture for the first time on *Abbey Road*.

Elbow released a fabulous cover version in 2017 – one of the best-ever, in our opinion. This reached number 29 in the UK single chart on the week of its release.

Streaming and downloads of The Beatles' version enabled another chart entry for them, too. 'Golden Slumbers' snuck into the UK top 50 for a single week in November 2017.

'Carry That Weight' (Lennon, McCartney)

Recorded 2-4, 30-31 July and 15 August 1969. Paul McCartney – vocals, piano, guitar; John Lennon – backing vocals; George Harrison – lead guitar, 6-string bass; Ringo Starr – backing vocals, drums, timpani; uncredited session musicians – 12 violins, four violas, four cellos, double bass, four horns, three trumpets, trombone, bass trombone.

As with 'Sun King' and 'Mean Mr Mustard', and with 'Polythene Pam' and 'She Came In Through The Bathroom Window', both 'Golden Slumbers' and 'Carry That Weight' were recorded together. The chorus of 'Carry That Weight' is as simple as it can be, all four Beatles singing in unison.

One must feel that they were fully aware that this was their last album and that they would, collectively, carry the weight of The Beatles for the rest of their lives. They all had successful solo careers in the years immediately after the split (and in some cases beyond), and even in 2026 as we write this book, Paul and Ringo continue to tour as they reach their mid-80s. Carry that weight, indeed.

It's a simple song. The clever part is when it switches back into a verse of 'You Never Give Me Your Money', gloriously enhanced by strings and brass. Despite hearing this song hundreds of times, that change still gives us goosebumps.

The 'Carry That Weight' chorus repeats, and we return again to arpeggiated guitars to close the track before the abrupt edit into 'The End'.

Trivia: the first official release of 'Golden Slumbers/Carry That Weight' was by the Scottish band White Trash, who recorded for Apple Records and were allowed to put out their not-quite-as-good carbon copy as a single a week ahead of *Abbey Road*. It reached number 35 in a three-week run in late October and early November 1969.

'The End' (Lennon, McCartney)

Recorded 23 July – 20 August 1969. Paul McCartney – lead and backing vocals, bass, piano, guitar solo; John Lennon – backing vocals, rhythm guitar, guitar solo; George Harrison – backing vocals, rhythm and lead guitar, guitar solo; Ringo Starr – backing vocals, drums, tambourine; uncredited session musicians – 12 violins, four violas, one double-bass, four horns, three trumpets, one trombone, one bass trombone

The end of the medley and the end of The Beatles. It was unlikely that any other Beatle than Paul McCartney could have (or would have) written The Beatles' own epitaph with one of the greatest-ever lines of lyrics in the history of popular music: 'And in the end, the love you take, is equal to the love you make...'

But first, each of The Beatles take a solo. Ringo's drums from 0:20-0:34 were recorded and mixed in stereo. His playing isn't big, showy, or complicated. Other drummers might have been flashier, but Ringo always played what was right and no more than that. This is why Ringo is one of the best drummers ever. He plays from the heart. We should never forget that John chose Paul and Paul brought in George, but they all picked Ringo. Ringo Starr is the blood that flowed through all of The Beatles' music and kept it going, right to 'The End'.

There's nothing you can add to those 14 seconds that would improve Ringo's solo. Take 3 of 'The End' is included on the *Abbey Road* box set and has a slightly different pattern of playing from Ringo. This sounds very odd after 50 years of the familiar take.

Fifty-four seconds into the song, we have 18 bars of lead guitar. McCartney, Harrison and Lennon play two bars each, in turn, a total of three times. It was George's idea to include a guitar solo, John suggested that they should alternate and, playing live against an existing backing track, Paul elected to go first.

0:54-0:57 Paul opens with a characteristically fluid and melodic sequence of notes
0:57-1:02 George responds loudly, soaring with sustain
1:02-1:04 John's choppy rhythm, hard and rowdy
1:05-1:09 Paul answers with a bluesy lick, spiralling upwards
1:09-1:13 George grunts some minor thirds, choppy and pulsing
1:13-1:17 John growls and throbs on his lowest string
1:17-1:21 Paul plays two notes, followed by a dramatic drop
1:21-1:24 George channels Eric Clapton with a sharply ascending sequence high up the neck
1:25-1:28 John finishes with a behind-the-beat string of insistent and heavily distorted power chords

The final 34 seconds are musical bliss. A four-square piano is joined by vocals.

> And in the end, the love you take, is equal to the love you make...

The orchestra soars on the second 'love', George drops a last, short, eloquent guitar solo, the wordless backing vocals swell and it finishes. Whether or not you speak English, you cannot fail to be moved by those words and the music that accompanies them.

'Her Majesty' (Lennon, McCartney)
Recorded 2 July 1969. Paul McCartney – vocals, acoustic guitar.
This delightful acoustic song was written and performed by Paul and originally placed into the long medley between 'Mean Mr Mustard' and 'Polythene Pam'. Paul, however, asked it to be removed and engineer John Kurlander, knowing better than to throw anything away, attached the track to the end of the master tape after 20 seconds of silence. The next day, mastering engineer Malcolm Davies cut an acetate including 'Her Majesty'. The Beatles liked the random effect and left it, uncredited, on the album.

Thus, the first 'hidden track'.

The song itself is pleasant enough. One can imagine Paul writing it in the morning and recording it in the afternoon with minimal effort.

'Something' b/w **'Come Together'** (Single)

UK: 31 October 1969. US: 6 October 1969.
Chart positions. UK: 4. US: 1.
Both were previously released on *Abbey Road*.

1970

Hey Jude (US album)

26 February 1970.
Chart position: 2.
'Can't Buy Me Love', 'I Should Have Known Better', 'Paperback Writer', 'Rain', 'Lady Madonna', 'Revolution', 'Hey Jude', 'Old Brown Shoe', 'Don't Let Me Down', 'The Ballad Of John And Yoko'

Hey Jude is a compilation of singles and B-sides from 1966 to 1969, plus, somewhat incongruously, two earlier songs that had yet to appear on a Capitol album ('Can't Buy Me Love', 'I Should Have Known Better').

This 33-minute album omits several other tracks not available on Capitol albums, namely 'Love Me Do' (single version), 'From Me To You', 'Misery', 'There's A Place', 'A Hard Day's Night', 'I'm Down' and 'The Inner Light' (this was a ridiculous omission as 'Lady Madonna' *is* included).

'Let It Be' b/w **'You Know My Name (Look Up The Number)'** (Single)

UK/US: 6 March 1970.
Chart positions. UK: 2 . US: 1.
'Let It Be' was the final Beatles single before Paul announced his departure from the band.

'Let It Be' (Lennon, McCartney)

Recorded 31 January and 30 April 1969, 4 January 1970. Paul McCartney – lead and backing vocals, piano, maracas, electric piano, bass; John Lennon – backing vocals; George Harrison – guitars, backing vocals; Ringo Starr – drums; Linda McCartney – backing vocals; Billy Preston – Hammond organ; uncredited session musicians – orchestration.

'Let It Be' is a stone-cold classic; it's impossible to imagine that, at one time, 'Let It Be' did not exist. It always seems to have been *there*. Not only that, the song was written late in The Beatles' career after they had already achieved so much. The title might seem like a symbol of closure for The Beatles' journey, but 'Let It Be' can be dated as early as September 1968. A rehearsal version, recorded the same day as 'While My Guitar Gently Weeps', was released in 2018.

By 3 January 1969, on the second day of the *Get Back* sessions, the song was much advanced with some lyrical variants ('in my darkest hour', instead of 'in my hour of darkness') and the familiar arrangement. Paul, John and George worked on the musical accompaniment at Twickenham on 9 January, returning to it across several days in the last week of sessions.

Paul said that he started to write 'Let It Be' after he had a dream about his mother, Mary Patricia McCartney, who had died of cancer in 1956 when he was fourteen. 'It was great to visit with her again', he said in *Anthology*. 'I felt very blessed to have that dream. So that got me writing 'Let It Be'.'

It uses the very common I, V, vi, IV chord progression, likely the most recycled chord progression in modern popular music history. In this case, the chords used are C, G, Am, F. This same progression had been used years previously in the band's cover of 'To Know Him Is To Love Him' by The Teddy Bears and was reused in many songs, notably Bob Marley's 'No Woman No Cry', 'Don't Stop Believing' by Journey and hundreds of others. It's probably the second-most performed chord progression ever, as it forms the basis for 'Auld Lang Syne', sung everywhere on New Year's Eve. Only 'Happy Birthday To You' can claim more.

This final version of 'Let It Be' was recorded on 31 January, the day after the famous rooftop performance. Paul plays piano, John plays six-string electric bass (later replaced by Paul), George plays guitar and Ringo plays drums. Billy Preston contributed a very soul/gospel accompaniment on Hammond organ.

This single mix has a different guitar solo, recorded three months after the original, and softer orchestration recorded in January 1970.

'You Know My Name (Look Up The Number)' (Lennon, McCartney)
Recorded 17 May, 7 and 8 June 1967, 30 April 1969. John Lennon – lead and backing vocals, guitar, maracas; Paul McCartney – lead vocals, piano, bass, handclaps, sound effects; George Harrison – lead guitar, vibraphone; Ringo Starr – drums, timbales, bongos; Brian Jones – alto saxophone.

Paul McCartney once claimed that 'You Know My Name (Look Up The Number)' was his favourite Beatles song. We assume that he affectionately recalls simply being silly with John, as even hardened Beatles fans would not listen to this with any frequency. Lennon said the phrase came from looking at the cover of a London telephone directory at Paul's house, with the slogan 'you know the name, look up the number'.

It's a fun piece, recorded in four separate sessions. The first three were in May and June 1967, during the sessions for *Magical Mystery Tour*. Vocals and sound effects were added in April 1969 during early sessions for *Abbey Road*, the day after 'Octopus's Garden' had been completed.

The song can be split thus:

0:00-0:46 standard rock instrumentation and loud vocals, with one line of lyrics repeated throughout the song.
0:46-2:18 'welcome to Slaggers', a cheesy cabaret number with a samba beat.
2:18-3:05 a clear homage to the silly voices of *The Goon Show*.
3:05-4:15 cool jazz with John and Paul grunting and straining their 'lead vocals' – saxophone and vibraphones take the song to a conclusion.

'You Know My Name (Look Up The Number)' was available only in mono until 1996, when an extended stereo mix was issued on *Anthology 2*. This mix restores trimmed portions of the song (a longer rock opening and an unheard reggae section) but removes or changes other parts that were issued on the original mono single, specifically *The Goon Show* section, which is almost completely different and several seconds shorter.

Section	Timings (mono)	Timings (stereo)
Standard rock	0:00-0:46 (46 seconds)	0:00-1:05 (65 seconds)
Reggae		1:05-2:17 (72 seconds)
Slaggers	0:46-2:18 (92 seconds)	2:17-3:49 (92 seconds)
The Goon Show	2:18-3:05 (47 seconds)	3:49-4:29 (40 seconds)
Jazz	3:05-4:15 (70 seconds)	4:29-5:45 (76 seconds)

Let It Be

UK/US: 8 May 1970.
Chart positions. UK: 1. US: 1.

The tense sessions that brought us *Let It Be* have been well-documented.

In summary, The Beatles reconvened on 2 January 1969 to be filmed writing and rehearsing new songs for a documentary. They chose Twickenham film studios, where they had recorded the promos for 'Hey Jude' and 'Revolution' on 4 September 1968, along with director Michael Lindsay-Hogg, who had helmed them, as well as earlier promo films for 'Paperback Writer' and 'Rain'.

Multi-track recordings of this first batch of sessions were not made because The Beatles were not attempting to record an album. Hundreds of hours of mono recordings from the filming were made and have been leaked to collectors. They make for miserable listening. George Harrison, in particular, was unhappy, complaining that his songs were either derided or ignored. The intrusive film cameras, the unfamiliar setting, the cold sound stage and the constant presence of Yoko Ono did not help. Eventually, on 10 January, George Harrison announced that he was 'leaving the band now'.

A few days later, the sessions were shifted to Apple Studios. George, after a little persuasion, agreed to rejoin, and the arrival of keyboardist Billy Preston on 22 January injected a fresh pulse into the band's sound – and, rather conveniently, smoothed over the lingering spats. What followed, from 22 to 31 January, was a blur of productivity. In that short span, they not only polished off their next single and album but also staged two memorable performances: the now-legendary rooftop concert on 30 January, and a quieter, more intimate set of songs the next day in the studio. Despite reservations, George seems relaxed and he smiles often. Paul, naturally, is cock-a-hoop. We can be thankful that the ideas to perform in a Tunisian amphitheatre or aboard the QE2 were quietly forgotten. Their simple solution would still resonate 50-plus years later.

Peter Jackson's peerless three-part documentary *The Beatles: Get Back*, first broadcast in 2021, tells us all we need to know. That documentary is essential viewing: a window allowing us to see The Beatles' processes in action. Like many other musicians, they tried riffs, chord progressions and dummy words until a song emerged.

Once the sessions had concluded, engineer and co-producer Glyn Johns was asked to compile an album to be called *Get Back*. Johns presented The Beatles with his first attempt in April 1969. This comprised:

Side One: 'One After 909' (30 January 1969), 'Rocker (Instrumental)' (22 January 1969), 'Save The Last Dance For Me' (22 January 1969), 'Don't Let Me Down' (22 January 1969), 'Dig A Pony' (22 January 1969), 'I've Got A Feeling' (22 January 1969), 'Get Back' (23 January 1969)
Side Two: 'For You Blue' (25 January 1969), 'Teddy Boy' (22 January 1969), 'Two Of Us' (24 January 1969), 'Maggie Mae' (24 January 1969), 'Dig It' (24 January 1969), 'Let It Be' (31 January 1969), 'The Long And Winding Road' (26 January 1969), 'Get Back (Reprise)' (23 January 1969)

The production of these songs is so at odds with the lush and luxuriant *Abbey Road* that it almost sounds like another band. Or at least as The Beatles might have sounded if they had skipped from *Beatles For Sale* to *Get Back* with nothing in between.

At The Beatles' request, the 23 January version of 'Get Back' (side one, track seven) was replaced by the single version. A longer edit of 'Dig It' was preferred, and some dialogue was added before 'The Long And Winding Road'. Fifty years later, this version of the *Get Back* album was released as part of the deluxe re-issue of *Let It Be* in 2021, although the version of 'For You Blue' used there is a later mix with a new vocal from George Harrison.

The album was originally slated for July 1969, only to be nudged back first to September, then December, to align with the planned theatrical release of the film. Once rough cuts were cobbled together, the producers noticed a problem: two songs featured in the movie weren't on the album. 'Across The Universe', laid down in February 1968, was dusted off and remixed by Johns for the new release. 'I Me Mine' needed a fresh recording, which happened in January 1970, while Johns also returned to remix much of the existing material yet again. At this stage, 'Teddy Boy' was quietly excised.

The third version of *Get Back* from January 1970 comprises:

Side One: 'One After 909' (30 January 1969), 'Rocker (Instrumental)' (22 January 1969), 'Save The Last Dance For Me' (22 January 1969), 'Don't Let Me Down' (22 January 1969), 'Dig A Pony' (22 January 1969), 'I've Got A Feeling' (22 January 1969), 'Get Back' (23 January 1969), 'Let It Be' (31 January 1969)
Side Two: 'For You Blue' (25 January 1969), 'Two Of Us' (24 January 1969), 'Maggie Mae' (24 January 1969), 'Dig It' (24 January 1969), 'The Long And Winding Road' (26 January 1969), 'I Me Mine' (3 January 1970), 'Across The Universe' (4 and 8 February 1968), 'Get Back (Reprise)' (23 January 1969)

Once again, this album was rejected by The Beatles. With a release date for the film finally scheduled, the session tapes were given to American producer Phil Spector in March 1970. Spector had produced 'Instant Karma!' for Plastic Ono Band on 27 January 1970 and would produce not only on The Beatles' final album but also the solo material released by George Harrison (*All Things*

Must Pass, including 'My Sweet Lord') and John Lennon ('Power To The People' and *Imagine*) in 1970-1971.

Spector re-ordered the tracks, added snippets of dialogue and chose several different takes for his version of the album, now called *Let It Be* after the newly-released single of the same name. Ultimately, just six tracks on *Let It Be* were wholly live performances in accordance with the original concept: 'I've Got A Feeling', 'One After 909' and 'Dig A Pony' from the rooftop performance, and 'Two Of Us', 'Dig It' and 'Maggie Mae' from studio sessions. These are given a bright, clean production, which is a testament to Glyn Johns' original engineering skills under difficult circumstances in a makeshift studio.

Spector added orchestra and choir to 'The Long And Winding Road', 'Across The Universe' and 'I Me Mine'. Paul McCartney was so deeply upset with the treatment of 'The Long And Winding Road' that he unsuccessfully attempted to halt the release of the *Let It Be* album. This was one of the contributing factors to Paul's public announcement on 10 April 1970 that he was leaving The Beatles.

Lennon, for his part, defended Phil Spector, saying in his famous *Playboy* interview in 1980, 'He was given the shittiest load of badly-recorded shit with a lousy feeling to it ever, and he made something of it.'

For our part, we agree with Paul. The excessive overdubs and the curious track sequencing take away much of the impact, especially now that we can listen to different takes, alternate mixes and less ornate production on *Let It Be ... Naked* and the deluxe edition of the original album. May we suggest an alternative running order, with a few different mixes?

Side One: 'Two Of Us', 'Across The Universe' (*Let It Be ... Naked* mix), 'I Me Mine', 'Let It Be' (single mix), 'For You Blue', 'The Long And Winding Road' (*Let It Be ... Naked* mix)
Side Two (the rooftop concert): 'I've Got A Feeling', 'One After 909', 'Dig A Pony', 'Don't Let Me Down' (studio version mixed with rooftop chatter), 'Get Back' (studio version mixed with rooftop chatter).

We think that's rather good. We'd take one home with us.

'Two Of Us' (Lennon, McCartney)

Recorded 31 January 1969. Paul McCartney – lead vocals, acoustic guitar; John Lennon – lead vocals, acoustic guitar; George Harrison – lead guitar; Ringo Starr – drums.

There's a purity about 'Two Of Us', the opening song on *Let It Be*. It certainly conforms to the 'back to basics' ethos of the *Get Back* project, comprising just guitars, drums and voices.

It started as a guitar-driven rocker and this was the arrangement they were working up when George quit the band on 10 January 1969.

A week or two later, it was reworked for acoustic guitars, with a finished version of the song recorded at Apple Studios on 31 January 1969. This is the performance that's included in both the *Let It Be* film and album, with dialogue added from ten days earlier. The band sound like they are enjoying themselves.

Although Paul wrote 'Two Of Us' about travelling with his then-girlfriend, Linda, and escaping the madness of Apple, it now takes on a new meaning: a gesture of affection to his long-time songwriting partner, John Lennon. They sing together, in harmony: two guys, two guitars, two voices, back in Forthlin Road in 1962.

'Dig A Pony' (Lennon, McCartney)

Recorded 30 January 1969. John Lennon – lead vocals, rhythm guitar; Paul McCartney – backing vocals, bass; George Harrison – lead guitar; Ringo Starr – drums; Billy Preston – electric piano.

John's obsessive 'Dig A Pony' was one of the first songs The Beatles ran through during the first day of the *Get Back* project, 2 January 1969, as the band showcased their latest songs. It was developed extensively over the next three weeks, and a studio take from 22 January was selected by Glyn Johns for each of his *Get Back* albums. This was released on *Anthology 3* and the deluxe *Let It Be*. It's ragged and entertaining but misses the power and intensity of the rooftop version chosen by Phil Spector for *Let It Be* in 1970, which is a proper rock song, with incredible singing and playing from everyone.

It opens and closes with a tricky guitar riff in 6/8 time, which requires accurate timing from everyone in the band. The lyrics are mostly nonsense, but seem to reference The Beatles' early moniker Johnny And The Moondogs ('I pick a moondog') and The Rolling Stones ('I roll a stoney').

'I was just having fun with words', John said in 1972. 'It was literally a nonsense song. You just take words and you stick them together, and you see if they have any meaning. Some of them do, and some of them don't.'

Even after four weeks of rehearsing the song, John needed the band's assistant, Kevin Harrington, to hold a clipboard in front of him with the lyrics on it.

We must also mention Billy Preston's electric piano, which sits under John's rhythm guitar and gives a pleasing soul-gospel touch to the instrumentation on 'Dig A Pony' and most of the other songs on the album.

'Across The Universe' (Lennon, McCartney)

Recorded 4 and 8 February 1968; 1 April 1970. John Lennon – lead vocals, acoustic and electric guitar; Paul McCartney – piano; George Harrison – tambura; Ringo Starr – drums, maracas; uncredited session musicians – choir, cellos, violas, harp, violins, trumpets, trombones.

'Across The Universe' was two years old when it was exhumed for official release on *Let It Be*. There is rehearsal footage from Twickenham in the film, possibly recalled by John as a new mono mix was made at that time for the aborted *Yellow Submarine* EP. The song was not even attempted at Apple Studios.

With that snippet included in the film, and therefore needed for the soundtrack, the only answer was to polish up an outtake from the 'Lady Madonna' sessions.

That recording, from February 1968, with its acoustic picking and Indian instrumentation, seems influenced by The Beatles' time with the Maharishi in Rishikesh. And yet it pre-dates all of the songs written there, dating back to late 1967.

Hunter Davies: 'John woke up at seven o'clock one morning and couldn't get back to sleep. He found the words 'pools of sorrow, waves of joy' going through his head. He got up and wrote them out, writing about ten lines in all, which eventually became 'Across The Universe'. In this first, early morning version, when he knew he was writing down some sloppy, corny phrases, just to get himself onto the next line, his handwriting got worse and more illegible, out of embarrassment, in case anyone should see lines he didn't like. This is what he did in his poems as a boy, or in letters to Stu, trying to cover up his soft sentimental thoughts in case Mimi or anyone should read them.'

As with many of John's songs, the structure is wholly unorthodox. The verses are either eight or seven measures long, with an extra half measure tacked on in some cases. There is a six-bar refrain split into four and two ('jai guru deva... om'), and the chorus is 16 bars. John's lyrics sound poetic in the way he sings them, but there is no real meaning. The 'jai guru deva om' mantra sounds at odds with the more direct songs written for the *Get Back* project. This doesn't detract from the quality of 'Across The Universe', but it sits uneasily on *Let It Be*, especially after extensive orchestral and choral overdubs added by Phil Spector in April 1970.

There are six officially released mixes available, in order:

- 1969 stereo mix. Released December 1969. *Nothing's Gonna Change Our World* charity album (more easily found on *Past Masters 2*).
- 1970 Phil Spector stereo mix. Released May 1970. *Let It Be.*
- 2003 stereo mix. Released November 2003. *Let It Be ... Naked.*
- 1969 mono mix. Released 2009. *Mono Masters.*
- 1970 Glyn Johns mix. Released October 2021. *Let It Be: Special Edition.*
- 2021 stereo mix. Released October 2021. *Let It Be: Special Edition.*

There are alternative takes on *Anthology 3* and *The Beatles: 50th Anniversary Edition*.

For us, the 2003 remix for *Let It Be ... Naked* is the best. It strips the song back to basics: acoustic guitar, vocals and tambura. It's one of those songs, like 'Something' and 'Dear Prudence', that can be played on a single guitar without losing any of the impact, such is the strength of the composition. The arrangement leans towards a mixture of folk and Indian music.

As for cover versions, David Bowie took on 'Across The Universe' in 1975, folding it into the restless, transitional glow of *Young Americans*. Cut at Electric Lady Studios in New York – on the same day as 'Fame' – the cover reshapes Lennon's meditation into something smoother and more terrestrial, filtered through Bowie's blue-eyed soul phase. Its most striking detail is also its most intimate: Lennon himself appears on guitar and backing vocals, quietly closing the circle. The song resurfaced in 2002 via Rufus Wainwright, whose version was recorded for the soundtrack to *I Am Sam*. Wainwright leans into the song's vulnerability, stripping it back into something tender and exposed, closer in spirit to the original's inward gaze. Liam Gallagher's band Beady Eye revisited the song in 2011, releasing it as a limited charity single in the wake of the Japan tsunami. Available briefly through the band's website, the cover directed all proceeds to the British Red Cross, charting modestly in the UK.

'I Me Mine' (Harrison)

Recorded 3 January and 1 April 1970. George Harrison – lead and backing vocals, acoustic guitars, lead guitars; Paul McCartney – backing vocals, bass, Hammond organ, electric piano; Ringo Starr – drums; uncredited session musicians – choir, 18 violins, four violas, four cellos, harp, three trumpets, three trombones

George's preachy 'I Me Mine' was the last song recorded during The Beatles' time together, the only track recorded during the 1970s. John was absent from the recording sessions, leading to George's quip, 'You all will have read that Dave Dee is no longer with us, but Mickey and Tich and I just like to carry on the good work that's always gone down in [studio] number two...'

Alternating between waltz-time verses and harder rock-style choruses, the original take lasted 94 seconds and comprised George on acoustic and electric guitar and vocals, Paul on bass guitar, Hammond organ and electric piano, and Ringo on drums.

Some studio trickery extended the song – from 1:20 of the released take, it repeats the chorus and second verse. These edits are hidden by subsequent orchestral overdubs (mostly strings, and quite subtle by Spector's standards) and add 51 seconds to the running time.

'Dig It' (Lennon, McCartney, Harrison, Starkey)

Recorded 26 January 1969. John Lennon – lead vocals, six-string bass; Paul McCartney – piano; George Harrison – lead guitar; Ringo Starr – drums; Billy Preston – Hammond organ; George Martin – maracas

This 51-second jam is about 50 seconds too long. The original was over 15 minutes, so be thankful for small mercies. They seem to be enjoying themselves, so there's that.

John's opening vocalising of 'like a rolling stone' is intriguing, as the chords are the same as, well, 'Like A Rolling Stone' (if in a different key).

'Let It Be' (Lennon, McCartney)

Phil Spector's album mix of the previously released 'Let It Be' has more echo and a harder, more aggressive guitar solo. It's one of George's best 'guitar hero' moments in the second half of The Beatles' career, along with 'Fixing A Hole', 'Old Brown Shoe' and his contributions to 'The End'.

'Maggie Mae' (Traditional arr. Lennon, McCartney, Harrison, Starkey)

Recorded 24 January 1969. John Lennon – vocals, acoustic guitar; Paul McCartney – vocals, acoustic guitar; George Harrison – electric guitar; Ringo Starr – drums

This is 40 seconds of The Beatles warming up with an old folk song.

If you really like it, then a longer edit can be heard on the *Fly On The Wall* bonus disc issued with early pressings of *Let It Be ... Naked.* Hint: don't bother.

'I've Got A Feeling' (Lennon, McCartney)

Recorded 30 January 1969. John Lennon – lead vocals, rhythm guitar; Paul McCartney – lead vocals, bass; George Harrison – lead guitar; Ringo Starr – drums; Billy Preston – electric piano.

The blues groove of 'I've Got A Feeling' marks the first of two more songs from the rooftop concert. It's a belter.

Each section of the song was written separately. John's 'Everybody Had A Hard Year', which he recorded at home twice in December 1968, was grafted onto Paul's 'I've Got A Feeling', first alternating, then sung simultaneously.

A powerful, intense bridge section has wailing guitars and Paul at full throttle.

> All these years I've been wandering around
> Wondering how come nobody told me
> All that I was looking for was somebody who looked like you!

The track was recorded live, in a single take – just *listen* to Paul's world-class bass-playing (despite his A string being out of tune).

Thrillingly, Paul performed the song live as a virtual duet with John in his live concerts between 2022 and 2025.

'One After 909' (Lennon, McCartney)

Recorded 30 January 1969. John Lennon – lead vocals, rhythm guitar; Paul McCartney – backing vocals, bass; George Harrison – lead guitar; Ringo Starr – drums; Billy Preston – electric piano.

If the *Get Back* sessions were stuffed full of oldies, it only seems right that they included an oldie of their own.

They dug up several of their early songs during the sessions: 'I Fancy Me Chances', 'I've Lost My Little Girl', even 'Love Me Do'. John's 'One After 909' dates from at least 1960 – there's a home recording from that year – and probably much earlier. It was recorded at EMI in March 1963 on the same day as 'From Me To You'. They were unhappy with the result, and it would be 1995 until that version was officially released (in a new edit) on *Anthology 1*.

The 1969 version rocks harder. Ringo really thumps the drums. There is a reframed introduction and a guitar solo from George, which drolly mixes Carl Perkins and Eric Clapton.

'The Long And Winding Road' (Lennon, McCartney)

Recorded 26 January 1969, 1 April 1970. Paul McCartney – vocals, piano; John Lennon – six-string bass; George Harrison – acoustic guitar; Ringo Starr – drums; Billy Preston – electric piano; uncredited session musicians – 18 violins, four violas, four cellos, harp, three trumpets, three trombones, two guitars, 14 female voices.

Paul McCartney makes it seem so easy, doesn't he?

As The Beatles were starting to fall apart in early 1969, he whipped this masterpiece from his back pocket. 'The Long And Winding Road' was written in Paul's Scottish bolt-hole, High Park Farm near Campbeltown, which he bought in 1966 and started to use in earnest in 1968 as a retreat from the day-to-day tension of The Beatles' personal and business relationships.

Paul spoke about the track when *Let It Be ... Naked* was released in 2003. 'I just sat down at my piano in Scotland,' he said, 'started playing and came up with that song, imagining it was going to be done by someone like Ray Charles. I have always found inspiration in the calm beauty of Scotland, and again, it proved to be the place where I found inspiration. When we're talking about the tensions between the music, unfortunately that sticks because it was a group breaking up. I can't say, 'Yeah, that was easy to deal with', or that it's a great memory because it was my favourite band in all the world breaking up.'

'The Long And Winding Road' is a balm that touches your soul. Its obvious sentimentality is a positive, and clear evidence, if it was needed, that he was one of the great composers of the 20th century.

At first glance, the song appears melodically straightforward, even conservative. A closer examination, however, reveals a carefully controlled and unusually restrained melodic design that plays a significant role in the song's emotional impact. Unlike many McCartney ballads, the verse melody is notably narrow in range, moving largely by step and avoiding dramatic leaps. This creates a conversational, almost tentative quality, reflecting the lyric's tone of fatigue and reflection rather than aspiration. Importantly, the melody avoids foreshadowing the chorus: there is little sense of a hook being prepared in advance, which delays the listener's expectation of release.

The song's true melodic apex occurs later, on the phrase 'still lead me back', where the vocal line reaches higher and sustains its pitch with greater emphasis. In melodic terms, the song owes more to the tradition of reflective standards than to the conventions of late-1960s rock, a choice that helps explain both its divisive reception and its enduring appeal. One expects that Burt Bacharach was a fan.

The basic track focuses on Paul's piano and vocals. When recording The Beatles' version a few days before the rooftop concert, Paul, presumably instinctively, uses the passaggio technique, whereby his voice settles in the transitional area between his chest and head vocal registers. McCartney spends most of the song hovering just below and through his passaggio, rather than smashing into it. In the verses, he uses his chest register, constantly preparing for the upper notes rather than reacting to them. In the chorus ('will never disappear...'), there is a clear mixed registration, and the head resonance is allowed ('still they lead me back') despite the heavy emotion. In late-1960s rock, this kind of singing was unusual. Most singers either belt through the break or jump to falsetto. McCartney instead blends through it, almost pop-crooner style. Other examples from this period include Steve Winwood on 'Can't Find My Way Home' (1969, *Blind Faith*), Robert Plant on 'Babe I'm Gonna Leave You' (1969, *Led Zeppelin*), David Bowie's 'Space Oddity' (1969) and Robin Gibb's fragile lead on The Bee Gees 'I Started A Joke' (1968). In each case, vocal instability, strain and head/chest register blur become expressive tools.

There were plans to gift 'The Long And Winding Road' to Tom Jones or Cilla Black, but in the end it was recorded during the sessions at Savile Row on 26 January 1969. Paul sings and plays piano, John is on six-string bass guitar, George plays electric guitar, Ringo Starr is on drums and Billy Preston plays electric piano. John's bass-playing is painfully bad – quite why Paul wasn't asked to redo it remains a mystery.

The song was released as a single in the US and was the band's 20th and last number one there. Phil Spector's overdubs angered McCartney so much that it was cited as one of six reasons for justifying the dissolution of The Beatles' legal partnership in early 1971. The *Let It Be ... Naked* version proves that these were not needed.

'For You Blue' (Harrison)

Recorded 25 January 1969, 8 January 1970. George Harrison – vocals, acoustic guitar; John Lennon – lap steel guitar; Paul McCartney – piano, bass; Ringo Starr – drums.

Ah, George. 'For You Blue' is a country blues, light-hearted and fun (even if it was recorded at a time of discord). After a tricky off-kilter introduction, it settles into the standard 12-bar pattern, a real rarity in The Beatles' catalogue.

It was recorded on 25 January 1969, with new lead vocals overdubbed on 8 January 1970. There's a snappy section for two solos. John plays an impressive lap steel solo (0:58-1:20), and Paul tinkles the piano (1:20-1:43). They all sound like they're having a lot of fun.

'Get Back' (Lennon, McCartney)
This is an abbreviated edit of the single version, cross-faded with dialogue from the rooftop concert: Paul's 'Thanks, Mo!' and John's hope that the group has 'passed the audition'.

Thus ends The Beatles' final album as an active band.

'The Long And Winding Road' b/w **'For You Blue'** (US single)
11 May 1970.
Chart position: 1.
Both were previously released on *Let It Be*.

Since 1970

The 1962 to 1970 discography tells only part of the story. A slew of compilation albums in the 1970s and 1980s kept the band in the charts, running in parallel to the solo careers of John, Paul, George and Ringo.

The Beatles' exclusive recording contract with EMI (and their Capitol subsidiary) expired on 30 April 1976, for both group and solo releases. EMI still retained the right to commercially exploit any songs that had been released up to that point and were obligated to pay royalties. The Beatles themselves had no say on what was released, both individually and collectively, but they were free to enter into contractual relationships with other record labels.

Over the next six years, from 1976 to 1982, EMI/Capitol released several compilation albums, mining their trove of available material whilst keeping the band's legacy visible.

John's death in 1980 ended any speculation that The Beatles would record together once more. However, the re-release of the back catalogue on CD in 1987-1988 proved that there was still a demand for Beatles product.

Ongoing legal cases between Apple, in effect The Beatles' management company, and EMI/Capitol were settled in 1989, and this gave the surviving Beatles and their representatives full control over future releases. Since 1994, a great many previously unreleased songs have been made available on several archive releases and box sets, along with 'new' songs in 1995, 1996 and 2023.

These, then, are the rest of the tracks of The Beatles on EMI and Apple.

1962-1966, 1967-1970

UK/US: 2 April 1973.

Chart positions. UK: 3/2. US: 3/3.

1962-1966: 'Love Me Do', 'Please Please Me', 'From Me To You', 'She Loves You', 'I Want To Hold Your Hand', 'All My Loving', 'Can't Buy Me Love', 'A Hard Day's Night', 'And I Love Her', 'Eight Days A Week', 'I Feel Fine', 'Ticket To Ride', 'Yesterday', 'Help!', 'You've Got To Hide Your Love Away', 'We Can Work It Out', 'Day Tripper', 'Drive My Car', 'Norwegian Wood (This Bird Has Flown)', 'Nowhere Man', 'Michelle', 'In My Life', 'Girl', 'Paperback Writer', 'Eleanor Rigby', 'Yellow Submarine'

1967-1970: 'Strawberry Fields Forever', 'Penny Lane', 'Sgt. Pepper's Lonely Hearts Club Band', 'With A Little Help From My Friends', 'Lucy In The Sky With Diamonds', 'A Day In The Life', 'All You Need Is Love', 'I Am The Walrus', 'Hello, Goodbye', 'The Fool On The Hill', 'Magical Mystery Tour', 'Lady Madonna', 'Hey Jude', 'Revolution', 'Back In The USSR', 'While My Guitar Gently Weeps', 'Ob-La-Di, Ob-La-Da', 'Get Back', 'Don't Let Me Down', 'The Ballad Of John And Yoko', 'Old Brown Shoe', 'Here Comes The Sun', 'Come Together', 'Something', 'Octopus's Garden', 'Let It Be', 'Across The Universe', 'The Long And Winding Road'

Both of these albums are chock full of great tracks, yes, but *1962-1966* is missing many classics, as it contains only Lennon-McCartney songs. Where are 'Twist And Shout', 'Roll Over Beethoven' and 'You Really Got A Hold On Me'? What about 'I Saw Her Standing There', 'This Boy', 'You Can't Do That', 'If I Needed Someone', 'Taxman', 'I'm Only Sleeping', 'Here, There And Everywhere', 'Got To Get You Into My Life' and 'Tomorrow Never Knows'? Wither 'Dear Prudence', 'Blackbird', 'Hey Bulldog', 'Oh! Darling'?

When the back catalogue was re-released in 1987-1988, ongoing legal problems prevented the inclusion of *1962-1966* and *1967-1970*, meaning that fans could not buy a CD of the hits (the mop-up albums *Past Masters* included tracks released as B-sides and from EPs that casual listeners would skip, and miss any singles that had been included on albums).

The eventual 1993 CD releases of *1962-1966* and *1967-1970* followed the same track lists as the vinyl release from 20 years before. It would be another 30 years before both albums were expanded to represent a true overview of the band's most popular songs, including all of those mentioned above.

Rock 'N' Roll Music

US: 7 June 1976. UK: 11 June 1976.
Chart positions. US: 2. UK: 11.
'Twist And Shout', 'I Saw Her Standing There', 'You Can't Do That', 'I Wanna Be Your Man', 'I Call Your Name', 'Boys', 'Long Tall Sally', 'Rock And Roll Music', 'Slow Down', 'Kansas City'/'Hey, Hey, Hey, Hey!', 'Money (That's What I Want)', 'Bad Boy', 'Matchbox', 'Roll Over Beethoven', 'Dizzy Miss Lizzy', 'Any Time At All', 'Drive My Car', 'Everybody's Trying To Be My Baby', 'The Night Before', 'I'm Down', 'Revolution', 'Back In The USSR', 'Helter Skelter', 'Taxman', 'Got To Get You Into My Life', 'Hey Bulldog', 'Birthday', 'Get Back'

This excellent collection of tracks highlights the band's strengths as rockers. It includes 16 originals and 12 cover versions of songs written by rock 'n' roll composers of the 1950s, including Chuck Berry, Little Richard, Carl Perkins and Larry Williams.

Some of the mixes on the original US pressing were tinkered with, so mix collectors need to obtain a copy for unavailable-elsewhere stereo variants of seven tracks.

At The Hollywood Bowl

UK/US: 4 May 1977.
Chart positions. UK: 1. US: 2.
Re-released 9 September 2016.
Chart positions. UK: 3. US: 7.
'Twist And Shout' (30 August 1965), 'She's A Woman' (30 August 1965), 'Dizzy Miss Lizzy' (Edited From 29 and 30 August 1965), 'Ticket To Ride' (29 August 1965), 'Can't Buy Me Love' (30 August 1965), 'Things We Said Today' (23 August 1964), 'Roll Over Beethoven' (23 August 1964), 'Boys' (23 August 1964), 'A Hard

Day's Night' (30 August 1965), 'Help!' (29 August 1965), 'All My Loving' (23 August 1964), 'She Loves You' (23 August 1964), 'Long Tall Sally' (23 August 1964)

Such was the demand for Beatles product in 1964 that Capitol proposed a live album. The Beatles' performance of 23 August at the Hollywood Bowl was recorded, but the sound quality of the tapes was deemed to be inadequate for commercial release. A year later, Capitol recorded a further two concerts, but again these remained unreleased. Keen collectors can hear all three concerts, complete and in stereo.

The imminent release of a poor-quality mono concert recording of the group performing in the Star-Club in Hamburg forced Capitol's hand. George Martin was asked to compile an official live album using tracks from the three available recordings. Whilst not as good as other concerts available (Stockholm, 24 October 1963; Melbourne, 16 June 1964; Blackpool,1 August 1965), it's certainly listenable as a microcosm of the pandemonium of Beatlemania.

The album was remixed and reissued in 2016 with four additional tracks: 'You Can't Do That' (23 August 1964), 'I Want To Hold Your Hand' (23 August 1964), 'Everybody's Trying To Be My Baby' (30 August 1965) and 'Baby's In Black' (30 August 1965).

Love Songs

UK: 19 November 1977. US: 21 October 1977.

Chart positions. UK: 7. US: 24.

'Yesterday', 'I'll Follow The Sun', 'I Need You', 'Girl', 'In My Life', 'Words Of Love', 'Here, There And Everywhere', 'Something', 'And I Love Her', 'If I Fell', 'I'll Be Back', 'Tell Me What You See', 'Yes It Is', 'Michelle', 'It's Only Love', 'You're Going To Lose That Girl', 'Every Little Thing', 'For No One', 'She's Leaving Home', 'The Long And Winding Road', 'This Boy', 'Norwegian Wood (This Bird Has Flown)', 'You've Got To Hide Your Love Away', 'I Will', 'P.S. I Love You'

This fascinating double album includes some great and not-so-obvious choices: 'Tell Me What You See', 'Every Little Thing', 'I Will', 'She's Leaving Home', 'This Boy', 'Yes It Is'. We can argue about the flow or whether it's really needed at all (perhaps not as it's never been re-released), but as compilations go, it's very fine indeed.

Rarities (UK version)

2 December 1978.

Chart position. 71.

'Across The Universe' ('Wildlife' Version), 'Yes It Is', 'This Boy', 'The Inner Light', 'I'll Get You', 'Thank You Girl', 'Komm, Gib Mir Deine Hand', 'You Know My Name (Look Up The Number)', 'Sie Liebt Dich', 'Rain', 'She's A Woman', 'Matchbox', 'I Call Your Name', 'Bad Boy', 'Slow Down', 'I'm Down', 'Long Tall Sally'

This compilation collects all of the officially-released Beatles songs that were not included (at that time) on any other Beatles album or on *1962-1966*, *1967-1970* and *Magical Mystery Tour*. We have several B-sides, the two German-language recordings, the four tracks from *Long Tall Sally* EP, a song recorded for the American market and a mix of 'Across The Universe' that had previously appeared on a charity record.

Rarities (US version)
Released 24 March 1980.
Chart position. 21.
'Love Me Do' (mono, single version; Ringo on drums), 'Misery', 'There's A Place', 'Sie Liebt Dich', 'And I Love Her' (stereo version with six-bar ending; originally issued in Germany), 'Help!' (mono mix), 'I'm Only Sleeping' (UK stereo mix), 'I Am The Walrus' (new edit; six note intro and extra beats before the 'Yellow matter custard' verse), 'Penny Lane' (new mix of stereo version and the US promo mono version with extra piccolo trumpet), 'Helter Skelter' (mono; ends at first fadeout), 'Don't Pass Me By' (mono; different violin in places), 'The Inner Light', 'Across The Universe' ('Wildlife' version), 'You Know My Name (Look Up The Number)', 'Sgt. Pepper Inner Groove'
This US version of *Rarities* includes tracks not previously issued on a Capitol or Apple LP and alternative versions or mixes of songs released outside the US.

The Beatles Ballads (UK album)
Released 20 October 1980.
Chart position. 17.
'Yesterday', 'Norwegian Wood (This Bird Has Flown)', 'Do You Want To Know A Secret', 'For No One', 'Michelle', 'Nowhere Man', 'You've Got To Hide Your Love Away', 'Across The Universe' ('Wildlife' Version), 'All My Loving', 'Hey Jude', 'Something', 'The Fool On The Hill', 'Till There Was You', 'The Long And Winding Road', 'Here Comes The Sun', 'Blackbird', 'And I Love Her', 'She's Leaving Home', 'Here, There And Everywhere', 'Let It Be' (Single version)
Coming three years after *Love Songs* and repeating ten songs found there, it's hard to find an argument for this album.

Reel Music
UK/US: 22 March 1982.
Chart positions. UK: 56. US: 19.
'A Hard Day's Night', 'I Should Have Known Better', 'Can't Buy Me Love', 'And I Love Her', 'Help!', 'You've Got To Hide Your Love Away', 'Ticket To Ride', 'Magical Mystery Tour', 'I Am The Walrus', 'Yellow Submarine', 'All You Need Is Love', 'Let It Be', 'Get Back', 'The Long And Winding Road'
This almost pointless compilation screams 'barrel scraping'. It comprises 14 songs from The Beatles' various films. And yet even here, the collector was rewarded with a unique stereo edit of 'I Should Have Known Better', which fixes

an error in the opening seconds. This version was issued only on the Capitol version of the *Reel Music* pressing and has never appeared on any other release.

The album was accompanied by the unnecessary single 'The Beatles' Movie Medley'.

20 Greatest Hits

Released 11 October 1982 (US version), 18 October 1982 (UK version).
Chart positions. US: 50. UK: 10.
US version: 'She Loves You', 'Love Me Do', 'I Want To Hold Your Hand', 'Can't Buy Me Love', 'A Hard Day's Night', 'I Feel Fine', 'Eight Days A Week', 'Ticket To Ride', 'Help!', 'Yesterday', 'We Can Work It Out', 'Paperback Writer', 'Penny Lane', 'All You Need Is Love', 'Hello, Goodbye', 'Hey Jude' (Fades Early), 'Get Back', 'Come Together', 'Let It Be', 'The Long And Winding Road'
UK version: 'Love Me Do', 'From Me To You', 'She Loves You', 'I Want To Hold Your Hand', 'Can't Buy Me Love', 'A Hard Day's Night', 'I Feel Fine', 'Ticket To Ride', 'Help!', 'Day Tripper', 'We Can Work It Out', 'Paperback Writer', 'Yellow Submarine', 'Eleanor Rigby', 'All You Need Is Love', 'Hello, Goodbye', 'Lady Madonna', 'Hey Jude', 'Get Back', 'The Ballad Of John And Yoko'

What felt like a final roll of the dice for new Beatles compilations, issued on the 20th anniversary of 'Love Me Do', gathers together 20 of their biggest hits, with different track listings for the US and UK markets. 'From Me To You', 'Day Tripper', 'Yellow Submarine', 'Eleanor Rigby', 'Lady Madonna' and 'The Ballad Of John And Yoko' on the UK version would be replaced with 'Eight Days A Week', 'Yesterday', 'Penny Lane', 'Come Together, 'Let It Be' and 'The Long And Winding Road' in the US. Both prove that any attempt to choose 20 tracks is prone to failure. The US edition fades 'Hey Jude' after five minutes.

Within five years, the CD revolution would persuade us all to re-buy the original albums.

Past Masters Volume One, Past Masters Volume Two

Released 7 March 1988.
Chart positions: Volume One – UK: 49. US: 149; Volume Two – UK: 46. US: 121
Volume One: 'Love Me Do' (Single Version), 'From Me To You', 'Thank You Girl', 'She Loves You', 'I'll Get You', 'I Want To Hold Your Hand', 'This Boy', 'Komm, Gib Mir Deine Hand', 'Sie Liebt Dich', 'Long Tall Sally', 'I Call Your Name', 'Slow Down', 'Matchbox', 'I Feel Fine', 'She's A Woman', 'Bad Boy', 'Yes It Is', 'I'm Down'
Volume Two: 'Day Tripper', 'We Can Work It Out', 'Paperback Writer', 'Rain', 'Lady Madonna', 'The Inner Light', 'Hey Jude', 'Revolution', 'Get Back', 'Don't Let Me Down', 'The Ballad Of John And Yoko', 'Old Brown Shoe', 'Across The Universe' ('Wildlife' Version), 'Let It Be' (Single Version), 'You Know My Name (Look Up The Number)'

Past Masters Volume One contains 11 tracks from British singles, both tracks from the German single 'Komm, Gib Mir Deine Hand'/'Sie Liebt Dich', all four tracks from the *Long Tall Sally* EP and the US-only track 'Bad Boy' from the album *Beatles VI. Past Masters Volume Two* contains 14 tracks from British singles and the 'Wildlife' version of 'Across The Universe' from the charity album *No One's Gonna Change Our World.*

Together, these albums gather all of the songs released commercially between 1962 and 1970 that were not available on the CD reissues of the 12 original UK albums and the US *Magical Mystery Tour.*

Live At The BBC

Released 30 November 1994.
Chart positions. UK: 1. US: 3.
'From Us To You', 'I Got A Woman', 'Too Much Monkey Business', 'Keep Your Hands Off My Baby', 'I'll Be On My Way', 'Young Blood', 'A Shot Of Rhythm And Blues', 'Sure To Fall (In Love With You)', 'Some Other Guy', 'Thank You Girl', 'Baby It's You', 'That's All Right (Mama)', 'Carol', 'Soldier Of Love', 'Clarabella', 'I'm Gonna Sit Right Down And Cry (Over You)', 'Crying, Waiting, Hoping', 'You Really Got A Hold On Me', 'To Know Her Is To Love Her', 'A Taste Of Honey', 'Long Tall Sally', 'I Saw Her Standing There', 'The Honeymoon Song', 'Johnny B. Goode', 'Memphis, Tennessee', 'Lucille', 'Can't Buy Me Love', 'Till There Was You', 'A Hard Day's Night', 'I Wanna Be Your Man', 'Roll Over Beethoven', 'All My Loving', 'Things We Said Today', 'She's A Woman', 'Sweet Little Sixteen', 'Lonesome Tears In My Eyes', 'Nothin' Shakin'', 'The Hippy Hippy Shake', 'Glad All Over', 'I Just Don't Understand', 'So How Come (No One Loves Me)', 'I Feel Fine', 'I'm A Loser', 'Everybody's Trying To Be My Baby', 'Rock And Roll Music', 'Ticket To Ride', 'Dizzy Miss Lizzy', 'Kansas City/Hey-Hey-Hey-Hey!', 'Matchbox', 'I Forgot To Remember To Forget', 'I Got To Find My Baby', 'Ooh! My Soul', 'Don't Ever Change', 'Slow Down', 'Honey Don't', 'Love Me Do'

Live At The BBC is a treasure trove of unreleased Beatles recordings made for the BBC between January 1963 and May 1965. There are robust covers written by the likes of Chuck Berry, Carl Perkins and Buddy Holly, and some delicious oddities by Ray Charles ('I Got A Woman'), Ann-Margaret ('I Just Don't Understand') and Arthur Alexander ('Soldier Of Love'). And, hidden amongst these, a Lennon-McCartney original, 'I'll Be On My Way', which rewrites Buddy Holly's 'Don't Ever Change'. It's worth recording that 'Baby It's You' from this album was released as a single, reaching number seven in the UK and number 67 in the US.

You might not listen to *Live At The BBC* very often, but it's an important historical artefact, nevertheless. A sequel followed in 2013 with cover versions of Chuck Berry's 'I'm Talking About You' and Tony Orlando's arrangement of 'Beautiful Dreamer'. This peaked at number 12 on the UK Albums Chart and number seven on the US *Billboard* 200 chart.

Anthology 1, 2, 3 and 4

Anthology 1:
Released 20 November 1995.
Chart positions. UK: 2. US: 1.

'Free As A Bird', 'That'll Be The Day', 'In Spite Of All The Danger', 'Hallelujah, I Love Her So', 'You'll Be Mine', 'Cayenne', 'My Bonnie', 'Ain't She Sweet', 'Cry For A Shadow', 'Searchin'', 'Three Cool Cats', 'The Sheik Of Araby', 'Like Dreamers Do', 'Hello Little Girl', 'Besame Mucho', 'Love Me Do', 'How Do You Do It', 'Please Please Me', 'One After 909 (takes 3, 4 & 5)', 'One After 909 (takes 4 & 5)', 'Lend Me Your Comb (Live At The BBC)', 'I'll Get You (Live)', 'I Saw Her Standing There (Live)', 'From Me To You (Live)', 'Money (That's What I Want) (Live)', 'You Really Got A Hold On Me (Live)', 'Roll Over Beethoven (Live)', 'She Loves You (Live)', 'Till There Was You (Live)', 'Twist And Shout (Live)', 'This Boy (Live)', 'I Want To Hold Your Hand (Live)', 'Moonlight Bay', 'Can't Buy Me Love (takes 1 & 2)', 'All My Loving (Live)', 'You Can't Do That (take 6)', 'And I Love Her (take 2)', 'A Hard Day's Night (take 1)', 'I Wanna Be Your Man (Live)', 'Long Tall Sally (Live)', 'Boys (Live)', 'Shout (Live)', 'I'll Be Back (take 2)', 'I'll Be Back (take 3)', 'You Know What To Do', 'No Reply (Demo)', 'Mr. Moonlight (takes 1 & 4)', 'Leave My Kitten Alone', 'No Reply (take 2)', 'Eight Days A Week (takes 1, 2 & 4)', 'Eight Days A Week (take 5)', 'Kansas City/Hey-Hey-Hey-Hey! (take 2)'

Anthology 2:

Released 18 March 1996.

Chart positions. UK: 1. US: 1.

'Real Love', 'Yes It Is (takes 2 & 14)', 'I'm Down (take 1)', 'You've Got To Hide Your Love Away (takes 1, 2 & 5)', 'If You've Got Trouble', 'That Means A Lot', 'Yesterday (take 1)', 'It's Only Love (takes 2 & 3)', 'I Feel Fine (Live)', 'Ticket To Ride (Live)', 'Yesterday (Live)', 'Help! (Live)', 'Everybody's Trying To Be My Baby (Live)', 'Norwegian Wood (This Bird Has Flown) (take 1)', 'I'm Looking Through You (take 1)', '12-Bar Original (take 2)', 'Tomorrow Never Knows (take 1)', 'Got To Get You Into My Life (take 5)', 'And Your Bird Can Sing (take 2)', 'Taxman (take 11)', 'Eleanor Rigby (Strings Only)', 'I'm Only Sleeping (Rehearsal)', 'I'm Only Sleeping (take 1)', 'Rock And Roll Music (Live)', 'She's A Woman (Live)', 'Strawberry Fields Forever (Demo Sequence)', 'Strawberry Fields Forever (take 1)', 'Strawberry Fields Forever (take 7 And Edit Piece)', 'Penny Lane (Remix)', 'A Day In The Life (takes 1, 2, 6 & Orchestra)', 'Good Morning Good Morning (take 8)', 'Only A Northern Song (takes 3 & 12)', 'Being For The Benefit Of Mr. Kite! (takes 1 & 2)', 'Being For The Benefit Of Mr. Kite! (take 7)', 'Lucy In The Sky With Diamonds (takes 6, 7 & 8)', 'Within You Without You (Instrumental)', 'Sgt. Pepper's Lonely Hearts Club Band (Reprise) (take 5)', 'You Know My Name (Look Up The Number) (Extended Remix)', 'I Am The Walrus (take 16)', 'The Fool On The Hill (Demo)', 'Your Mother Should Know (take 27)', 'The Fool On The Hill (take 4)', 'Hello, Goodbye (take 16)', 'Lady Madonna (takes 3 & 4)', 'Across The Universe (take 2)'

Anthology 3:

Released 28 October 1996.

Chart positions. UK: 4. US: 1.

'A Beginning', 'Happiness Is A Warm Gun (Home Demo)', 'Helter Skelter (take 2)', 'Mean Mr. Mustard (Home Demo)', 'Polythene Pam (Home Demo)', 'Glass

Onion (Home Demo)', 'Junk (Home Demo)', 'Piggies (Home Demo)', 'Honey Pie (Home Demo)', 'Don't Pass Me By (takes 3 & 5)', 'Ob-La-Di, Ob-La-Da (take 5)', 'Good Night (Rehearsal & take 34)', 'Cry Baby Cry (take 1)', 'Blackbird (take 4)', 'Sexy Sadie (take 6)', 'While My Guitar Gently Weeps (Demo)', 'Hey Jude (take 2)', 'Not Guilty (take 102)', 'Mother Nature's Son (take 2)', 'Glass Onion (Original Mono Mix)', 'Rocky Raccoon (take 8)', 'What's The New Mary Jane (take 4)', 'Step Inside Love/Los Paranoias', 'I'm So Tired (takes 3, 6 & 9)', 'I Will (take 1)', 'Why Don't We Do It In The Road? (take 4)', 'Julia (take 2)', 'I've Got A Feeling', 'She Came In Through The Bathroom Window', 'Dig A Pony', 'Two Of Us', 'For You Blue', 'Teddy Boy', 'Medley: Rip It Up/Shake, Rattle And Roll/ Blue Suede Shoes', 'The Long And Winding Road', 'Oh! Darling', 'All Things Must Pass (Demo)', 'Mailman, Bring Me No More Blues', 'Get Back (Live)', 'Old Brown Shoe (Demo)', 'Octopus's Garden (takes 2 & 8)', 'Maxwell's Silver Hammer (take 5)', 'Something (Demo)', 'Come Together (take 1)', 'Come And Get It (Demo)', 'Ain't She Sweet', 'Because', 'Let It Be', 'I Me Mine (take 16)', 'The End (Remix)'

Anthology 4:

Released 21 November 2025 as a stand-alone album and as part of The Anthology Collection.

Chart positions. UK: 9. US: 48.

'I Saw Her Standing There (take 2)', 'Money (That's What I Want) (RM7 Undubbed)', 'This Boy (takes 12 & 13)', 'Tell Me Why (takes 4 & 5)', 'If I Fell (take 11)', 'Matchbox (take 1)', 'Every Little Thing (takes 6 & 7)', 'I Need You (take 1)', 'I've Just Seen A Face (take 3)', 'In My Life (take 1)', 'Nowhere Man (First Version – take 2)', 'Got To Get You Into My Life (Second Version – Unnumbered Mix)', 'Love You To (take 7)', 'Strawberry Fields Forever (take 26)', 'She's Leaving Home (take 1 – Instrumental)', 'Baby, You're A Rich Man (takes 11 & 12)', 'All You Need Is Love (Rehearsal For BBC Broadcast)', 'The Fool On The Hill (take 5 – Instrumental)', 'I Am The Walrus (take 19 – Strings, Brass, Clarinet Overdub)', 'Hey Bulldog (take 4 – Instrumental)', 'Good Night (take 10 With A Guitar Part From take 5)', 'While My Guitar Gently Weeps (Third Version – take 27)', '(You're So Square) Baby I Don't Care (Studio Jam)', 'Helter Skelter (Second Version – take 17)', 'I Will (take 29)', 'Can You Take Me Back? (take 1)', 'Julia (Two Rehearsals)', 'Get Back (take 8)', 'Octopus's Garden (Rehearsal)', 'Don't Let Me Down (First Rooftop Performance)', 'You Never Give Me Your Money (take 36)', 'Here Comes The Sun (take 9)', 'Something (take 39 – Instrumental – Strings Only)', 'Free As A Bird (2025 Mix)', 'Real Love (2025 Mix)', 'Now And Then'

The Beatles Anthology **TV series, which purported to tell The Beatles' story 'in their own words' and was broadcast in November 1995, was accompanied by a 'new' single and a double album of outtakes and live tracks. Beyond a few curios, however, it offers little of any substance. If** ***Anthology 1*** **offered slim pickings, then** ***Anthology 2*** **is a different story. Everything there is fascinating for scholars and die-hard fans – it's like**

picking through Tutankhamun's tomb for golden relics – but the three previously unheard songs, all outtakes from 1965, are far from essential. *Anthology 3* is a hodge-podge of sessions from 1968 to 1970. We get a few gems, such as George's demos of 'While My Guitar Gently Weeps' and 'All Things Must Pass', Paul's chirpy 'Come And Get It' and the rejected 'Not Guilty'. 'What's The New Mary Jane' is, however, best forgotten.

An extended version of the original series would be broadcast by Disney in 2025. This includes remasters of the three *Anthology* albums from 1995-1996, along with a new *Anthology 4* comprising 37 tracks, all of which are variants of previously-released songs. Who knows if we'll ever get to hear 'Carnival Of Light'...?

'Free As A Bird' (Lennon, McCartney, Harrison, Starkey)
Released as a single, 4 December 1995.
Chart positions. UK: 2. US: 6.
'Free As A Bird' originated as a home demo by John Lennon in 1977. This is available online and reveals the song's beautiful structure, with some unconventional chords, even if it's unfinished and badly recorded.

The surviving Beatles reunited in 1994 to complete the track using Lennon's original vocal and piano recording. ELO's Jeff Lynne was employed to produce.

It was their first 'new' release in 25 years and a symbolic reunion. The song blends Lennon's lo-fi demo with new instrumental and vocal layers. McCartney and Harrison contributed new verses and harmonies.

Upon its 1995 release, the song reached the top ten in both the UK and the US, reigniting global interest in The Beatles. It was accompanied by a widely praised music video filled with visual references to Beatles lyrics and history. The track served as a poignant tribute to Lennon and a rare instance of posthumous collaboration.

Opinions on its musical merits might vary, but, along with 'Real Love' and 'Now And Then', it remains an emotionally resonant piece for fans. In this case, it's a nice song, produced well in the 1969 style (with ELO gloss), but we feel it shouldn't sit alongside any of their original output. As a postscript for fans, yes. But as statements in their own right, maybe not.

The track was remixed in 2023 for the expanded re-release of *1967-1970.* This has been tinkered with and, in our view, is much less effective than the 1995 mix. The 2015 version from *1+* is very good, though.

Your authors heard the song in very different circumstances. One of us, who had been a fan for 20 years or more, first heard it as the last song played on Chris Evans' BBC Radio 1 breakfast show on 20 November 1995. He was late for work as the happy tears flowed. The other, who was only 13 in 1995, didn't hear the song for another ten years, by which time it was already part of The Beatles' past history.

Where were you when you first heard it?

'That'll Be The Day' (Allison, Petty, Holly)
'In Spite Of All the Danger' (McCartney, Harrison)
This two-sided acetate dates from 12 July 1958. It's a curio, nothing more. 'That'll Be The Day' is a youthful cover of a song by The Crickets.

Despite its shortcomings, 'In Spite Of All The Danger' is historically significant as The Beatles' first-known original composition. Paul McCartney and George Harrison are credited as co-writers, and the song shows clear influences from 1950s rock 'n' roll, particularly Elvis Presley and Buddy Holly.

Inevitably, it has a raw, live-in-one-take sound.

A single copy was pressed, and this was kept in the possession of pianist Duff Lowe for decades. McCartney eventually bought it from him in the 1980s. Despite its roughness, the song has much charm. Paul McCartney has performed it live on occasion.

'Hallelujah, I Love Her So' (Charles)
'You'll Be Mine' (Lennon, McCartney)
'Cayenne' (McCartney)
These three songs are home recordings, most likely made in spring 1960 at the McCartney home in Forthlin Road on a borrowed reel-to-reel.

'Hallelujah, I Love Her So' is a cover of a Ray Charles song. It was a mainstay of The Beatles' live set from 1960 to 1962. Other versions from 1961 (with Tony Sheridan) and 1962 (from the Star-Club) are available.

'You'll Be Mine' is a tongue-in-cheek parody of doo-wop love songs. Lennon handles the spoken lead vocals in a theatrical, mock-sincere voice, an early indication of the nonsense lyrics that would come later in 'I Am The Walrus' and 'Sun King'.

'Cayenne' is an instrumental track, loosely structured with a Latin flair and a touch of The Shadows.

These rough, informal recordings – the only three officially available with Stu Sutcliffe on bass – give a glimpse of the pre-fame Beatles' creativity, humour and early songwriting chops. The Beatles were developing a unique personality and sound, even before setting off for Hamburg a few weeks after these recordings.

'My Bonnie' (trad, arr. Sheridan)
'My Bonnie' occupies a quietly pivotal place in The Beatles' story, not because it's a great performance, but because it's the one that started the paper trail. Recorded in Hamburg in June 1961 with Tony Sheridan on lead vocal, it captures the group still functioning as a hard-working club band, adaptable to whatever the job required. John, Paul and George recede into the role of backing musicians, locking into a sturdy, disciplined rhythm while Sheridan takes centre stage.

The arrangement is brisk and purposeful. The band display tight timing, confident playing and an instinctive grasp of rock 'n' roll dynamics, even when they aren't the main attraction. This is the sound of a group earning its stripes, learning professionalism under pressure.

Released in Germany in late 1961, the news of the release found its way to Liverpool, prompting Brian Epstein to enter the story. In that sense, 'My Bonnie' matters enormously. It isn't the moment they arrived, but it is the moment they start to become visible.

'Ain't She Sweet' (Ager, Yellen)

The Beatles' version of 'Ain't She Sweet' is a fascinating relic of their early days, showcasing their raw energy, adaptability and ambition. It was recorded in Hamburg on 22 June 1961, a full year before their first sessions for EMI. John Lennon's peerless singing provides a gritty, rock 'n' roll edge that transforms this 1927 Tin Pan Alley standard into something tough.

The tempo is brisk and the backbeat is tight, very much in the style of Gene Vincent or Eddie Cochran. This nicely-recorded curio exemplifies their Hamburg period. Play it loud, and you have an idea of how they would have sounded in the Top Ten and Star-Club.

It was released as a single during the height of Beatlemania in 1964, reaching number 19 on the *Billboard* Hot 100 and number 29 in the UK.

'Cry For A Shadow' (Lennon, Harrison)

During sessions in Hamburg for Tony Sheridan, for which The Beatles had been hired as a backing band, they were given a bit of free studio time, during which they recorded the instrumental 'Cry For A Shadow'. It's a playful tribute to the British instrumental rock group The Shadows, who were Cliff Richard's backing band and hugely popular in the UK at the time. The twangy, echo-drenched guitar tones mimic The Shadows' style.

It was first released in Germany in 1962 as the B-side to Tony Sheridan's 'Why', credited to Tony Sheridan & The Beat Brothers.

'Like Dreamers Do' (Lennon, McCartney)
'Hello Little Girl' (Lennon, McCartney)

These two songs are taken from The Beatles' unsuccessful audition for Decca on 1 January 1962. 'Like Dreamers Do' is a polished pop ballad with a bouncy rhythm and melodic sweetness. Principally written by Paul McCartney, it shows his romantic side. The song has a complex construction which shows advanced songwriting technique (Paul was 19 years old at the time), and his singing sounds very mature, as though he was faking it – putting on an act to sound sophisticated. Nevertheless, this was the tune that prompted their first music publishing contract, which in turn secured them a record deal for a single with EMI, although no one knew it at that time. The song was later given to The Applejacks, whose 1964 version became a top 20 UK hit.

'Hello Little Girl' is an upbeat, Everly Brothers-style pop tune with harmonies and a light rock 'n' roll feel. It's one of John's earliest known compositions, written in the late 1950s. Even here, it sounds like *them*. The song was eventually recorded by The Fourmost in 1963 and reached number nine in the UK.

That neither of these original songs was deemed suitable to present to George Martin six months later shows how quickly they were moving in 1962.

'Bésame Mucho' (Velázquez)

'Bésame Mucho' is one of those performances that really shouldn't work, which is perhaps why it does. It finds The Beatles reaching far beyond their years and experience, tackling a Latin standard better known from polite orchestras and crooners. Paul McCartney takes the lead vocal, delivering it with an earnest intensity that's both fearless and faintly absurd, his schoolboy Spanish barely disguising the emotional ambition behind it.

The arrangement is brisk and heavily backbeat-driven (Pete Best on drums, acquitting himself well). This refashions the song as a piece of urgent, sweaty club rock. It's raw, slightly ungainly and completely sincere.

This recording now stands as a vivid reminder of a young band prepared to take risks, overshoot the mark and keep going anyway.

'How Do You Do It' (Murray)

Recorded on 4 September 1962, 'How Do You Do It' had been chosen by George Martin as The Beatles' first single for Parlophone. The Beatles themselves, however, felt that 'How Do You Do It' was too lightweight and poppy, lacking the grit and personal touch they wanted in their music. They pushed to release 'Love Me Do' instead, even though George Martin thought 'How Do You Do It' had more commercial potential (which it did).

Though reluctantly, The Beatles re-worked Mitch Murray's demo to suit their style, with tight harmonies and an edgier arrangement. But their lack of enthusiasm is evident – they didn't put their full energy into it.

The song was eventually recorded by Gerry And The Pacemakers, using The Beatles' arrangement, scoring a UK number one in the spring of 1963.

The Beatles' insistence that their version of 'How Do You Do It' should not be released was a defining early moment in their artistic journey, showing their desire to control their sound and assert themselves as serious songwriters. Full marks to George Martin for capitulating. Choosing 'Love Me Do' was an early stand for creative control – a move that ultimately helped to define their career.

'One After 909 (takes 3, 4 & 5) (Lennon, McCartney)
'One After 909 (takes 4 & 5)' (Lennon, McCartney)

'One After 909' has a long history. It was one of the earliest Lennon-McCartney compositions, dating from around 1958, when they were teenagers. It was recorded for Parlophone on the same day as 'From Me To You' in March 1963, but was never finished to their satisfaction. Their performance was uncharacteristically ragged.

Almost six years later, as their career came to a close, it was dusted off during the *Get Back* sessions in January 1969, adding back-to-basics rock 'n' roll spirit and a sense of fun amidst the tension of that period. The definitive version was recorded live on the rooftop of Apple Corps on 30 January 1969.

Anthology 1 presents a series of false starts (in take 3, Paul has lost his plectrum; in take 4, George fluffs his solo and John misses his cue) and a reconstructed version, which edits takes 4 and 5.

'You Know What To Do' (Harrison)

Here is one of the unexpected gems from *Anthology 1*.

This was one of three demos recorded on 3 June 1964, alongside John's 'No Reply' and Paul's 'It's For You'. Ringo had been hospitalised with tonsillitis and, with a session booked, they made the best use of an hour of free time.

Featuring George on vocals and electric guitar and someone on tambourine, 'You Know What To Do' is his second-known composition for The Beatles (after 'Don't Bother Me' in 1963). It is a sort of passive-aggressive farewell, which shows early signs of George's melodic instinct, though much simpler than Lennon-McCartney songs of the time. The verses switch from E to A, but the bridge drops into an unexpected Bm, and George feels his way back to the tonic. It doesn't quite work, but it clearly reflects George's quiet ambition to be taken seriously as a songwriter. 'You Know What To Do' represents an increasing desire to contribute creatively to The Beatles' catalogue, even if, as yet, the technique needs polish.

'Leave My Kitten Alone' (John, Turner, McDougal)

'Leave My Kitten Alone' is one of The Beatles' most electrifying tracks from the early years, and its omission from *Beatles For Sale* in 1964 remains one of the great 'what if' questions in Beatles history.

It was recorded in five takes on 14 August 1964 and was given a raw, R&B-infused rock treatment, with John Lennon delivering a fiery vocal and the band backing with tight, driving energy. Despite its power and polish, it was left off the album, possibly because it was too similar in tone to other tracks such as 'Rock And Roll Music' or 'Kansas City/Hey-Hey-Hey-Hey!'.

A proposed album of unreleased Beatles tracks called *Sessions* was compiled in 1982, and 'Leave My Kitten Alone' would have been a part of that. The album was scrapped before release, reportedly due to objections from George Harrison and others over quality and context.

'Leave My Kitten Alone' finally saw official release on *Anthology 1*, to strong fan and critical acclaim. It stands out as one of the highlights of that collection, capturing their live energy at its peak. This is rare for an EMI recording. EMI was obsessed with clean tones, controlled dynamics, no audible distortion and tight arrangements that would translate to radio, so even when the songs came from the band's live set, they were usually tamed once they hit tape. 'Leave My Kitten Alone', we think, comes closest, along with 'Twist And Shout', 'I Saw Her Standing There', 'There's A Place', 'Hold Me Tight' and 'Long Tall Sally'. With its aggressive rhythm guitar, snarling vocal and pounding drums, 'Leave My Kitten Alone' sounds like a Hamburg-era rock band that were accidentally given studio time. If this had been released in 1964, it would have reset people's idea of how hard The Beatles could go.

'Real Love' (Lennon)
Released as a single, 4 March 1996.
Chart positions. UK: 4. US: 11.
'Real Love' originated as a series of solo demos by John Lennon, recorded in the late 1970s at his home in New York. In 1995, Paul McCartney, George Harrison and Ringo Starr reunited to complete the song using one of Lennon's heartfelt, delicate, exquisite original vocal and piano tracks.

It's a melodic ballad with a straightforward verse-chorus structure. Lennon's intimate, introspective lyrics explore themes of emotional connection and commitment. The Beatles added full instrumentation, swelling vocal harmonies and sympathetic arrangement enhancements, transforming the demo into a polished, mid-tempo track with a 1967 *Magical Mystery Tour* feel, while retaining its gentle, reflective tone. As fans, we can be sentimental about the song and its message.

Released on 4 March 1996 as the second 'new' Beatles single after 'Free As A Bird', 'Real Love' reached number four on the UK Singles Chart and received considerable airplay worldwide. Though not universally acclaimed, 'Real Love' laid the groundwork for the 2023 track 'Now And Then'.

The remix for 2015's *1+* is far superior to our ears. No need to be alone. No need to be afraid. It's real love.

'If You've Got Trouble' (Lennon, McCartney)
'That Means A Lot' (Lennon, McCartney)
'12-Bar Original' (Lennon, McCartney, Harrison, Starkey)
Rejected recordings were rare in the Beatles' canon, but here we have three from 1965. These tracks reveal The Beatles' increasing focus on audit and compliance – by now, they were willing to discard anything they felt wasn't up to standard, even after putting work into it. Their rapid artistic evolution in 1965 and 1966 meant that quality control was everything.

The first of these, 'If You've Got Trouble', dates from 18 February 1965 during sessions for *Help!* It was intended as Ringo's vocal feature on the album, but it's clunky, lyrically awkward and Ringo sounds decidedly uncomfortable. It was eventually replaced by 'Act Naturally', a lively country cover that better suited Ringo's personality and voice.

Despite multiple takes, Paul's 'That Means A Lot' was never recorded to the satisfaction of the band or George Martin. Paul's vocal is overwrought, and the production feels distant, messy and unclear. The song was handed to P.J. Proby, who released it as a single later in 1965. It reached number 30. The Beatles' version is an interesting failure: ambitious but not fully realised.

'12-Bar Original' is a lifeless instrumental blues jam which was recorded during the *Rubber Soul* sessions. The Beatles were moving rapidly toward more sophisticated songwriting and experimentation with 'Norwegian Wood' and 'In My Life', and '12-Bar Original' didn't meet the high creative standards of *Rubber Soul*, nor did it align with their direction in late 1965. Even in this edited version, it seems overlong.

'A Beginning' (Martin)

'A Beginning' is a short orchestral piece composed by George Martin as an introduction to 'Don't Pass Me By'. It comprises strings, woodwinds and brass in a light, pastoral arrangement, originally recorded on 22 July 1968. It's delightful: George Martin was a genius, and his association with The Beatles was one of those amazing, serendipitous coincidences that recur throughout the story of this band.

'A Beginning' serves as the opening track on *Anthology 3,* but sits better in the deluxe edition of *The Beatles*, where it serves its original function.

'Junk' (McCartney)

'Junk' is one of Paul McCartney's purest and quietest songs, and its absence from the *White Album* says a great deal about the mood of the band in 1968. It reveals McCartney retreating from confrontation into miniature, domestic reflection. The lyric is built from small, discarded objects – buttons, bicycles, broken toys – observed with a tenderness that stops short of sentimentality. McCartney's vocal is gentle and unguarded, and the melody unfolds with a natural, almost childlike grace. There's no attempt to impress, no studio cleverness, just a songwriter sketching a mood and trusting its weight to carry.

In the context of The Beatles' late period, 'Junk' feels almost out of time. Its modesty runs counter to the scale and tension of the sessions around it, which perhaps explains why it was set aside.

This demo dates from May 1968 at George Harrison's house, Kinfauns, in Esher, Surrey. Paul later recorded a more polished version on *McCartney*, his first solo album.

'Not Guilty' (Harrison)

'Not Guilty' is one of the most revealing casualties of the *White Album* sessions, and the *Anthology 3* version lets you hear exactly why it failed to make the cut – and why it mattered anyway. Recorded in August 1968, it finds George Harrison pushing back, lyrically and musically, against the pressures of life inside The Beatles. The song is a defence statement set to music, brittle with resentment. It is widely interpreted as George's response to tensions within The Beatles, especially after their trip to India and his growing frustration with his place in the band. George is asserting his independence here: defending his choices and expressing irritation over being criticised or misunderstood by the other Beatles. It's a turning point in his songwriting confidence, leading into *Abbey Road* and eventually *All Things Must Pass*.

The performance is taut and obsessive, built around a staccato guitar figure, a harpsichord and an arrangement that never quite settles. You can hear the band worrying away at it, take after take, tightening the screws rather than loosening them.

Harrison's vocal is controlled but edgy, his words circling the same grievances until they start to feel less like explanation and more like accusation. This is not a song reaching for universality; it's personal, inward-looking and deliberately uncomfortable.

'Not Guilty' reflects a group no longer instinctively pulling in the same direction, expending enormous effort on a track that seems to underline division rather than disguise it. Left off the album, it nonetheless stands as an unusually candid snapshot of Harrison asserting himself – not yet liberated, but no longer prepared to stay quiet.

The version released on *Anthology 3* is a 3:22 edited version of take 102. A longer 4:28 version can be heard on the 2019 deluxe edition of *The Beatles*. A solo version by Harrison, smoother and laid-back and more introspective in tone, appears on his 1979 album *George Harrison*.

'What's The New Mary Jane' (Lennon, McCartney)

'What's The New Mary Jane' is not so much a song as a test of endurance. We tried to pretend that it simply doesn't exist.

It is discordant, avant-garde, psychedelic and full of absurd lyrics, random sound effects and a deliberately chaotic arrangement. It quickly reveals itself as an exercise in chaos, sustained well beyond the point at which the joke – if there ever was one – has worn thin.

'Step Inside Love'/'Los Paranoias' (Lennon, McCartney/Lennon, McCartney, Harrison, Starkey)

This is a relaxed and comfortable recording of Paul, John and Ringo larking about during sessions for 'I Will'.

'Step Inside Love' is all poise and melodic assurance, its circular structure designed to draw the listener in rather than push outward. Even in fragmentary form, it carries the stamp of McCartney's professionalism and his instinct for elegant pop architecture. Listen out for the 'Gretty' chord, re-used from 'Till There Was You', at 0:36 and 1:20-1:21.

'Los Paranoias' undercuts the calm of 'Step Inside Love' with a burst of playfulness. It feels forced, however, as if Paul is trying just too hard to maintain John's attention.

'Teddy Boy' (McCartney)

'Teddy Boy' was written by Paul McCartney in India in 1968 and re-visited during the *Get Back* sessions in January 1969. It was included in Glyn Johns' early versions of the *Get Back* album, but was cut from the final *Let It Be* album released in 1970.

The lyric, with its tale of maternal devotion and gentle moral framing, is earnest to the point of inertia. McCartney delivers it with confidence and clarity, but the others sound unconvinced, offering half-hearted contributions that suggest compliance rather than commitment. 'Teddy Boy' ultimately reveals more about the band dynamic than the song itself. It highlights McCartney's increasing need for structure and purpose, set against a backdrop of disengagement from the rest of the group. Later recast successfully on his *McCartney* album, the song finally found the context it required. In Beatles form, however, it stands as a reminder that not every good idea survives contact with a band that no longer wants to be one.

The *Anthology 3* version combines two takes from the 1969 sessions. It's rough, with minimal arrangement – mostly acoustic guitar, Paul's vocal and some background interjections from John. Despite Paul's fondness for it, John can be heard mocking the song with sarcastic commentary and rhythm during some of the takes.

'Mailman, Bring Me No More Blues' (Roberts, Katz, Clayton)
'Rip It Up'/'Shake, Rattle And Roll'/'Blue Suede Shoes' (Blackwell, Marascalco, Calhoun, Perkins)

'Mailman, Bring Me No More Blues' is a slow and loose cover of a Buddy Holly B-side, a casual jam during a long day of rehearsals and run-throughs for the *Get Back* project. It was scheduled for the unreleased *Sessions* album in 1984-85. John takes the lead vocal, relaxed and conversational. Musically, it's loose but assured, driven by a rolling groove that never strains for effect. The pleasure lies in the playing itself. For a few minutes, the baggage of January 1969 is left at the door.

The rock 'n' roll medley is pure muscle memory. They revert to their most basic instincts, tearing through three foundational songs with speed, volume and barely contained glee. The transitions are messy, but the tempos are aggressive: rock 'n' roll as physical release, played too fast and slightly out of control, just as it would have been in Hamburg a decade earlier.

'All Things Must Pass' (Harrison)

Can it be true that The Beatles rejected one of George's best songs?

The Beatles rehearsed 'All Things Must Pass' multiple times at Twickenham and Apple Studios in January 1969, with vocal harmonies and full-band arrangement. For whatever reason, it went no further at this stage. A rough and tentative version recorded at the *Get Back* sessions can be heard on the deluxe edition of *Let It Be* (2021).

Stripped back to acoustic guitar and voice, this demo, recorded on 25 February 1969, reveals a song of poise, maturity and emotional balance that sits uncomfortably alongside the turmoil of that period. George sounds calm, reflective and entirely self-contained – which, in itself, tells you everything.

The melody unfolds with unforced grace, and the lyric carries a philosophical acceptance that feels hard-won rather than vague. There's no bitterness here, no pleading for attention, just an understanding that cycles end and attachments loosen. Heard in this skeletal form, the song doesn't need arrangement or embellishment to make its point; it arrives fully formed.

What gives the demo its weight is the knowledge of where it was heard – and where it wasn't taken seriously. Played for bandmates who were largely preoccupied elsewhere, 'All Things Must Pass' stands as evidence that Harrison had outgrown the space available to him. When he finally recorded it on his own terms in 1970, its scale expanded, but its core remained unchanged. In this early version, you hear not a work in progress, but an artist already preparing to move on.

'Come And Get It' (McCartney)

During the sessions for the *Abbey Road* medley, Paul McCartney recorded a minor classic, 'Come And Get It', playing all the instruments and singing the lead vocal in a session lasting less than one hour.

This is Paul McCartney operating with ruthless efficiency; it's less a Beatles outtake than a masterclass in professional songwriting, delivered with such clarity that it almost renders the band redundant. From the opening piano figure, the song arrives fully assembled, structure, melody and hook all firmly in place.

McCartney's vocal is bright and persuasive, pitched perfectly between urgency and charm. There's no flab here: every section does its job, every lyric points the listener toward the chorus. It's pop craftsmanship without apology, and without any apparent need for collaboration.

Paul subsequently produced the song for Badfinger, whose copycat version (with added Beatles-esque harmonies) went to number four in early 1970. You can hear why it was handed over to Badfinger essentially intact – the blueprint required no revision. Crucially, 'Come And Get It' shows Paul applying his instincts to projects that no longer depended on group consensus.

Efficient, confident and faintly impersonal, the song stands as evidence that by mid-1969, at least one Beatle was already functioning as a solo hit factory – whether the others liked it or not.

The *Anthology 3* mix is presented in fake stereo, which sounds like Paul is playing at the end of a long corridor. There is a lovely true stereo mix on the 2019 deluxe version of *Abbey Road*.

Yellow Submarine Songtrack

Released 13 September 1999.
Chart positions. UK: 8. US: 15.
'Yellow Submarine', 'Hey Bulldog', 'Eleanor Rigby', 'Love You To', 'All Together Now', 'Lucy In The Sky With Diamonds', 'Think For Yourself', 'Sgt. Pepper's Lonely Hearts Club Band', 'With A Little Help From My Friends', 'Baby, You're A Rich Man', 'Only A Northern Song', 'All You Need Is Love', 'When I'm Sixty-Four', 'Nowhere Man', 'It's All Too Much'
This album of new mixes was to coincide with a re-release of the animated film *Yellow Submarine*. The mixes are very good, but most have been improved in subsequent box sets.

1

Released 13 November 2000.
Chart positions. UK: 1. US: 1.
'Love Me Do', 'From Me To You', 'She Loves You', 'I Want To Hold Your Hand', 'Can't Buy Me Love', 'A Hard Day's Night', 'I Feel Fine', 'Eight Days A Week', 'Ticket To Ride', 'Help!', 'Yesterday', 'Day Tripper', 'We Can Work It Out', 'Paperback Writer', 'Yellow Submarine', 'Eleanor Rigby', 'Penny Lane', 'All You Need Is Love', 'Hello, Goodbye', 'Lady Madonna', 'Hey Jude', 'Get Back', 'The Ballad Of John And Yoko', 'Something', 'Come Together', 'Let It Be', 'The Long And Winding Road'
This massive-selling greatest hits CD – the best-selling CD of the 2000s – gathers the band's number one singles in the UK and US. Purists might argue that the omissions of 'Please Please Me' (number one in most UK charts, and the band's first massive hit) and 'Strawberry Fields Forever' (not a number one but their best single) are unforgivable.

Let It Be ... Naked

Released 17 November 2003.
Chart positions. UK: 7. US: 5.
'Get Back', 'Dig A Pony', 'For You Blue', 'The Long And Winding Road', 'Two Of Us', 'I've Got A Feeling', 'One After 909', 'Don't Let Me Down', 'I Me Mine', 'Across The Universe', 'Let It Be'
This vanity release reshapes *Let It Be* with composite edits, new mixes, different takes and digital corrections. The stripped back 'Across The Universe' and 'The Long And Winding Road' are wonderful, but the rest is, well, *Let It Be* in new (or fewer) clothes.

A bonus disc called *Fly On The Wall* adds 22 minutes of song excerpts and dialogue from the sessions.

Love

Released 20 November 2006.
Chart positions. UK: 3. US: 4.

'Because', 'Get Back', 'Glass Onion', 'Eleanor Rigby' (with 'Julia' transition), 'I Am The Walrus', 'I Want To Hold Your Hand', 'Drive My Car/The Word/What You're Doing', 'Gnik Nus', 'Something' (with 'Blue Jay Way' transition), 'Being For The Benefit Of Mr. Kite!/I Want You (She's So Heavy)/Helter Skelter', 'Help!', 'Blackbird/Yesterday', 'Strawberry Fields Forever', 'Within You Without You/ Tomorrow Never Knows', 'Lucy In The Sky With Diamonds', 'Octopus's Garden', 'Lady Madonna', 'Here Comes The Sun' (with 'The Inner Light' transition), 'Come Together/Dear Prudence' (with 'Cry Baby Cry' transition), 'Revolution', 'Back In The USSR', 'While My Guitar Gently Weeps', 'A Day In The Life', 'Hey Jude', 'Sgt. Pepper's Lonely Hearts Club Band (Reprise)', 'All You Need Is Love'. Digital bonus tracks: 'The Fool On The Hill', 'Girl'

Question: Should masterpieces like these be messed about with? We think that most Beatles fans would answer, 'yes'. It's possible to enjoy the remixes and mash-ups on *Love*, and, should you wish, go back and listen to the original versions.

Love stands as a remarkable sonic tapestry, weaving together elements from 130 individual Beatles recordings, both commercial releases and demos alike. This intricate remix is best understood as a sophisticated mash-up, a genre that found its early 2000s stride through audacious reworkings of familiar material. As Alexis Petridis has noted, The Beatles proved a favoured source for such ventures: Danger Mouse's *The Grey Album* (2004) famously stitched Jay-Z's verses to the *White Album*'s musical canvas, while Go Home Productions' 'Paperback Believer' seamlessly blended 'Paperback Writer' with The Monkees' 'Daydream Believer'.

More than a mere remix, *Love* functions as a sprawling sound collage. Its 26 tracks dissolve into a perfect, blissful ambient flow. The amount of work involved is almost beyond comprehension. And it was wholly worth it.

The album's opening track, 'Because', incorporates bird sounds lifted from 'Across The Universe' and 'Free As A Bird', augmented by a freshly recorded British wood pigeon to add local colour. 'Get Back' melds the opening chord from 'A Hard Day's Night' with drum and guitar solos from 'The End', percussion from 'Sgt. Pepper (Reprise)' and the orchestral swell from 'A Day In The Life'.

Throughout *Love*, such alchemical combinations give fresh colour to familiar songs: 'Glass Onion' brings together guitar from 'Things We Said Today', horns from 'Penny Lane' and vocals from 'Hello Goodbye'; 'I Want To Hold Your Hand' marries studio and live elements; and the medley 'Drive My Car/The Word/What You're Doing' brilliantly fuses the 'Taxman' guitar solo with two lesser-known Beatles songs.

'Lady Madonna' skilfully blends drums from 'Why Don't We Do It The Road?' and, thrillingly, the loud guitars from both 'Hey Bulldog' and 'While My Guitar Gently Weeps'. The re-imagined 'Strawberry Fields Forever' grows from an acoustic demo to incorporate early takes with restored harmonies, interlaced with orchestral and instrumental snippets from across The Beatles' catalogue. George Harrison's 'While My Guitar Gently Weeps' appears here in an acoustic demo version enhanced by George Martin's final orchestral arrangement for The Beatles.

Best of all, the fusion of 'Within You Without You' and 'Tomorrow Never Knows' brilliantly layers Eastern instrumentation with a propulsive rhythm section. Instead of chaos, something uncanny emerges. The original spiritual solemnity of 'Within You Without You' is preserved in microcosm, but suddenly undercut and expanded by the relentless, swirling percussion and studio trickery of 'Tomorrow Never Knows'. The effect is disorienting in the best possible way: you're floating in Harrison's contemplative world one moment, then plunged into Lennon's acid-fuelled sonic kaleidoscope the next. Yet somehow, the transitions feel inevitable, as if these two seemingly opposed visions were always part of the same cosmic blueprint. Musically, it's a triumph of juxtaposition – sitars, tamburas, looped drums and Mellotrons all coexisting without a hint of compromise. More than a remix, it's a revelation: The Beatles' late 1960s experimentation reframed, compressed and clarified.

Love is as much a celebration of legacy as a radical reinvention. It's a monumental work that breathlessly lays out the genius of the greatest band of all time. It's not about novelty for novelty's sake. The songs themselves remain intact at their core, their melodies, hooks and emotions fully recognisable, even as the context is altered. The album is playful, dazzling, occasionally jarring and, above all, a testament to the elasticity of The Beatles' music. If you meet a little green guy from space and want to demonstrate, in one hour, how great The Beatles were, then you could do worse than starting with *Love*: a perfect snapshot of the band's career.

The Beatles Bootleg Recordings 1963

Released 17 December 2013.
Did not chart.
Studio Outtakes: 'There's A Place (takes 5, 6, 8, 9)', 'Do You Want To Know A Secret (take 7)', 'A Taste Of Honey (take 6)', 'I Saw Her Standing There (take 2)', 'Misery (takes 1 & 7), 'From Me To You' (takes 1, 2 & 5), 'Thank You Girl' (takes 1 & 5), 'One After 909' (takes 1 & 2)', 'Hold Me Tight (take 21)', 'Money (That's What I Want) (Mono Mix)'
BBC Radio Recordings: 'Some Other Guy', 'Love Me Do', 'Too Much Monkey Business', 'I Saw Her Standing There', 'Do You Want To Know A Secret', 'From Me To You', 'I Got To Find My Baby', 'Roll Over Beethoven', 'A Taste Of Honey', 'Love Me Do', 'Please Please Me', 'She Loves You', 'I Want To Hold Your Hand', 'Till There Was You', 'Roll Over Beethoven', 'You Really Got A Hold On Me', 'The Hippy Hippy Shake', 'Till There Was You', 'A Shot Of Rhythm And Blues', 'A Taste Of Honey', 'Money (That's What I Want)', 'Anna (Go To Him)', 'Love Me Do', 'She Loves You', 'I'll Get You', 'A Taste Of Honey', 'Boys', 'Chains', 'You Really Got A Hold On Me', 'I Saw Her Standing There', 'She Loves You', 'Twist And Shout', 'Do You Want To Know A Secret', 'Please Please Me', 'Long Tall Sally', 'Chains', 'Boys',

'A Taste Of Honey', 'Roll Over Beethoven', 'All My Loving', 'She Loves You', 'Till There Was You'
Home demos: 'Bad To Me', 'I'm In Love'
This compilation album of 59 previously unreleased recordings was released on iTunes for a matter of hours in December 2013. The release extended the copyright of the band's 1963 recordings under EU law. It includes 15 studio outtakes and 42 recordings for BBC radio, all of which have been circulating for years on bootlegs.

Of most interest are two unheard (or much improved) John Lennon demo recordings.

'Bad To Me' (Lennon, McCartney)
'I'm In Love' (Lennon, McCartney)
'Bad To Me' was written in the spring of 1963 by John Lennon, reportedly while he was on holiday in Barcelona and Torremolinos with his manager, Brian Epstein (the rest of The Beatles were on holiday in Tenerife in the Canary Islands at the same time). 'Bad To Me' was intended from the outset as a song for Billy J. Kramer with The Dakotas, another act managed by Epstein and produced by George Martin. The demo recording dates from May 1963 and features Lennon singing and playing acoustic guitar. It was available on bootlegs for decades before its legitimate release on *The Beatles Bootleg Recordings 1963*.

'Bad To Me' was recorded by Billy J. Kramer with The Dakotas at Abbey Road on 26 June 1963. It was released as a single on 26 July 1963 in the UK and went to number one the following month. The song was released in the US in 1964, where it reached number nine on the *Billboard* Hot 100.

'I'm In Love' was composed in mid-1963, again for Billy J. Kramer, who turned it down (or didn't record it properly, accounts vary). It was eventually recorded by The Fourmost, another Liverpool group managed by Brian Epstein. Their version was produced by George Martin and recorded on 6 October 1963 at Abbey Road Studios. It was released as a single on 15 November 1963 and peaked at number 17 on the UK Singles Chart. The demo version by John Lennon (again, just voice and guitar) surfaced on bootlegs and was officially released as part of *The Beatles Bootleg Recordings 1963*.

Both of these songs reflect the early 1960s period of Lennon-McCartney's prolific songwriting, when they were not just writing hits for The Beatles but for other Merseybeat acts. 'Bad To Me' remains the most successful of these, showing The Beatles' brand power even through other performers.

1+
Released 6 November 2015.
Chart positions. UK: 1. US: 3.
This deluxe version of the *1* album includes remixes of most of the tracks by Giles Martin from the original multi-track masters. There are surround sound

5.1 mixes, as well as 50 promotional films and performances, plus commentary and introductions from Paul McCartney and Ringo Starr.

The remix of 'Real Love' is quite different, especially in the opening moments. Intriguingly, the new mix of 'Free As A Bird' includes either an alternative vocal take or a deft edit for George's solo vocals. This same edit was retained for Jeff Lynne's new 2025 mix, which also employs the MAL software to clean up John's voice – he now sounds like he's in the room and not in the bathroom down the hall.

Sgt. Pepper's Lonely Hearts Club Band: 50th Anniversary Edition
Released 26 May 2017.
Chart positions. UK: 1. US: 3.
Includes original mono and new stereo remixes of *Sgt. Pepper's Lonely Hearts Club Band* and the following session outtakes:

'Strawberry Fields Forever (takes 1, 4, 7 & 26)', 'Strawberry Fields Forever (2015 Stereo Mix)', 'When I'm Sixty-Four (take 2)', 'Penny Lane (take 6), 'Penny Lane (Vocal Overdubs)', 'Penny Lane (2017 Stereo Mix)', 'A Day In The Life (takes 1 & 2)', 'A Day In The Life (Orchestra Overdub)', 'A Day In The Life (Hummed Last Chord)' (takes 8, 9, 10 & 11), 'A Day In The Life (The Last Chord)', 'Sgt. Pepper's Lonely Hearts Club Band (takes 1 & 9)', 'Good Morning Good Morning (takes 1 & 8)', 'Fixing A Hole (takes 1 & 3)', 'Being For The Benefit Of Mr. Kite! (takes 4 & 7)', 'Lovely Rita (take 9)', 'Lucy In The Sky With Diamonds (takes 1 & 5), 'Getting Better (takes 1 & 12)', 'Within You Without You (take 1 And George Coaching The Musicians)', 'She's Leaving Home (takes 1 & 6)', 'With A Little Help From My Friends (takes 1 & 2)', 'Sgt. Pepper's Lonely Hearts Club Band (Reprise) (take 8)', 'Strawberry Fields Forever (Original Mono Mix)', 'Penny Lane (Original Mono Mix)', 'A Day In The Life (First Mono Mix)', 'Lucy In The Sky With Diamonds (Unreleased Mono Mix)', 'She's Leaving Home (First Mono Mix)', 'Penny Lane (Capitol Records US Promo Single – Mono Mix)'

This deluxe re-issue has a very good new stereo mix of the original album, plus many session outtakes, which are a fascinating listen.

The Christmas Records
Released 15 December 2017.
Did not chart.
'The Beatles Christmas Record', 'Another Beatles Christmas Record', 'The Beatles Third Christmas Record', 'Pantomime: Everywhere It's Christmas', 'Christmas Time Is Here Again!', 'The Beatles 1968 Christmas Record', 'The Beatles Seventh Christmas Record'
Each year between 1963 and 1969, The Beatles released an exclusive flexi-disc to members of their fan clubs. These comprise spoken messages, skits and

some original compositions. They're goofy, self-indulgent, often incomprehensible, but fascinating precisely because they reveal the band unfiltered: playful, absurd and occasionally sharp-edged.

They were made generally available, on vinyl, in 2017. Anyone who wants to hear these will have had one of various bootlegs for years.

'The Beatles Christmas Record' (1963)
The inaugural Christmas flex is charmingly chaotic. It's part sketch, part song, part improvised nonsense. The lads are brimming with mischief: John's sarcasm, Paul's melodrama, George's dry wit and Ringo's deadpan contributions all collide. It's early evidence of their ability to dominate attention without any conventional structure, a miniature, private riot for fans.

'Another Beatles Christmas Record' (1964)
By the second year, the sketches are longer, the gags sharper and the jokes more meta. The boys lean into parody, lampooning themselves, the media and the mania. It's audibly looser than the first, less polished, and the humour occasionally teeters on the edge of grotesque. But underneath the nonsense, there's a remarkable cohesion – the group's instinct for timing, tension and audience awareness remains flawless.

'The Beatles Third Christmas Record' (1965)
The 1965 edition is more polished and scripted, featuring comic sketches, sound effects and surreal humour, showing The Beatles moving away from traditional messages. Lennon's sarcasm is fully deployed; McCartney experiments with melody; Harrison drops in sideways jokes. The record is a hodgepodge, but in its patchwork absurdity, you can trace their growing interest in the studio as a playground rather than a mere recording space.

It includes original songs such as 'Yesterday' parodied in humorous ways.

'Pantomime: Everywhere It's Christmas' (1966)
This is a fully produced audio pantomime with quirky characters, musical interludes and avant-garde storytelling, highlighting The Beatles' growing experimentalism. Here, the Christmas record starts to resemble a proto-psychedelic sketch, an eccentric pantomime of their public personas. It's mostly wordplay, surreal soundscapes and deliberately fragmented songs. The group's humour is now sly, self-referential and occasionally cruel. Musically, it's thin – the point is narrative chaos – but as a document of Lennon and McCartney's creative interplay, it's brilliant in its audacious weirdness.

'Christmas Time Is Here Again!' (1967)
Built around a repetitive original song titled 'Christmas Time (Is Here Again)!', this 1967 record includes satirical skits and mock interviews. It reflects the band's psychedelic era and was their longest and most complex Christmas

message. The refrain is catchy, cheerful and unmistakably Beatles, but it's surrounded by skits, vocal experiments and absurd announcements.

'The Beatles 1968 Christmas Record' (1968)
With the band increasingly working separately, this record features individual contributions, especially from John and Yoko, and a poem from George. Paul offers a brief musical number, and Ringo adds a festive message. Like the band in 1968, it feels fragmented.

'The Beatles Seventh Christmas Record' (1969)
The final Christmas fan club release consists of separately recorded segments edited together, including John and Yoko's experimental audio and George's minimal appearance. It reflects The Beatles' impending breakup and stands as a farewell of sorts.

The Beatles 50th Anniversary Deluxe Edition
Released 9 November 2018.
Chart positions. UK: 4. US: 6.
Includes a remix of *The Beatles* and the following:

> Esher Demos: 'Back In The USSR', 'Dear Prudence', 'Glass Onion', 'Ob-La-Di, Ob-La-Da', 'The Continuing Story Of Bungalow Bill', 'While My Guitar Gently Weeps', 'Happiness Is A Warm Gun', 'I'm So Tired', 'Blackbird', 'Piggies', 'Rocky Raccoon', 'Julia', 'Yer Blues', 'Mother Nature's Son', 'Everybody's Got Something To Hide Except Me And My Monkey', 'Sexy Sadie', 'Revolution', 'Honey Pie', 'Cry Baby Cry', 'Sour Milk Sea', 'Junk', 'Child Of Nature', 'Circles', 'Mean Mr. Mustard', 'Polythene Pam', 'Not Guilty', 'What's The New Mary Jane'
> Session Outtakes: 'Revolution 1 (take 18)', 'A Beginning (take 4)/Don't Pass Me By (take 7)', 'Blackbird (take 28)', 'Everybody's Got Something To Hide Except Me And My Monkey (Unnumbered Rehearsal)', 'Good Night (Unnumbered Rehearsal)', 'Good Night (take 10 With A Guitar Part From take 5)', 'Good Night (take 22)', 'Ob-La-Di, Ob-La-Da (take 3)', 'Revolution (Unnumbered Rehearsal)', 'Revolution (take 14)', 'Cry Baby Cry (Unnumbered Rehearsal)', 'Helter Skelter (take 2)', 'Sexy Sadie (take 3)', 'While My Guitar Gently Weeps (Acoustic Version, take 2)', 'Hey Jude (take 1)', 'Saint Louis Blues', 'Not Guilty (take 102)', 'Mother Nature's Son (take 15)', 'Yer Blues (take 5 With Guide Vocal)', 'What's The New Mary Jane (take 1)', 'Rocky Raccoon (take 8)', 'Back In The USSR (take 5)', 'Dear Prudence (Vocal, Guitar & Drums)', 'Let It Be (Unnumbered Rehearsal)', 'While My Guitar Gently Weeps (take 27)', '(You're So Square) Baby I Don't Care', 'Helter Skelter (take 17)', 'Glass Onion (take 10)', 'I Will (take 13)', 'Blue Moon', 'I Will (take 29)', 'Step Inside Love', 'Los Paranoias', 'Can You Take Me Back? (take 1)', 'Birthday' (take 2), 'Piggies (take 12)', 'Happiness Is A Warm Gun (take 19)', 'Honey Pie (Instrumental Backing Track)', 'Savoy Truffle (Instrumental

Backing Track)', 'Martha My Dear (Without Brass & Strings)', 'Long, Long, Long (take 44)', 'I'm So Tired' (takes 7 And 14)', 'I'm So Tired (take 14)', 'The Continuing Story Of Bungalow Bill (take 2)', 'Why Don't We Do It In The Road? (take 5), 'Julia (Two Rehearsals)', 'The Inner Light (take 6)', 'Lady Madonna (take 2)', 'Lady Madonna (Backing Vocals From take 3)', 'Across The Universe (take 6)'

This is possibly too much of a good thing. Nevertheless, there are several previously unreleased songs here.

'Child Of Nature' (Lennon)
'Sour Milk Sea' (Harrison)
'Circles' (Harrison)

'Child Of Nature' was written by John Lennon in early 1968 during The Beatles' stay in Rishikesh, India, inspired by a lecture from the Maharishi Mahesh Yogi. It's a gentle acoustic ballad with pastoral lyrics. Although considered for *The Beatles*, the band never recorded it in full as a group. John eventually reworked the song into 'Jealous Guy', replacing the lyrics and keeping the melody; it appeared on his 1971 solo album *Imagine*, becoming one of his most beloved solo tracks.

'Circles' was likewise written in India in 1968. It's a meditative, philosophical ballad about reincarnation and the impermanence of life, reflecting composer George Harrison's deepening spiritual focus. The demo features George on electric keyboard and vocals. It has a hypnotic, circular chord structure. The Beatles never formally recorded 'Circles'. George finally recorded it for his 1982 solo album *Gone Troppo* with a fuller arrangement.

'Sour Milk Sea' was also composed by George Harrison in India in 1968. The lyrics are based on the teachings of Lahiri Mahasaya, a yogi in the Kriya Yoga tradition. The demo features George on acoustic guitar and vocals, delivering an upbeat and bluesy message about spiritual transformation. Harrison gave the song to Apple artist Jackie Lomax, producing the studio version himself with a backing band comprising Eric Clapton, Paul McCartney, Ringo Starr and Nicky Hopkins. Released as Lomax's debut Apple single in August 1968, it was not a commercial hit but is now praised for its hard-driving rock energy.

Some clever people have married George's Esher demo to the Lomax backing track, re-creating what could have been a standout Beatles track.

'St. Louis Blues' (Handy)

Written by WC Handy in 1914, 'St. Louis Blues' is a foundational American blues classic. It has been covered by many major artists, from Bessie Smith to Louis Armstrong and Nat King Cole. The Beatles casually jammed on 'St. Louis Blues' 'for 50 seconds during a break in rehearsal sessions for 'Hey Jude' on 30 July 1968.

'Blue Moon' (Rodgers, Hart)
'Blue Moon' is a classic pop standard written by Richard Rodgers and Lorenz Hart in 1934. It was famously covered by Elvis Presley, whose version was a major influence on The Beatles, who performed it in their pre-fame club sets. This off-the-cuff 16 September 1968 performance lasts just over one minute, busked during sessions for 'I Will'.

'Can You Take Me Back?' (Lennon, McCartney)
'Can You Take Me Back?' was improvised by Paul McCartney during the studio session for 'I Will' on 16 September 1968 at Abbey Road. McCartney strummed and sang this melancholy tune spontaneously between takes. A snippet of this performance was inserted between 'Cry Baby Cry' and 'Revolution 9' on the *White Album*. This full-length version is a long 2:22.

'(You're So Square) Baby I Don't Care' (Leiber, Stoller)
Written by Jerry Leiber and Mike Stoller, this was first recorded by Elvis Presley in 1957 for the film *Jailhouse Rock*. It was a favourite of both John Lennon and Paul McCartney, who admired Elvis deeply. This loud, raucous 42-second jam was recorded on 9 September 1968 during sessions for 'Helter Skelter'.

Abbey Road – 2019 Deluxe Edition
Released 27 September 2019.
Chart positions. UK: 1. US: 3.
Includes a remix of *Abbey Road* and the following session outtakes:

> 'I Want You (She's So Heavy) (Trident Recording Session And Reduction Mix)', 'Goodbye (Home Demo)', 'Something (Studio Demo)', 'The Ballad Of John And Yoko (take 7)', 'Old Brown Shoe (take 2)', 'Oh! Darling (take 4)', 'Octopus's Garden (take 9)', 'You Never Give Me Your Money (take 36)', 'Her Majesty (takes 1-3)', 'Golden Slumbers/Carry That Weight (takes 1-3)', 'Here Comes The Sun (take 9)', 'Maxwell's Silver Hammer (take 12)', 'Come Together (take 5)', 'The End (take 3)', 'Come And Get It (Studio Demo)', 'Sun King (take 20)', 'Mean Mr. Mustard (take 20)', 'Polythene Pam (take 27)', 'She Came In Through The Bathroom Window (take 27)', 'Because (take 1)', 'The Long One (Trial Edit And Mix)', 'Something (take 39, Strings Only)', 'Golden Slumbers/Carry That Weight' (take 17, Strings & Brass Only)'

'Goodbye' (Lennon, McCartney)
The song 'Goodbye' is a Paul McCartney composition written specifically for Mary Hopkin in early 1969, shortly after Hopkin's huge success with her debut single 'Those Were The Days'. McCartney's demo of the song was recorded at his home on Cavendish Avenue in early 1969. Paul plays guitar and sings. This demo surfaced on bootlegs in the mid-1990s.

Mary Hopkin's version was produced by Paul and recorded at EMI Studios in March 1969. It was released as a single on 28 March 1969 on Apple Records and reached number two on the UK Singles Chart, held off the top spot by The Beatles' own 'Get Back'. It also reached number 13 on the *Billboard* Hot 100 in the US.

Let It Be – 2021 Special Edition
Released 15 October 2021.
Chart positions. UK: 2. US: 5.
Includes a new remix of *Let It Be* and the following tracks:

Session Outtakes And Rehearsals: 'Morning Camera (Speech)/Two Of Us (take 4)', 'Maggie Mae/Fancy My Chances With You', 'Can You Dig It?', 'I Don't Know Why I'm Moaning (Speech)', 'For You Blue (take 4)', 'Let It Be/ Please Please Me/Let It Be (take 10)', 'I've Got A Feeling (take 10)', 'Dig A Pony (take 14)', 'Get Back (take 19)', 'Like Making An Album? (Speech)', 'One After 909 (take 3)', 'Don't Let Me Down (First Rooftop Performance)', 'The Long And Winding Road (take 19)', 'Wake Up Little Susie/I Me Mine (take 11)', 'On The Day Shift Now (Speech)/All Things Must Pass (Rehearsals)', 'Concentrate On The Sound (Speech)', 'Gimme Some Truth (Rehearsals)', 'I Me Mine (Rehearsals)', 'She Came In Through The Bathroom Window (Rehearsals)', 'Polythene Pam (Rehearsals)', 'Octopus's Garden (Rehearsals)', 'Oh! Darling (Jam)', 'Get Back (take 8)', 'The Walk (Jam)', 'Without A Song', 'Something (Rehearsals)', 'Let It Be (take 28)'
Glyn Johns' 1969 Mix (Sic): 'One After 909', 'I'm Ready (Rocker)/Save The Last Dance For Me/Don't Let Me Down', 'Don't Let Me Down', 'Dig A Pony', 'I've Got A Feeling', 'Get Back', 'For You Blue', 'Teddy Boy', 'Two Of Us', 'Maggie Mae', 'Dig It', 'Let It Be', 'The Long And Winding Road', 'Get Back (Reprise)'
Alternative Mixes: 'Across The Universe (Unreleased Glyn Johns 1970 Mix)', 'I Me Mine (Unreleased Glyn Johns 1970 Mix)', 'Don't Let Me Down (New Mix Of Original Single Version)', 'Let It Be' (New Mix Of Original Single Version)

Beatles fanatics have been diligently trawling through the hundreds of hours of available tapes from four weeks of sessions in January 1969 for many years. People have written books about them. The recordings are mostly horrible, but the best of them are included here, and in Peter Jackson's *The Beatles: Get Back* documentary.

'Fancy My Chances With You' (Lennon, McCartney)
'Fancy My Chances With You' is an early Lennon-McCartney composition which is simple, bluesy and playful. This is the only known recording captured during sessions for 'Two Of Us' on 24 January 1969. John and Paul perform it casually as a duet, with both on vocals and acoustic guitar.

'Gimme Some Truth' (Lennon)
This recording of John's 'Gimme Some Truth' dates from the Twickenham rehearsals for *Get Back*. John first ran through the song on 3 January 1969, and revisited it again, heard here, four days later. The lyrics reflect John's growing political frustration, anti-establishment views and disillusionment with the media and government. Though never fully developed by The Beatles, John Lennon re-recorded 'Gimme Some Truth' for his 1971 album *Imagine*, with George Harrison on slide guitar. It became one of Lennon's most scathing political tracks and remains a standout on the *Imagine* album.

'The Walk' (McCracklin, Garlic)
Written by Jimmy McCracklin and Bob Garlic, 'The Walk' was a 1958 R&B hit by McCracklin, known for its catchy groove and bluesy swagger. It was a favourite among early rock 'n' roll and R&B performers and clearly remembered by The Beatles when they performed it spontaneously on 27 January 1969 during a break in recording the song 'Let It Be' at Apple Studios. Paul McCartney takes lead vocals, and the rest of the band join in rhythmically.

'Without A Song' (Youmans, Rose, Eliscu)
Billy Preston takes the lead on 'Without A Song', written in 1929 by Vincent Youmans, Billy Rose and Edward Eliscu. It's a classic American standard, covered by artists like Perry Como, Frank Sinatra and Tony Bennett. Preston performs the song in a soulful, jazzy style. Recorded on 24 January 1969.

'Rocker'/'Save The Last Dance for Me'/'Don't Let Me Down'
(Domino, Lewis, Bradford/Pomus, Shuman/Lennon, McCartney)
This sequence of songs, recorded on 22 January 1969, was planned for release on the initial *Get Back* album, mixed between 10 and 13 March 1969, and presented to The Beatles in April 1969. This same sequence was also present in the revamped version of *Get Back,* which dates from January 1970, but was dropped from the final running order when the project was handed to Phil Spector.

'Rocker' is, in fact, Fats Domino's 'I'm Ready'. 'Save The Last Dance For Me' was written by Doc Pomus and Mort Shuman for The Drifters. Phil Spector made the right decision to chop them from *Let It Be,* as 'rough' doesn't quite describe these performances.

Get Back – The Rooftop Performance

Streaming audio, 28 January 2022.
'Get Back (take 1)', 'Get Back (take 2)', 'Don't Let Me Down (take 1)', 'I've Got A Feeling (take 1)', 'One After 909', 'Dig A Pony', 'God Save The Queen', 'I've Got A Feeling (take 2)', 'Don't Let Me Down (take 2)', 'Get Back (take 3)'
This is the almost-complete rooftop performance. An opening soundcheck run-through of 'Get Back' is omitted.

It's wonderful.

'I've Got a Feeling (take 1)', 'One After 909' and 'Dig A Pony' (with some backing vocals mixed out) were used on the album *Let It Be* in 1970. The final performance of 'Get Back' is included on *Anthology 3*. Edits of the two takes of 'Don't Let Me Down' and the two takes of 'I've Got A Feeling' can be heard on *Let It Be ... Naked*.

Revolver: Special Edition

Released 28 October 2022.

Chart positions. UK: 2. US: 4.

Includes the original mono mix and a new stereo remix of *Revolver* and the following tracks.

> Session Outtakes: 'Tomorrow Never Knows (take 1)', 'Tomorrow Never Knows (Mono Mix RM 11)', 'Got To Get You Into My Life (take 5)', 'Got To Get You Into My Life (Second Version, Unnumbered Mono Mix)', 'Got To Get You Into My Life (take 8)', 'Love You To (take 1)', 'Love You To (Unnumbered Rehearsal)', 'Love You To (take 7)', 'Paperback Writer (takes 1 & 2)', 'Rain (take 5 – Actual Speed)', 'Rain (take 5 – Slowed Down For Master Tape)', 'Doctor Robert (take 7)', 'And Your Bird Can Sing (take 2)', 'And Your Bird Can Sing (take 2 Vocals Overdub)', 'And Your Bird Can Sing (take 5)', 'Taxman (take 11)', 'I'm Only Sleeping (Rehearsal Fragment)', 'I'm Only Sleeping (take 2)', 'I'm Only Sleeping (take 5)', 'I'm Only Sleeping (Mono Mix RM1)', 'Eleanor Rigby (Speech Before take 2)', 'Eleanor Rigby (take 2)', 'For No One (take 10)', 'Yellow Submarine (Songwriting Work Tape #1)', 'Yellow Submarine (Songwriting Work Tape #2)', 'Yellow Submarine (take 4)', 'Yellow Submarine (Sound Effects)', 'I Want To Tell You (take 4)', 'Here, There And Everywhere (take 6)', 'She Said She Said (Demo)', 'She Said She Said (take 15)'
>
> Mixes: 'Paperback Writer (New Stereo Mix)', 'Rain (New Stereo Mix)', 'Paperback Writer (Original Mono Mix)', 'Rain (Original Mono Mix)'

Peerless and magnificent. Every moment.

'Now And Then' b/w **'Love Me Do'** (Single)

Released 2 November 2023.

Chart positions. UK: 1. US: 7.

Paul had often told of his desire to finish up the third of the three 'new' Beatles songs that had been worked on in 1994-1995. It was only when audio technology had sufficiently advanced that work was able to proceed.

Paul, 81 when 'Now And Then' was released, was finally reunited with Ringo (83 and still kicking), John (who had by now been dead for longer than he was alive) and George (22 years deceased).

'Now And Then' (Lennon)
Also released on *The Beatles 1967-1970* (2023 expanded edition).

'Now And Then' was written and recorded as a rough piano-and-voice demo by John Lennon, probably in 1977 at his Dakota apartment in New York. The demo was not completed nor formally recorded during Lennon's lifetime. It features introspective, melancholic lyrics, typical of Lennon's late-1970s solo style and was leaked to bootleggers in the mid-1990s, after the *Anthology* project. By then, Paul McCartney, George Harrison and Ringo Starr had worked on a 'Beatles' version of 'Now And Then', but abandoned it because the sound quality of the original demo was poor (John's voice was buried in electrical hum and piano bleed) and because George reportedly disliked the song.

Once again, The Beatles pioneered invention in their production techniques. The deployment of AI-driven audio separation technology developed by Peter Jackson's team during the making of *The Beatles: Get Back* (2021) allowed Lennon's voice to be cleanly extracted from the demo. In 1966-1967, they used backwards tapes, artificial double tracking, varispeed, tape loops, flanging, classical instrumentation and tape splicing. If the four Beatles were alive recording today, they would surely use AI as a tool in the studio. Following this breakthrough, Paul and Ringo returned to the project in 2022 and finished it, incorporating John's original vocal and piano, George Harrison's acoustic and electric rhythm guitars from the 1995 sessions and new contributions from Paul (bass, piano, slide guitar) and Ringo (drums).

Gone are the gimmicks of 'Free As A Bird': no synthesised keyboards, no layered sound effects, no artificial ornamentation. What remains is the skeleton of the song – Lennon's home demo, McCartney's intuitive production and instrumental embellishments, and the band's hallmark harmonic interplay – given space to breathe.

Harmony vocals were borrowed, *Love*-style, from 'Here, There And Everywhere', 'Because' and 'Eleanor Rigby'. A new string arrangement by Paul, recorded at Abbey Road with Giles Martin and Ben Foster, echoes George Martin's style. This session took place in May 2022 with the decoy name 'Give & Take' to hide the song's true identity. The strings are clean, unprocessed and arranged to support rather than dominate, offering warmth and colour without calling attention to themselves.

The recording dates for the various elements are:

6 June 1966	backing vocals from 'Eleanor Rigby'
14 June 1966	backing vocals from 'Here, There And Everywhere'
4 August 1969	backing vocals from 'Because'
c. 1977	Lennon's lead vocals
2 February 1995	George Harrison's acoustic and electric guitars
2 February 2021	Paul McCartney's guitar solo

9 July 2021 McCartney's basslines
12 July 2021 McCartney's vocals
9 April 2022 Ringo Starr's drums
1 May 2022 orchestra

The choice of organic simplicity in the production does more than evoke nostalgia; it humanises the performance. 'Now And Then' doesn't aim to impress or overwhelm – it insists that the music itself, stripped of artifice, is enough. In an era of endless layering and manipulation, it's a quiet, almost radical statement: The Beatles at their most direct, their most vulnerable, and somehow, their most alive.

'Now And Then' was released on 2 November 2023 as a double A-side single with a new mix of 'Love Me Do' marketed as 'The Last Beatles Song'. It went to number one in the UK, their first in 54 years.

The response to 'Now And Then' was overwhelmingly positive, both critically and emotionally. At the very least, the reunion of The Beatles, despite two of them having died, was symbolic. *The Guardian* called 'Now And Then' 'a ghostly triumph of technology and love'. *Rolling Stone* praised its emotional heft and said it 'may be their saddest song'. *NME* declared it 'an emotional final chapter – and a beautiful tribute to their brotherhood'.

Fans, us included, were deeply moved and the accompanying music video by Peter Jackson – showing archival and newly created footage of all four Beatles – added to the song's powerful impact. We defy any Beatles fan to watch the video and not have a little weep.

'Now And Then' closes the story of The Beatles.

So many bands have come and gone and will eventually be forgotten.

But The Beatles will be remembered forever. Nobody even comes close.

Bibliography

Babiuk, A., *Beatles Gear* (Backbeat, San Francisco, 2002).
Badman, K., *The Beatles After The Break-Up 1970-2000* (Omnibus Press, London, 1993).
Bassols, G., *The Musical Instruments Of Progressive Rock* (Grupo Editorial Círculo Rojo, self-pub, 2019).
Beatles, The, *The Complete Beatles Scores* (Hal Leonard, Wisconsin, 2000).
Beatles, The, *The Beatles Anthology* (Cassell & Co, London, 2000).
Bramwell, T. & Kingsland, R., *Magical Mystery Tours* (St. Martin's Press, New York, 2005).
Braun, M., *'Love Me Do' The Beatles' Progress* (Penguin, London, 1994).
Carrera, M., 'The Beatles *Let It Be* 50th Deluxe Box Set – What's New' (unpublished notes).
Clayson, A. & Sutcliffe, P., *Stuart Sutcliffe: The Lost Beatle* (Pan, London, 1994).
Coleman, R., *Brian Epstein* (Penguin, London, 1990).
Davies, H., *The Beatles: The Authorised Biography* (Heinemann, London, 1968).
Davies, H., *The Quarrymen* (Omnibus Press, London, 2001).
Davies, H., *The Beatles Lyrics: The Stories Behind The Music* (Little Brown, London, 2014).
Egan, S. [ed], *The Mammoth Book Of The Beatles* (Constable & Robinson, London, 2009).
Englehardt, K., *Beatles Undercover* (Collector's Guide Publishing, Burlington, 1998).
Everett, W., *The Beatles As Musicians: Revolver Through The Anthology* (Oxford University Press, Oxford, 1999).
Everett, W., *The Beatles As Musicians: The Quarry Men Through Rubber Soul* (Oxford University Press, Oxford, 2001).
Frame, P., *The Beatles And Some Other Guys* (Omnibus Press, London, 1997).
Friede, G., Titone, R. and Weiner, S., *Beatles A-Z* (Eyre Methuen, London, 1980).
Goldman, A., *The Lives Of John Lennon* (Bantam, London, 1988).
Hammack, J., *The Beatles Recording Reference Manual: Volume 1: My Bonnie Through Beatles For Sale (1961-1964)* (CreateSpace, 2017).
Hammack, J., *The Beatles Recording Reference Manual: Volume 2: Help! Through Revolver (1965-1966)* (CreateSpace, 2018).
Hammack, J., *The Beatles Recording Reference Manual: Volume 3: Sgt. Pepper's Lonely Hearts Club Band Through Magical Mystery Tour (late 1966-1967)* (CreateSpace, 2018).
Hammack, J., *The Beatles Recording Reference Manual: Volume 4: The Beatles Through Yellow Submarine (late 1966-1967)* (CreateSpace, 2019).
Hammack, J., *The Beatles Recording Reference Manual: Volume 5: Let It Be Through Abbey Road (1969-1970)* (CreateSpace, 2020).
Harrison, G., *I Me Mine* (Weidenfeld & Nicholson, London, 2002).

Harry, B., *The Encyclopaedia Of Beatles People* (Blandford, London, 1997).
Hertsgaard, M., *A Day In The Life – The Music And Artistry Of The Beatles* (Delacorte Press, New York, 1995).
Hepworth, D., *Abbey Road: The Inside Story Of The World's Most Famous Recording Studio* (Penguin, London, 2023).
Herzogenrath, W. & Hansen, D., *John Lennon Drawings Performances Films* (Thames and Hudson, London, 1995).
Leslie, I., *John And Paul: A Love Story In Songs* (Faber & Faber, London, 2025).
Lewisohn, M., *The Beatles Recording Sessions* (Hamlyn, London, 1988).
Lewisohn, M., *The Complete Beatles Chronicle* (Pyramid Books, London, 1992).
Lewisohn, M., *All These Years: Volume 1 'Tune In'* [Extended version] (Little Brown, London, 2013).
McCartney, P., *Blackbird Singing – Poems And Lyrics 1965-1999* (Faber and Faber, London, 2001).
Lewisohn, M., *The Lyrics: 1956 To The Present* (Penguin, London, 2021).
MacDonald, I., *Revolution In The Head – The Beatles' Records And The Sixties* (Pimlico, London, 1998).
Maconie, S., *With A Little Help From Their Friends* (HarperNorth, Glasgow, 2025).
Madinger, C. & Easter, M, *Eight Arms To Hold You* (44. 1 Productions Inc., USA, 2001).
Miles, B., *Many Years From Now* (Secker & Warburg, London, 1997).
Norman, P., *Shout!* (Corgi, London, 1981).
O'Donnell, J., *The Day John Met Paul* (Penguin, London, 1996).
Patterson, R.H., *The Walrus Was Paul* (Simon & Schuster, 1996).
Peebles, A., *The Lennon Tapes* (BBC, London, 1981).
Pedler, D., *The Songwriting Secrets Of The Beatles* (Omnibus Press, London, 2003/2017).
Reeve, A., *Turn Me On Dead Man: The Beatles And The Paul Is Dead Hoax* (AuthorHouse, Bloomington, 2004).
Riley, T., *Tell Me Why – A Beatles Commentary* (Vintage, New York, 1988).
Riley, T., *Lennon – The Man, The Myth, The Music* (Hyperion, New York, 2011).
Rosnow, R.L. and Fine, G.A., *Rumour And Gossip: The Social Psychology Of Hearsay* (Elsevier, New York, 1976).
Schaffner, N., *Beatles Forever* (McGraw-Hill, New York, 1977).
Schultze, E., *Carry That Weight: The Story Of The Beatles* (Xlibris, Bloomington, 1997).
Spignesi, S., *The Beatles Book Of Lists* (Citadel, Secaucus, 1998).
Spizer, B., *The Beatles Records On Vee-Jay* (498, New Orleans, 1998).
Spizer, B., *The Beatles Story On Capitol Records – Part One: Beatlemania & The Singles* (498, New Orleans, 2000).
Spizer, B., *The Beatles Story On Capitol Records – Part Two: The Albums* (498, New Orleans, 2000).
Sulpy, D. & Schweighardt, R., *Get Back – The Beatles' Let It Be Disaster [Drugs, Divorce And A Slipping Image]* (Helter Skelter, London, 1998).

Sulpy, D., *The 910's Guide To The Beatles' Outtakes [3rd Edition]* (Poptomes, Jackson, 1999).
Sulpy, D., *The 910's Guide To The Beatles' Outtakes: Part One [4th Edition]* (The 910, Jackson, 2001).
Sulpy, D., *The 910's Guide To The Beatles' Outtakes: Part Two – The Complete Get Back Sessions* (The 910, Jackson, 2001).
Sulpy, D., *The 910's Guide To The Beatles' Outtakes: Part Three – The Core Collection* (The 910, Jackson, 2002).
Sulpy, D., *The 910's Guide To The Beatles' Outtakes 2004 Edition* (The 910, Jackson, 2004).
Uharriet. T.E, *The Memoirs Of Billy Shears* (CreateSpace Independent Publishing Platform, 2009).
Weiner, A. J., *The Beatles: The Ultimate Recording Guide* (Facts on File, New York, 1992).
Winn, J., *Lifting Latches: The Beatles' Recorded Legacy, Volume Three, Inside The Beatles Vaults* (Multiplus Books, Sharon VT, 2005).
Winn, J., *Way Beyond Compare: The Beatles' Recorded Legacy, Volume One, 1957-1965* (Three Rivers Press, New York, 2008).
Winn, J., *That Magic Feeling: The Beatles' Recorded Legacy, Volume Two, 1966-1970* (Three Rivers Press, New York, 2009).
Wenner, J., *Lennon Remembers* (Penguin, Harmondsworth, 1973).
Williams, A. & Marshall, W., *The Man Who Gave The Beatles Away* (Coronet, London, 1976).
Womack, K., *Maximum Volume: The Life Of Beatles Producer George Martin The Early Years 1926-1966* (Orphans Publishing, Leominster, 2017).
Womack, K., *Sound Pictures: The Life Of Beatles Producer George Martin The Later Years 1966-2016* (Orphans Publishing, Leominster, 2018).